LONGMAN PREPARATION SERIES FOR THE TOEIC® TEST

INTRODUCTORY COURSE 5TH EDITION

LISTENING AND READING

Lin Lougheed

Longman Preparation Series for the TOEIC® Test: Listening and Reading, Introductory Course, Fifth Edition

Pearson Education, 10 Bank Street, White Plains, NY 10606

Staff credits: The people who made up the ***Longman Preparation Series for the TOEIC® Test: Listening and Reading*** team—representing editorial, production, design, and manufacturing—are Aerin Csigay, Dave Dickey, Pam Fishman, Mike Kemper, Barbara Perez, Liza Pleva, Robert Ruvo, and Adina Zoltan.

Development: Helen B. Ambrosio Publishing Services, Inc.
Text composition: ElectraGraphics, Inc.
Text font: Palatino
Cover photograph: Shutterstock.com
Cover design: Barbara Perez

Photo Credits: All photos are from Instructional Design International, Inc., Washington D.C., except for the following: **Page 2** Copyright © Educational Testing Service. Reprinted with permission; **p. 10** Shutterstock.com; **p. 23** Shutterstock.com; **p. 26** Shutterstock.com; **p. 29** Shutterstock.com; **p. 34** (both) Shutterstock.com; **p. 37** (top) Shutterstock.com; **p. 38** (top) Shutterstock.com; **p. 105** Copyright © Educational Testing Service. Reprinted with permission; **p. 108** (bottom) Shutterstock.com; **p. 109** (top) Royalty-Free/Corbis; **p. 110** (bottom) Royalty-Free/Corbis; **p. 226** Copyright © Educational Testing Service. Reprinted with permission; **p. 228** (bottom) Shutterstock.com; **p. 230** (bottom) Shutterstock.com; **p. 264** Copyright © Educational Testing Service. Reprinted with permission; **p. 266** (bottom) Shutterstock.com; **p. 267** (top) Royalty-Free/Corbis, (bottom) Shutterstock.com; **p. 268** (bottom) Shutterstock.com; **p. 304** Copyright © Educational Testing Service. Reprinted with permission; **p. 305** (both) Shutterstock.com; **p. 306** (both) Shutterstock.com; **p. 307** (both) Shutterstock.com; **p. 308** (both) Shutterstock.com; **p. 309** (both) Shutterstock.com.

Library of Congress Cataloging-in-Publication Data

Lougheed, Lin
Longman preparation series for the TOEIC test: listening and reading. Introductory course / Lin Lougheed.—5th ed.
p. cm.
ISBN 978-0-13-286148-9 (with answer key)—ISBN 0-13-286148-8 (with answer key)—ISBN 978-0-13-286151-9 (without answer key)—ISBN 0-13-286151-8 (without answer key)—ISBN 0-13-286142-9—ISBN 0-13-286146-1—ISBN 0-13-286152-6—ISBN 0-13-286143-7—ISBN 0-13-286145-3 1. Test of English for International Communication—Study guides. 2. English language—Business English—Examinations—Study guides. 3. English language—Textbooks for foreign speakers. I. Lougheed, Lin, 1946– Longman preparation series for the TOEIC test. Introductory course. II. Title.

PE1128.L646 2012
428.0076—dc23

2011037693

Printed in the United States of America

ISBN 10: 0-13-286148-8 (with answer key)
ISBN 13: 978-0-13-286148-9 (with answer key)

2 3 4 5 6 7 8 9 10—V001—17 16 15 14 13 12

ISBN 10: 0-13-286151-8 (without answer key)
ISBN 13: 978-0-13-286151-9 (without answer key)

2 3 4 5 6 7 8 9 10—V001—17 16 15 14 13 12

CONTENTS

READING 119

INTRODUCTION

TO THE STUDENT

The TOEIC® (Test of English for International Communication) test measures your ability to understand English. It also measures your ability to take a standardized, multiple-choice test. In order to score well on the TOEIC test, you must have two goals: to improve your proficiency in English and improve your test-taking skills. The *Longman Preparation Series for the TOEIC® Test: Listening and Reading* will help you do both. This book will teach you *language strategies* and *test strategies* that will help you do well on the TOEIC test.

Goals

IMPROVING YOUR PROFICIENCY IN ENGLISH

The *Longman Preparation Series for the TOEIC® Test: Listening and Reading* will help you build your vocabulary. It will introduce you to words that are often used on the TOEIC test. These are words that are used frequently in general English and also in business English contexts. You will learn words used by businesspeople involved in making contracts, marketing, planning conferences, using computers, writing letters, and hiring personnel. You will learn the words to use when shopping, ordering supplies, examining financial statements, and making investments. You will also learn general English terms often found in business contexts. This includes words used for travel and entertainment and for eating out and taking care of one's health.

The *Longman Preparation Series for the TOEIC® Test: Listening and Reading* will help you review English grammar. The grammar items commonly tested on the TOEIC test are reviewed here. You will learn grammar structures in TOEIC contexts.

IMPROVING YOUR TEST-TAKING SKILLS

The *Longman Preparation Series for the TOEIC® Test: Listening and Reading* will teach you to take the TOEIC test efficiently. It will help you understand what a question asks. It will help you analyze the test items so you will know what tricks and traps are hidden in the answer choices. It will familiarize you with the format of the test so you will feel comfortable when taking the test. You will know what to expect. You will know what to do. You will do well on the TOEIC test.

TOEIC Study Contract

A contract is a type of agreement. It is a document that describes work you agree to do. You can make a contract with yourself that describes how much time you will spend studying English each week. When you sign the contract, it means that you promise to do the work.

Complete the contract below with your name and the number of hours you plan to study English each week. Sign and date the contract. This is a promise to yourself to follow your study plan. Keep track of the hours that you study every day to make sure that you fulfill the terms of your contract.

STUDY CONTRACT

I, ____________________________, make a promise to study for the TOEIC test by following a regular study plan. I will use *Longman Preparation Series for the TOEIC® Test: Listening and Reading, Introductory Course* and, in addition, I will study English on my own.

I will study English for ____ hours a week. I will divide my study time as follows.

Listening to English: ____ hours a week

Writing in English: ____ hours a week

Speaking English: ____ hours a week

Reading English: ____ hours a week

________________________________ ________________________________

Signed Date

On Your Own

There are a variety of ways you can study English on your own. Here are some suggestions. Add some of your own ideas to the list.

INTERNET-BASED ACTIVITIES

Listening

____ YouTube
____ Pod casts
____ Movies (Trailers)
____ TV shows
____ News channels (BBC, CNN, NBC)
____ ______________________________

Speaking

____ Talk to English speakers with Skype
____ Chat with other users of social websites, like Facebook, Yahoo, etc.
____ ______________________________

Writing

____ Write a blog
____ Post comments on blogs
____ Post comments on an online forum
____ Start a Facebook page in English
____ Use Twitter in English
____ ______________________________

Reading

____ Read blogs
____ Read online newspaper articles
____ Look for information on topics that interest you
____ ______________________________

OTHER WAYS TO STUDY ON YOUR OWN

Listening

____ Listen to English language radio broadcasts
____ Watch English language movies and TV in English
____ Watch English language TV programs
____ Listen to songs in English
____ ______________________________

Speaking

____ Find a friend to practice conversations with
____ Summarize your daily activities to yourself aloud
____ ______________________________

Writing

____ Write to an English-speaking pen pal
____ Keep a journal in English
____ Write essays on topics of importance to you
____ Write lists of things you see, do, and want to do
____ ______________________________

Reading

____ Read books in English
____ Read newspaper articles in English
____ Read magazine articles in English
____ ______________________________

SAMPLE SELF-STUDY ACTIVITIES

You can use any kind of study material to practice English in a variety of ways. Websites, books, magazine articles, and TV shows, for example, can all be used for listening, speaking, reading, and writing activities. Here are some ways you can use different resources to practice your English skills.

Shop for a product

Think of a product you would like to buy. Try www.amazon.com or another shopping site in English and look for the product you are interested in. Read the descriptions and the reviews. (*Read*) Based on what you read, decide whether or not you want to buy the product. Now write about the product. (*Write*) Pretend you are writing an article for a magazine. Write a description of the product. Tell why you want (or do not want) to buy it. Next, talk about the product. (*Speak*) Record yourself as you describe it. Listen to your recording, correct your mistakes, and record yourself again. Some websites have video reviews on a product (e.g., www.cnet.com). Watch these video reviews. (*Listen*) Then choose a different kind of product and repeat the activities.

Plan a vacation

Go to www.tripadvisor.com or another travel website in English. Choose a city you would like to visit and fill in the dates for your imaginary trip. Look at the suggested hotels and read the reviews, then choose which hotel you would like to stay at. Read about the different things to do and see in the city and choose some that you are interested in. (*Read*) Now write about the city. Pretend that you are writing an article for a travel magazine and describe your imaginary trip for tourists. (*Write*) Next, give a presentation about the city. Record yourself as you describe your imaginary trip to the city. (*Speak*) Listen to your recording, correct your mistakes, and record yourself again. (*Listen*) Then choose a different city and repeat the activities.

Find out about any subject

Think of a topic you would like to know more about and look for information about it online. One place to look is http://simple.wikipedia.org/wiki/Main_Page. This website is written in simple English. Read information about your topic on this or other websites. (*Read*) Now write a short essay about your topic. (*Write*) Next, talk about your topic. Record yourself as you speak. (*Speak*) Listen to your recording, correct your mistakes, and record yourself again. (*Listen*) Then choose a different topic and repeat the activities.

Report the news

Listen to an English language news report on the radio, watch a news program on TV, or read the news in English online. (*Listen and read*) Take notes as you listen or read and use them to write a short summary of the news. (*Write*) Next, record yourself as you give a spoken summary of the news. (*Speak*) Listen to your recording, correct your mistakes, and record yourself again. Then choose a different news story and repeat the activities.

Summarize a TV show or movie

Watch a TV show or movie in English. (*Listen*) Take notes as you watch and use them to write a summary of the show or movie. (*Write*) Include your opinion. Say whether or not you liked it and why. Next, record yourself as you give a spoken summary of the show or movie. (*Speak*) Listen to your recording, correct your mistakes, and record yourself again. (*Listen*) Then watch another TV show or movie and repeat the activities.

Review a book

Read a book in English. (*Read*) Then pretend that you are writing a book review for a magazine. Write a short summary of the book and explain your opinion of it. Explain what you liked and did not like about the book and why. Compare it to other books you have read. (*Write*) Next, talk about the book. Record yourself as you give a spoken review of the book. (*Speak*) Listen to your recording, correct your mistakes, and record yourself again. (*Listen*) Then read another book and repeat the activities.

TO THE TEACHER

As a teacher, you want your students to become proficient in English, but you know your student's first goal is to score well on the TOEIC test. Fortunately, with the *Longman Preparation Series for the TOEIC® Test: Reading and Listening,* both your goals and the students' goals can be met. All activities in the Longman Preparation Series match those on the actual TOEIC test. Every practice exercise a student does prepares him or her for a similar question on the test. You do not, however, have to limit yourself to this structure. You can take the context of an item and adapt it to your own needs. I call this teaching technique "LIPP service:" Look at; Identify; Paraphrase; Personalize. LIPP service makes the students repeat the target words and ideas in a variety of ways. Repetition helps students learn English. Variety keeps them awake. Here are some examples on how LIPP service can "serve" you in your classroom for each of the seven parts of the TOEIC test.

LIPP Service Examples

PART 1: PHOTOS

L Have the students look at the photo.

I Have the students identify all the words in the photo. Have them determine who is in the photo, what they are doing, and where they are standing. If there are no people, have them determine what is in the photo and describe it.

P Have the students paraphrase the sentences they used when identifying the people or objects in the photo. This can be very simple, but it teaches the versatility and adaptability of language. For example, the students identify in the picture a man getting on the bus. Paraphrase: *A passenger is boarding the bus.* The students can also enrich the sentence by adding modifiers: *A young man is about to get on the city bus.*

P Have the students personalize their statements. Start with simple sentences such as *I am getting on the bus* and expand to short stories: *Every morning, I wait for the bus on the corner. The bus stop is between Fifth and Sixth Street on the west side of the street. There are often many people waiting for the bus, so we form a line.*

PART 2: QUESTION-RESPONSE

L Have the students listen to the question and three responses.

I Have the students identify all the words in the question and three responses. They can take dictation from the audio program or from you.

P Have the students paraphrase the question or statement they hear. *You're coming, aren't you?* can be paraphrased as *I hope you plan to come.* Options such as, *Yes, of course,* can be paraphrased as *Sure.*

P Have the students personalize their statements. The students can work in pairs and develop small dialogues: *You're coming to my house tonight, aren't you? No, I'm sorry. I have to study.*

PART 3: CONVERSATIONS

L Have the students listen to the conversations and look at the three questions and answer options in the book.

I Have the students identify all the words in the short conversations, the three written questions, and possible answers.

P Have the students paraphrase the sentences. The method is the same as for Parts 1 and 2. The students will demonstrate their understanding of the individual sentences by providing a paraphrase.

P Have the students personalize their statements. If the conversation is about dining out, the students can make up their own short conversation about a dining experience that they had. They should work in pairs or small groups for this exercise.

PART 4: TALKS

L Have the students listen to the talks and look at the question(s) and answer options in the book.

I Have the students identify all the words in the talks, the written question(s), and possible answers.

P Have the students paraphrase the sentences.

P Have the students personalize their statements. Have them work in pairs or groups to create a similar talk. Have different individuals from the same group stand and give the talk. It will be interesting to see which vocabulary and grammar patterns they choose to share.

PART 5: INCOMPLETE SENTENCES

L Have the students look at the statement and four responses.

I Have the students identify all the words in the statement and four responses.

P Have the students paraphrase the statement. They can also create sentences with the answer options that did not complete the blank in the original statement.

P Have the students personalize their statements. The students may find it difficult to find something in common with the whole statement, but they might be able to isolate one word and create some personal attachment. For example, in *Our clients are satisfied with their computer system*, your students may not have clients, but they will probably have a computer: *I am satisfied with my personal computer.*

PART 6: TEXT COMPLETION

L Have the students look at the statement and four answer options.

I Have the students identify all the words in the statement and the four answer options.

P Have the students paraphrase the statement. They can also create sentences with the answer options that did not complete the blank in the original statement.

P Have the students personalize their statements. For example, in *Our offices are modern and spacious*, your students may not work in offices, but they probably live in apartments: *My apartment is modern, but it's not very spacious.*

PART 7: READING COMPREHENSION

L Have the students look at the passage or passages.

I Have the students identify all the words in the passage(s).

P Have the students paraphrase the passage(s). If a passage is an advertisement, have them create a new advertisement for the same product. If a passage is a timetable, have them put the timetable in a different format.

P Have the students personalize the passage(s). An advertisement can be turned into a student's personal classified ad. A diary can be turned into a student's own schedule. A report can be turned into a student's essay on the same subject. With a little imagination, you can find a way to personalize almost any reading passage.

ABOUT THE TOEIC TEST

The Test of English for International Communication (TOEIC) is a multiple-choice test of English for adult, nonnative speakers of the language. The test uses the language of international business. It has two sections: Listening Comprehension and Reading.

Section	Part	Questions	Time
Listening Comprehension	Part 1 Photos	10	45 minutes
	Part 2 Question-Response	30	
	Part 3 Conversations	30	
	Part 4 Talks	30	
	TOTAL	100	
Reading	Part 5 Incomplete Sentences	40	75 minutes
	Part 6 Text Completion	12	
	Part 7 Reading Comprehension		
	• Single Passages	28	
	• Double Passages	20	
	TOTAL	100	

The TOEIC test is scored on a scale of 10 to 990. Only correct responses count toward your score. These correct responses are added and converted to a TOEIC score.

Tips for Taking the TOEIC Test

- **Be familiar with the directions before you take the exam.**
  The directions are the same on every exam. If you study the directions in this book, which are identical to those on the actual TOEIC test, you don't need to read them on the day of the exam. Instead you can study the photos, read the answer options, and take more time to answer the questions themselves.
- **Work rapidly, but carefully.**
  Train yourself to work quickly. Train yourself to be thorough.
- **Guess.**
  If you do not know the answer, guess. You are not penalized for wrong answers, and you may get it right.
- **Mark only one answer per question.**
  Any question with more than one answer blackened will be counted as wrong.
- **Use the strategies and tips that you learned in this book.**
  This book was written so you can score higher on the TOEIC test. Use these strategies and tips for success.

TOEIC TEST DIRECTIONS AND ANSWER SHEETS

General Directions

These directions are provided by the Educational Testing Service (ETS) and are reprinted here with their permission. Read them and make sure you understand them. These directions are the same on every test.

Test of English for International Communication

General Directions

This test is designed to measure your English language ability. The test is divided into two sections: Listening and Reading.

You must mark all of your answers on the separate answer sheet. For each question, you should select the best answer from the answer choices given. Then, on your answer sheet, you should find the number of the question and fill in the space that corresponds to the letter of the answer that you have selected. If you decide to change an answer, completely erase your old answer and then mark your new answer.

Specific Directions

Each part of the TOEIC test begins with specific directions for that part. In this book, you will find these directions at the beginning of each study section and in the Practice Tests. Read them and be sure you understand them.

TOEIC Test Answer Sheets

The Answer Sheets used in this book are similar to those used in the TOEIC test. The precise format of the Answer Sheets varies from test site to test site.

To record a response to a test question, find the number on the answer sheet that corresponds to the test question and make a solid mark with a pencil, filling in the space that corresponds to the letter of the answer they have chosen.

PROVEN TIPS FOR DOING WELL ON THE TEST

Scientists from many U.S. universities, such as Purdue University, University of North Texas, St. Lawrence University, University of Chicago, and Trinity College, Hartford, have conducted research on the best ways to prepare for standardized tests like the TOEIC test. Here is a summary of some of the results of their research:

1. **Take a lot of practice tests.**
   Taking a lot of practice tests will train your brain to retrieve the information it needs from your memory. It will also improve your test-taking skills.

2. **Study in a quiet place.**
   You might think that listening to music or talking to your friends will help you relax, but distractions make it more difficult to retain the information that you are studying.

3. **Review the night before the test.**
   On the night before the test, review and practice the most difficult material. This will keep it fresh in your mind.

4. **Keep your regular hours the week before the test.**
   Go to sleep and wake up at your normal time. Staying up too late or waking up too early to study can interfere with your memory.

5. **Eat right.**
   During the week leading up to the test, make sure to eat well-balanced meals with plenty of fruit and vegetables. On the morning of the test, eat a high fiber, low sugar breakfast, such as whole grain cereal. Good food will provide your brain with the energy it needs to function well.

6. **Relax.**
   Try to remove stress from your life. Before the day of the test, make sure you are very familiar with the test procedures. Know what you can bring with you and what you have to leave at home. Make sure you know how to go to the test center. If you can, go to the test center, find the room, locate the restroom, water fountains, or coffee bar. Know how to get there and how long it takes to get there.

7. **Be confident.**
   If you have studied and practiced regularly, slept well, and eaten right, then you know that you will do your best on the day of the test.

Source: Shellenbarger, Sue. "Toughest Exam Question: What Is the Best Way to Study?" *Wall Street Journal* 26 October 2011. Online.

LISTENING COMPREHENSION

In the first section of the TOEIC® test, you will be tested on how well you understand spoken English. There are four parts to this section with special directions for each part:

Part 1	Photos
Part 2	Question-Response
Part 3	Conversations
Part 4	Talks

In this part of the *Introductory Course* for the TOEIC test, you will learn strategies to help you on the Listening Comprehension section. Each part contains activities to help you practice these strategies. Each part ends with a Strategy Review consisting of questions similar to those on the TOEIC test.

NOTE: The TOEIC test directions for each part of the TOEIC test will be given at the beginning of the section. Read the directions carefully to be sure you understand them.

Part 1: Photos

These are the directions for Part 1 of the TOEIC® test. Study them now. If you understand these directions now, you will not have to read them during the test.

LISTENING TEST

In the Listening test, you will be asked to demonstrate how well you understand spoken English. The entire Listening test will last approximately 45 minutes. There are four parts, and directions are given for each part. You must mark your answers on the separate answer sheet. Do not write your answers in the test book.

PART 1

Directions: For each question in this part, you will hear four statements about a picture in your test book. When you hear the statements, you must select the one statement that best describes what you see in the picture. Then find the number of the question on your answer sheet and mark your answer. The statements will not be printed in your test book and will be spoken only one time.

Example

Sample Answer

  ● 

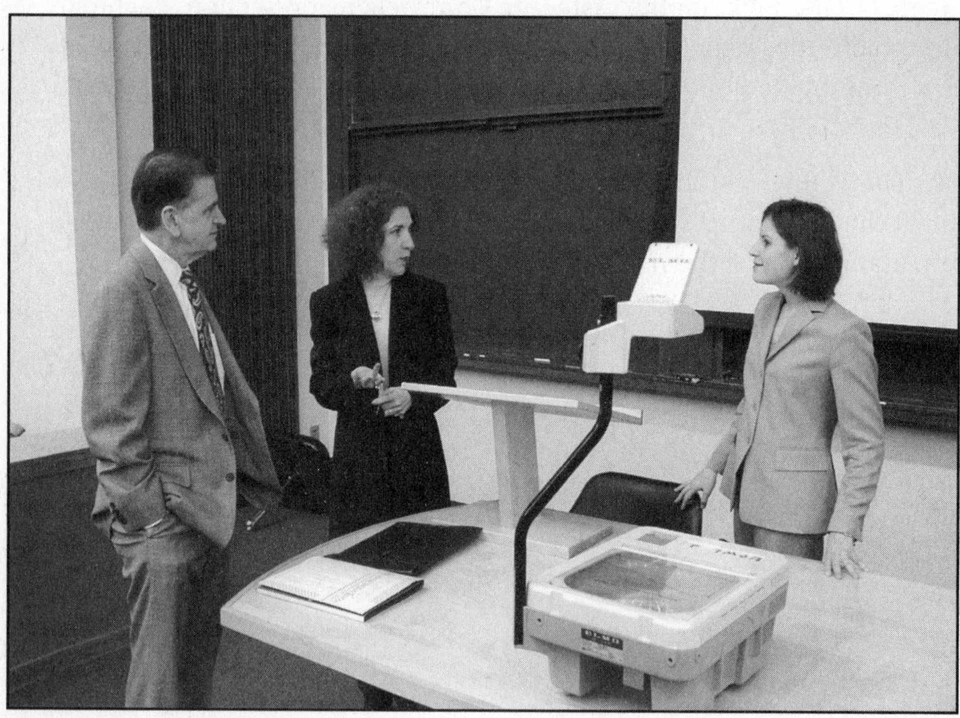

Statement (C), "They're standing near the table," is the best description of the picture, so you should select answer (C) and mark it on your answer sheet.

STRATEGY OVERVIEW

LANGUAGE STRATEGIES

In the chapter, you will learn how to look at photographs. These are two types of photographs you will see on Part 1 of the TOEIC test:

- photos of people
- photos of things

In Part 1 if you see photos of people, you will hear statements that may answer these questions about the people:

- Who are they?
- Where are they?
- What are they doing?
- What do they look like?

In Part 1 if you see photos of things, you will hear statements that may answer these questions about the things:

- What are they?
- Where are they?
- What was done to them?
- What do they look like?

TEST STRATEGIES

Some answer choices are designed to trick you. They are written to seem like the correct answer. You must learn to recognize the way the answer choices may seem correct:

- Some choices have words that sound similar to the correct answer.
- Some choices have words related to the correct answer.
- Some choices have words used in a different context.
- Some choices have incorrect details.
- Some choices make incorrect inferences.

The two examples on the following pages will help you develop test strategies to avoid answer choices that seem correct.

Example 1

(A)	The carpenter is hammering a nail.	(correct answer)
(B)	The snail is crawling up the wall.	(similar sound *snail/nail*)
(C)	The carpet is nailed to the wall.	(similar sound *carpet/carpenter; nail* and *wall* used in a different context)
(D)	The handyman is putting away his tools.	(*handyman* and *tools* related to correct answer)

Example 2

(A)	The tourist is buying some postcards.	(*tourist* used in a different context)
(B)	The passenger is checking his bags.	(incorrect inference)
(C)	The traveler is pushing his luggage ahead of him.	(incorrect detail)
(D)	The man is pulling his suitcase behind him.	(correct answer)

PHOTOS OF PEOPLE

LANGUAGE STRATEGIES

You will hear statements that may answer these questions:

- Who are they?
- Where are they?
- What are they doing?
- What do they look like?

TEST STRATEGIES

You will hear statements that may seem correct.

- Some choices have words that sound similar to the correct answer.
- Some choices have words related to the correct answer.
- Some choices have words used in a different context.
- Some choices have incorrect details.
- Some choices make incorrect inferences.

Use these strategies when you do the exercises. They will help you choose the right answer.

PHOTO 1

A. Who are the people? Look at the photo above. Make assumptions about the occupation or relationship of the people in the photo.

Write Y (Yes), N (No), or ? (Unsure) beside the following relationships or occupations.

1. _____ brother and sister

2. _____ father and son

3. _____ boss and worker

4. _____ employees

5. _____ colleagues

6. _____ workers

7. _____ clerks

8. _____ repair personnel

9. _____ landlords

10. _____ shipping agents

11. _____ dentists

12. _____ mechanic and customer

B. Where are the people? Try to determine the setting. Pay attention to the prepositions such as *next to, in front of,* and *at.*

Write Y (Yes), N (No), or ? (Unsure) beside the following locations.

1. _____ in an office
2. _____ on the job
3. _____ at home
4. _____ next to a school
5. _____ on the bus
6. _____ at work
7. _____ in the street
8. _____ in a hallway
9. _____ behind a desk
10. _____ by a work station
11. _____ in front of a window
12. _____ in a conference room

C. What are the people doing? Identify the appropriate action.

Use these words to complete the sentences:

facing giving sitting taking touching

1. The man on the right is _______________ a box from the man on the left.
2. The man on the left is _______________ a box to the man on the right.
3. Both men are _______________ one another.
4. Neither man is _______________ down.
5. Both men are _______________ the box.

D. What do the people look like? How would you describe these people?

Write Y (Yes) if the description is true. If it is not, rewrite the sentence to make it true.

1. _____ Both men are wearing jackets.

   ____

2. _____ The man on the right is wearing a tie.

   ____

3. _____ Both men are wearing glasses.

   ____

4. _____ One man has a watch on his right hand.

   ____

5. _____ There are a lot of people in the office.

   ____

6. _____ Both men are wearing dark shirts.

   ____

7. _____ The box is big and heavy.

   ____

8. _____ The man on the left is wearing a vest.

   ____

PHOTO 2

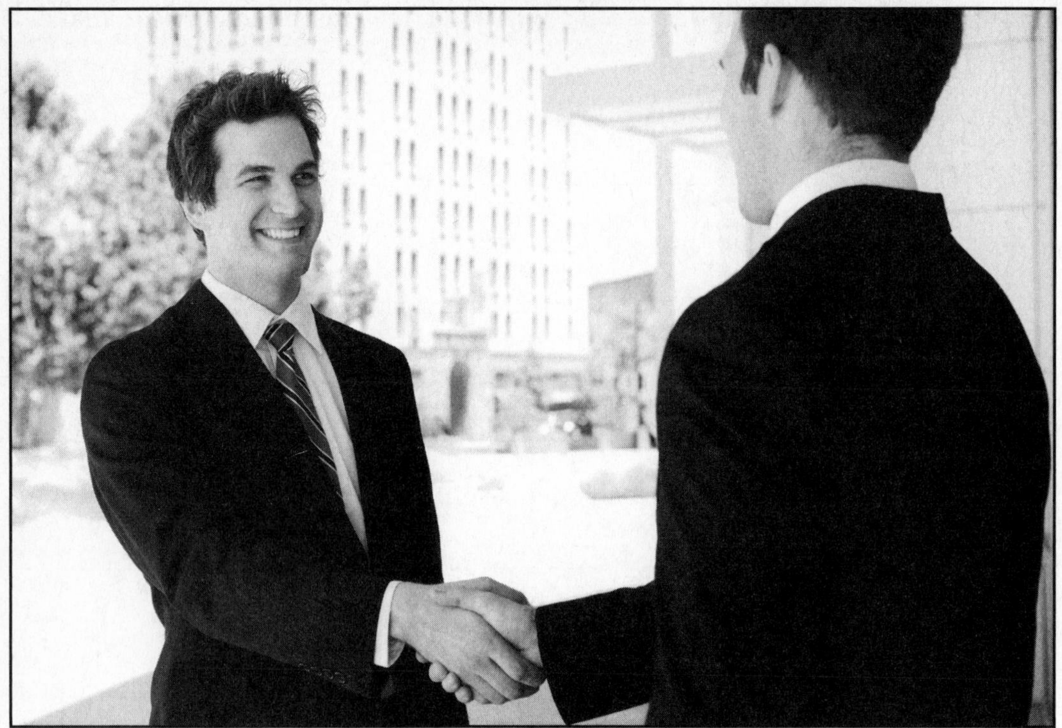

A. Who are the people? Look at the photo above. Make assumptions about the occupation or relationship of the people in the photo.

Write Y (Yes), N (No), or ? (Unsure) beside the following relationships or occupations.

1. _____ father and son
2. _____ brothers
3. _____ colleagues
4. _____ doctor and patient
5. _____ waiter and customer
6. _____ employer and employee
7. _____ political opponents
8. _____ construction managers
9. _____ architects
10. _____ service technicians
11. _____ teacher and administrator
12. _____ teacher and student

B. Where are the people? Try to determine the setting. Pay attention to the prepositions such as *next to, in front of,* and *at.*

Write Y (Yes), N (No), or ? (Unsure) beside the following locations.

1. _____ inside the building
2. _____ outside the building
3. _____ under the tree
4. _____ on the sidewalk
5. _____ in front of the window
6. _____ next to each other
7. _____ across the street from a tall building
8. _____ between the trees
9. _____ inside the door
10. _____ next to a sign
11. _____ near the building
12. _____ in the office

C. What are the people doing? Identify the appropriate action.

Use these words to complete the sentences:

shaking standing smiling looking wearing

1. Both men are __________ business clothes.
2. They are __________ at each other.
3. We can see one man's face. He is __________ at the other man.
4. The men are __________ hands with each other.
5. They are __________ outside on the sidewalk.

D. WHAT DO THE PEOPLE LOOK LIKE? How would you describe these people?

Write Y (Yes) if the description is true. If it is not, rewrite the sentence to make it true.

1. _____ Both men are wearing suits.

   ____

2. _____ Both men are wearing glasses.

   ____

3. _____ Only one man is wearing a white shirt.

   ____

4. _____ Both men have long beards.

   ____

5. _____ One man is dressed casually.

   ____

6. _____ Both men are wearing dark suits.

   ____

7. _____ One man is bald.

   ____

8. _____ One man has a handkerchief in his pocket.

   ____

PHOTO 3

A. Who are the people? Look at the photo above. Make assumptions about the occupation or relationship of the people in the photo.

Write Y (Yes), N (No), or ? (Unsure) beside the following relationships or occupations.

1. _____ husband and wife
2. _____ brothers
3. _____ construction workers
4. _____ file clerks
5. _____ lawyer and client
6. _____ metal workers
7. _____ computer technicians
8. _____ doctor and patient
9. _____ building inspectors
10. _____ assembly line workers
11. _____ circus performers
12. _____ dock hands

B. Where are the people? Try to determine the setting. Pay attention to the prepositions such as *next to, in front of,* and *at.*

Write Y (Yes), N (No), or ? (Unsure) beside the following locations.

1. _____ at a construction site
2. _____ in a basement
3. _____ on the roof
4. _____ on a girder
5. _____ at the drug store
6. _____ at the payroll office
7. _____ on a support beam
8. _____ in a clinic
9. _____ by a telephone pole
10. _____ near a bridge
11. _____ on a trolley
12. _____ around back

C. What are the people doing? Identify the appropriate action.

Use these words to complete the sentences:

constructing following holding walking watching

1. The construction workers are ______________ where they are going.
2. They are ______________ a new building.
3. They are ______________ on to a support wire.
4. One man is ______________ the other.
5. The workers are ______________ across the support beam.

D. WHAT DO THE PEOPLE LOOK LIKE? How would you describe these people?

Write Y (Yes) if the description is true. If it is not, rewrite the sentence to make it true.

1. _____ Both men are wearing hard hats.

   ____

2. _____ Both men are wearing similar construction uniforms.

   ____

3. _____ One man is not wearing shoes.

   ____

4. _____ One man is wearing gloves.

   ____

5. _____ The man in front is wearing a sport coat.

   ____

6. _____ The man behind is wearing light colored pants.

   ____

7. _____ Both men have dark hard hats.

   ____

8. _____ Both men are wearing shorts.

   ____

PHOTO 4

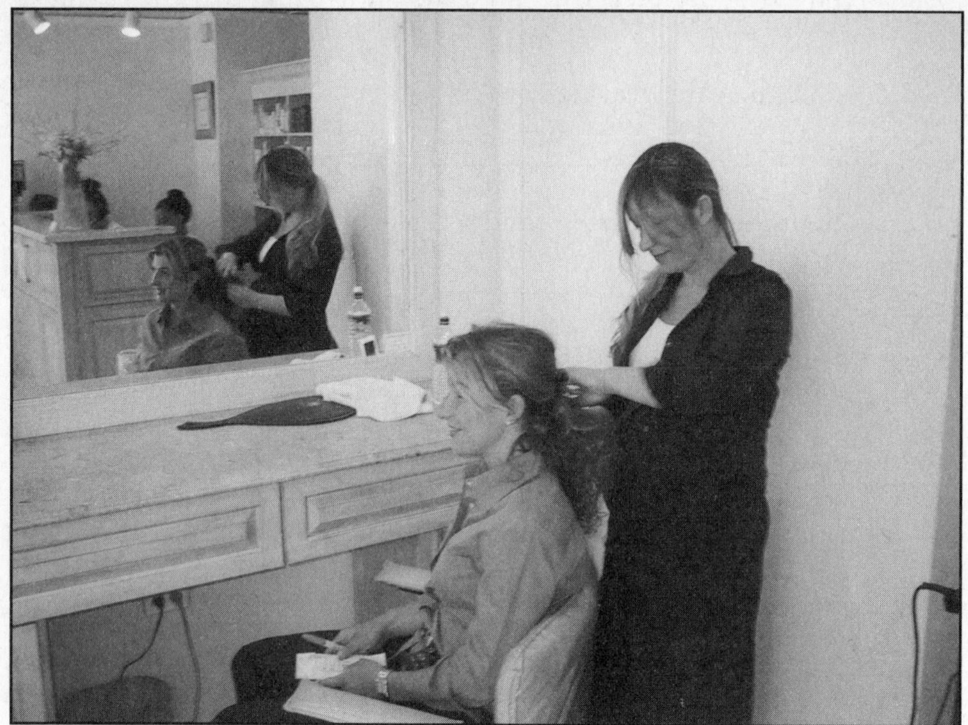

A. WHO ARE THE PEOPLE? Look at the photo above. Make assumptions about the occupation or relationship of the people in the photo.

Write Y (Yes), N (No), or ? (Unsure) beside the following relationships or occupations.

1. _____ aunt and niece
2. _____ mother and daughter
3. _____ customer and salesperson
4. _____ pharmacist and client
5. _____ doctor and patient
6. _____ TV technician and actress
7. _____ student and teacher
8. _____ security guard and electrician
9. _____ insurance salesperson and health care provider
10. _____ hairstylist and client
11. _____ strangers
12. _____ carpenter and homeowner

B. Where are the people? Try to determine the setting. Pay attention to the prepositions such as *next to, in front of, behind,* and *at.*

Write Y (Yes), N (No), or ? (Unsure) beside the following locations.

1. _____ in a chair
2. _____ behind the client
3. _____ in front of the mirror
4. _____ behind the door
5. _____ in the corner
6. _____ on top of the cabinet
7. _____ next to the shelf
8. _____ under the drawers
9. _____ beside the stylist
10. _____ at the hair salon
11. _____ inside the supermarket
12. _____ across the aisle

C. What are the people doing? Identify the appropriate action.

Use these words to complete the sentences:

having holding looking sitting styling

1. The stylist is _______________ the client's hair.
2. The client is _______________ her hair styled.
3. The woman is _______________ a pen and paper.
4. The haircutter is _______________ at her client.
5. The customer is _______________ in the chair.

D. What do the people look like? How would you describe these people?

Write Y (Yes) if the description is true. If it is not, rewrite the sentence to make it true.

1. _____ Both women are wearing white dresses.

   ____

2. _____ The stylist is wearing a dark skirt.

   ____

3. _____ Both women have hair across their eyes.

   ____

4. _____ Only one woman has long hair.

   ____

5. _____ The woman on the right is wearing a dark shirt.

   ____

6. _____ The woman on the left is wearing white pants.

   ____

7. _____ Both women are wearing glasses.

   ____

8. _____ The woman sitting down has dark hair.

   ____

PHOTOS OF THINGS

LANGUAGE STRATEGIES

You will hear statements that may answer these questions:

- What are they?
- Where are they?
- What was done to them?
- What do they look like?

TEST STRATEGIES

You will hear statements that may seem correct.

- Some choices have words that sound similar to the correct answer.
- Some choices have words related to the correct answer.
- Some choices have words used in a different context.
- Some choices have incorrect details.
- Some choices make incorrect inferences.

Use these strategies when you do the exercises. They will help you choose the right answer.

PHOTO 5

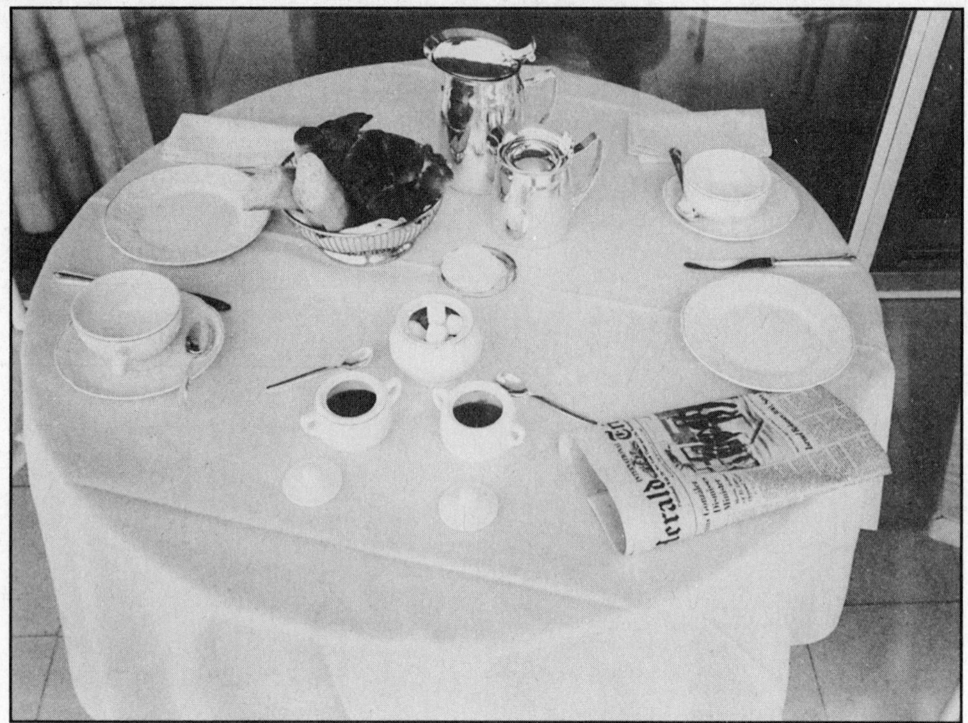

A. WHAT ARE THE THINGS? Look at the photo above. Make assumptions about what you see.

Write Y (Yes), N (No), or ? (Unsure) beside the following assumptions.

1. ______ There are flowers on the table.

2. ______ The newspaper is beside a plate.

3. ______ There are two napkins on the table.

4. ______ The coffee cups are to the left of the plates.

5. ______ There are three coffee cups.

6. ______ There is no tablecloth on the table.

7. ______ The table is set for breakfast.

8. ______ There is a basket of bread on the table.

9. ______ There are two lids on the table.

10. ______ There is a fork by the coffee cup.

11. ______ There is only one spoon on the table.

12. ______ There is a sugar bowl near the center of the table.

B. Where are the things? Pay attention to the prepositions such as *next to, in front of,* and *at.*

Write Y (Yes), N (No), or ? (Unsure) beside the following locations.

1. _____ The cups and saucers are on the table.
2. _____ The spoons are under the saucer.
3. _____ The newspaper is beside the coffeepot.
4. _____ The place settings are opposite one another.
5. _____ The bread basket is close to the newspaper.
6. _____ The sugar bowl is between two pots of jam.
7. _____ The lids are on the jam pots.
8. _____ The small pitcher is beside the large one.
9. _____ The tablecloth is beside the table.
10. _____ The knife is between the plate and the saucer.
11. _____ The napkins are both to the right of the saucers.
12. _____ The sugar bowl is near the center of the table.

C. What was done to these things?

Use these words to complete the sentences:

filled folded placed set took off

1. The ______________ newspaper is on the table.
2. Someone ______________ the lids to the jam pots.
3. The table is ______________ for breakfast.
4. The basket is ______________ with bread.
5. The spoons were ______________ on the saucers.

D. What do the things look like? How would you describe these things?

Write Y (Yes) if the description is true. If it is not, rewrite the sentence to make it true.

1. _____ The saucers are smaller than the plates.

   ____

2. _____ Both cups are the same size.

   ____

3. _____ The pitchers are the same size.

   ____

4. _____ The table is square.

   ____

5. _____ The tablecloth is a dark color.

   ____

6. _____ The bread basket is full.

   ____

7. _____ The coffee cups are empty.

   ____

8. _____ The plates are dirty.

   ____

PHOTO 6

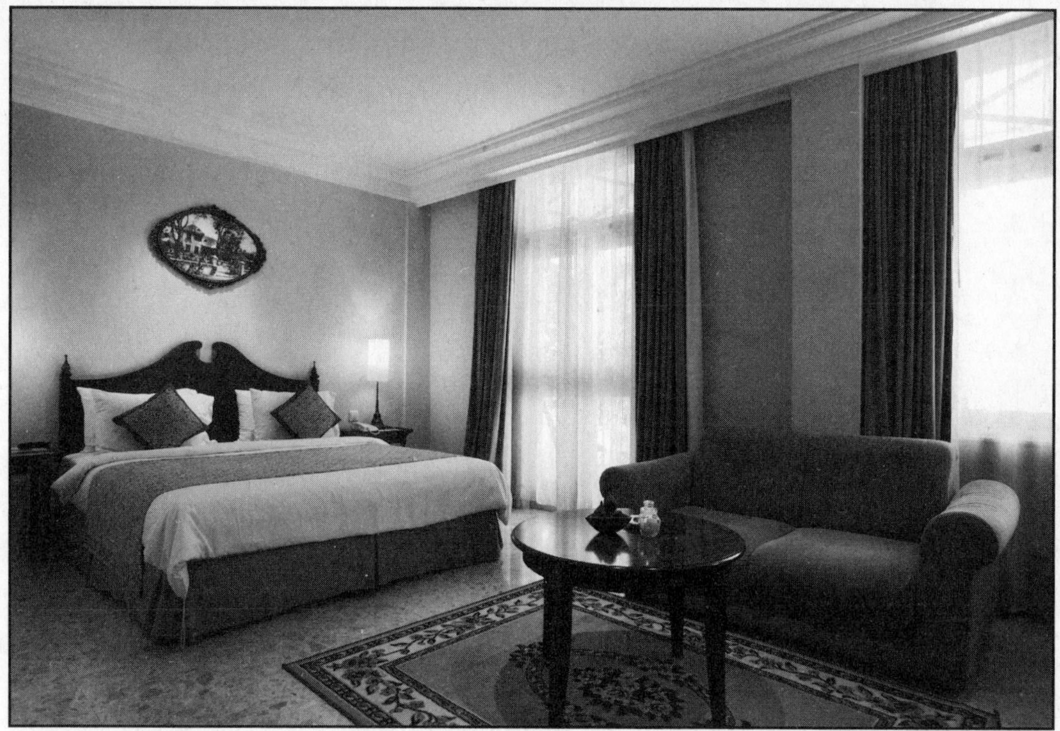

A. What are the things? Look at the photo above. Make assumptions about what you see.

Write Y (Yes), N (No), or ? (Unsure) beside the following assumptions.

1. ______ A television is in the corner.
2. ______ There are pillows on the bed.
3. ______ There is a small table in front of the sofa.
4. ______ A small rug is on the floor.
5. ______ The windows are open.
6. ______ A picture is on the wall.
7. ______ The bed is unmade.
8. ______ Someone is sitting on the sofa.
9. ______ The room has a view of the city.
10. ______ There are curtains on the windows.
11. ______ There is a floor lamp by the bed.
12. ______ There are clothes on the floor.

B. Where are the things? Pay attention to the prepositions such as *next to, in front of,* and *at.*

Write Y (Yes), N (No), or ? (Unsure) beside the following locations.

1. _____ A lamp is next to the bed.
2. _____ The picture is over the sofa.
3. _____ The rug is under the coffee table.
4. _____ The pillows are on the floor.
5. _____ The sofa is between the windows.
6. _____ The bed is behind the sofa.
7. _____ There are clothes on the sofa.
8. _____ The bed is between two small tables.
9. _____ There is a lamp hanging from the ceiling.
10. _____ A book is on the coffee table.
11. _____ The blankets are on the bed.
12. _____ The bed is near the window.

C. What was done to these things?

Use these words to complete the sentences:

washed   opened   turned on   made   placed

1. The bed was _______________ by the housekeeper.
2. The lamp was _______________ by the guests.
3. The floor was _______________ before the guests arrived.
4. The blankets were _______________ on the bed.
5. The curtains were _______________ in the morning.

D. What do the things look like? How would you describe these things?

Write Y (Yes) if the description is true. If it is not, rewrite the sentence to make it true.

1. _____ The coffee table is made of wood.

   ____

2. _____ The bed is not made.

   ____

3. _____ The rug covers the entire floor.

   ____

4. _____ The lamp is on.

   ____

5. _____ The sofa has arms.

   ____

6. _____ The windows are tall.

   ____

7. _____ The sofa can seat six people comfortably.

   ____

8. _____ The curtains are covered with a bright design.

   ____

PHOTO 7

A. What are the things? Look at the photo above. Make assumptions about what you see.

Write Y (Yes), N (No), or ? (Unsure) beside the following assumptions.

1. _____ Two bicycles are parked outside.

2. _____ There are flowers on the tree branches.

3. _____ The tree has many leaves.

4. _____ The tree is near a building.

5. _____ The building is an apartment building.

6. _____ The door is open.

7. _____ The bicycles belong to two sisters.

8. _____ One bicycle is much smaller than the other.

9. _____ It's a rainy day.

10. _____ The bicycles have baskets.

11. _____ There are curtains in some of the windows.

12. _____ The ground is covered with grass.

B. Where are the things? Pay attention to the prepositions such as *next to, in front of,* and *at.*

Write Y (Yes), N (No), or ? (Unsure) beside the following locations.

1. _____ The bicycles are parked next to each other.
2. _____ The door is between two windows.
3. _____ The bicycles are in front of the door.
4. _____ The bicycles are inside a garage.
5. _____ The baskets are in back of the bicycles.
6. _____ There are windows over the door.
7. _____ The bicycles are under the tree.
8. _____ The tree is beside the door.
9. _____ There are flowers in the windows.
10. _____ There is a streetlamp in front of a window.
11. _____ There are flowers next to the door.
12. _____ There is a sidewalk in front of the building.

C. What was done to these things?

Use these words to complete the sentences:

hanging leaning attached left closed

1. The bicycles are _______________ against the tree.
2. The windows are _______________.
3. The baskets are _______________ to the bicycles.
4. The curtains are _______________ in the windows.
5. The bicycles were _______________ outside.

D. WHAT DO THE THINGS LOOK LIKE? How would you describe these things?

Write Y (Yes) if the description is true. If it is not, rewrite the sentence to make it true.

1. _____ The windows are different styles.

   ____

2. _____ The road is a dirt road.

   ____

3. _____ The street is crowded with people.

   ____

4. _____ The bicycles are child-sized.

   ____

5. _____ The bicycles look similar to each other.

   ____

6. _____ The building is one story high.

   ____

7. _____ The building is made of bricks.

   ____

8. _____ The bicycles are dark in color.

   ____

PHOTO 8

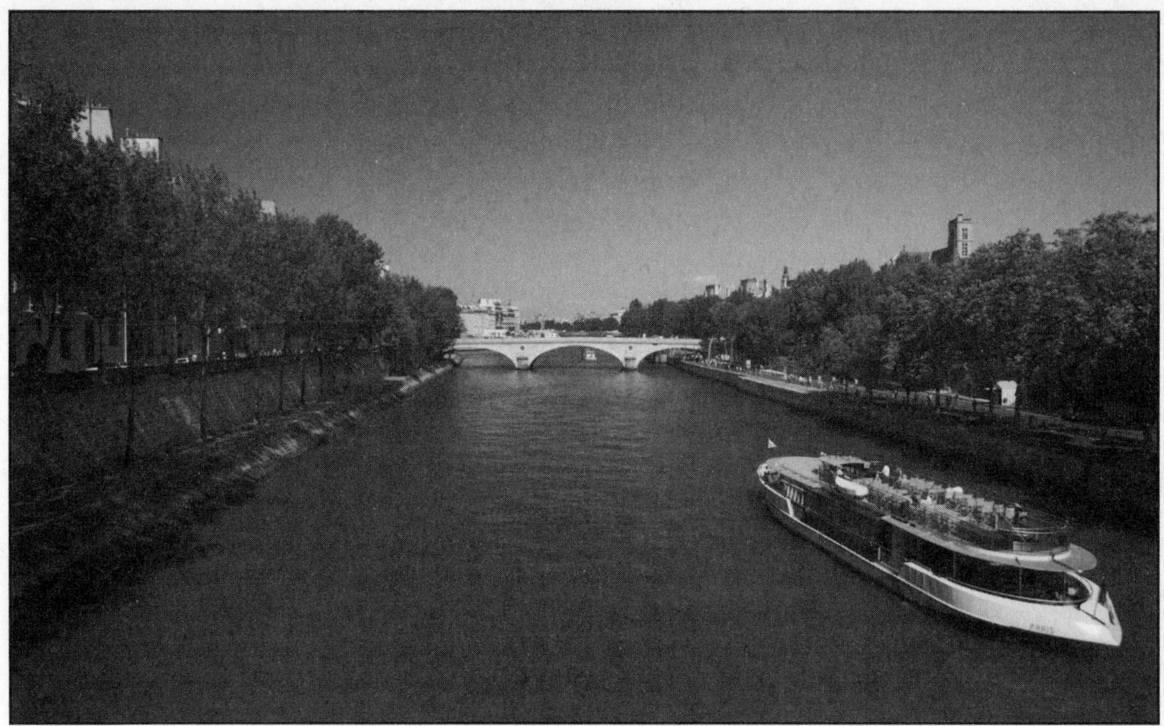

A. WHAT ARE THE THINGS? Look at the photo above. Make assumptions about what you see.

Write Y (Yes), N (No), or ? (Unsure) beside the following assumptions.

1. _____ There is a bridge across a river.

2. _____ There is a parking lot beside the river.

3. _____ A boat is traveling in the river.

4. _____ There are a lot of passengers in the boat.

5. _____ The river is lined with trees on both sides.

6. _____ People are swimming in the water.

7. _____ There are a lot of cars on the bridge.

8. _____ Some of the buildings are taller than the trees.

9. _____ There aren't any clouds in the sky.

10. _____ The water is very deep.

11. _____ The river runs through a city.

12. _____ The boat is moving very fast.

B. Where are the things? Pay attention to the prepositions such as *next to, in front of,* and *under.*

Write Y (Yes), N (No), or ? (Unsure) beside the following locations.

1. _____ The river passes under the bridge.
2. _____ The trees are between the river and the buildings.
3. _____ There is a small park to the right of the river.
4. _____ There are buildings beyond the bridge.
5. _____ There are buildings behind the trees.
6. _____ The boat is under the bridge.
7. _____ There are no buildings on the left side of the river.
8. _____ The boat is next to a tall building.
9. _____ The bridge is in front of the boat.
10. _____ The boat is under a tree.
11. _____ The boat is near the right side of the river.
12. _____ The bridge is in the distance.

C. What was done to these things?

Use these words to complete the sentences:

moves planted painted separates built

1. Trees were ______________ along the river.
2. Houses were ______________ near the river.
3. A wall ______________ the river from the street.
4. The boat ______________ down the river.
5. The boat was ______________ white.

D. What do the things look like? How would you describe these things?

Write Y (Yes) if the description is true. If it is not, rewrite the sentence to make it true.

1. _____ The bridge has three arches.

   ____

2. _____ The leaves have fallen off the trees.

   ____

3. _____ The river is straight.

   ____

4. _____ The boat has several large sails.

   ____

5. _____ There are big waves in the river.

   ____

6. _____ The bow of the boat is pointed.

   ____

7. _____ The river is crowded with boats.

   ____

8. _____ It's a rainy day.

   ____

GRAMMAR TIP

Same Sound, Different Meaning

Be careful of words that sound the same but have different meanings and different grammatical functions.

Word	Meaning
there	in that place
they're	contraction of *they are*
their	belonging to them

There are glasses on the table.
They're waiting for us.
Their car is in the driveway.

VOCABULARY TIP

Jobs

Listen for words that identify a person by occupation or activity. When you add *-er* to a verb, you form a noun that names a person's job. An *-er* noun refers to a person who does a particular thing.

Verb	Noun	Definition
paint	painter	a person who paints
speak	speaker	a person who speaks
work	worker	a person who works

The *painters* are painting the walls blue.
Mary is a good *worker*.
The *speaker* is standing at the front of the room.

STRATEGY REVIEW

Language Strategies

In the exercises for Part 1, you learned what to ask yourself when analyzing a photo. Knowing what to ask yourself will help you choose the right answer.

For photos of people, ask yourself:

- Who are they?
- Where are they?
- What are they doing?
- What do they look like?

For photos of things, ask yourself:

- What are they?
- Where are they?
- What was done to them?
- What do they look like?

Test Strategies

In the exercises for Part 1, you saw and heard how certain answer choices try to confuse you.

Knowing the ways these choices seem correct will help you choose the right answer.

- Some choices have words that sound similar to the correct answer.
- Some choices have words related to the correct answer.
- Some choices have words used in a different context.
- Some choices have incorrect details.
- Some choices make incorrect inferences.

STRATEGY PRACTICE

DIRECTIONS: Look at these photos and listen to the four statements. Choose the statement that most closely matches the photo. Listen again and see if you can recognize how an answer choice tries to confuse you.

1. Ⓐ Ⓑ Ⓒ Ⓓ

2. Ⓐ Ⓑ Ⓒ Ⓓ

3. Ⓐ Ⓑ Ⓒ Ⓓ

4. Ⓐ Ⓑ Ⓒ Ⓓ

5. (A) (B) (C) (D)

6. (A) (B) (C) (D)

7. (A) (B) (C) (D)

8. (A) (B) (C) (D)

9. (A) (B) (C) (D)

10. (A) (B) (C) (D)

PART 2: QUESTION-RESPONSE

These are the directions for Part 2 of the TOEIC® test. Study them now. If you understand these directions now, you will not have to read them during the test.

PART 2

Directions: You will hear a question or statement and three responses spoken in English. They will not be printed in your test book and will be spoken only one time. Select the best response to the question or statement and mark the letter (A), (B), or (C) on your answer sheet.

Sample Answer

Example

You will hear: Where is the meeting room?

You will also hear: (A) To meet the new director.
(B) It's the first room on the right.
(C) Yes, at two o'clock.

Your best response to the question "Where is the meeting room?" is choice (B), "It's the first room on the right," so (B) is the correct answer. You should mark answer (B) on your answer sheet.

STRATEGY OVERVIEW

LANGUAGE STRATEGIES

In this chapter, you will learn how certain words will help you identify the purpose of a question. These are the purposes you will learn about:

- identifying time
- identifying people
- identifying an opinion
- identifying a choice
- identifying a suggestion
- identifying a reason
- identifying a location

The words you will learn in this chapter will help you develop strategies to choose the correct answer.

TEST STRATEGIES

In Part 2, like in Part 1, some answer choices are designed to trick you. They are written to seem like the correct answer. You must learn to recognize the way the answer choices may seem correct:

- Some choices have words that sound similar to the correct answer.
- Some choices have words related to the correct answer.
- Some choices have words used in a different context.
- Some choices use an incorrect verb tense or person.
- Some choices are an inappropriate response to the type of question.

Look at these examples:

Example 1

Mrs. Smith is never late for her meetings.

(A) He is always on time. (incorrect person)
(B) Her meeting is running late. (words used in a different context)
(C) She's very punctual. (correct answer)

Example 2

Are you hiring an assistant or a secretary?

(A) I need both. (correct answer)
(B) Yes, I am. (inappropriate response to an "*or*" question)
(C) I was hired yesterday. (incorrect verb tense)

Example 3

How can I get to the train station from here?

(A) The radio station is a block away. (word used in a different context)
(B) You can take the A-4 bus. (correct answer)
(C) The plane leaves in ten minutes. (words that sound similar)

IDENTIFYING TIME

You will hear questions or statements about time. Some questions will begin with *When* or *How long*. Others will be *yes/no* questions. The answer to a *yes/no* question is sometimes a statement without *yes* or *no*.

Example 1

When did she leave for work?
(A) About an hour ago.
(B) It doesn't work.
(C) As soon as he's ready.

The correct answer is (A). Choice (B) tries to confuse you by repeating the word *work*. Choice (C) tries to confuse you by changing the tense to present and the person to *he*.

Example 2

Haven't you filled out the application yet?
(A) They filled the jet with fuel.
(B) I've been too busy.
(C) I applied it over the surface.

The correct answer is (B). The *no* is implied in the response. The person was too busy to take the time to complete the application. Choice (A) tries to confuse you by repeating the word *filled* and using the similar-sounding word *jet* for *yet*. Choice (C) tries to confuse you by using *applied* with a different meaning.

Example 3

We'll leave at 5, so try to be on time.
(A) That leaves five of us.
(B) I'm never late. I'll be there at 4:59.
(C) The plane is on time.

The correct answer is (B). The speaker suggests that the listener will not be on time, but the listener responds that he/she is never late and will in fact be there one minute early. Choice (A) tries to confuse you by repeating the word *leave* but with a different meaning. The word *five* is repeated, but here it means *people* not *time of day*. Choice (C) repeats the phrase *on time* but in a different context.

These are some words you might hear in questions about time:

when	on time
early	at 1:00, 2:30 . . .
late	morning, noon, afternoon, evening, night
how long	yesterday, last week, last month, last year
what time	today, this week, this month, this year
yet	tomorrow, next week, next month, next year
still	

Practice: Identifying Time

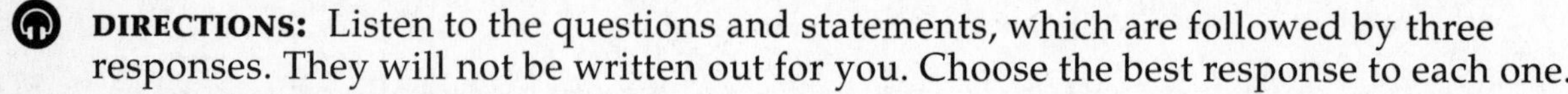

DIRECTIONS: Listen to the questions and statements, which are followed by three responses. They will not be written out for you. Choose the best response to each one.

1. Ⓐ Ⓑ Ⓒ
2. Ⓐ Ⓑ Ⓒ
3. Ⓐ Ⓑ Ⓒ
4. Ⓐ Ⓑ Ⓒ
5. Ⓐ Ⓑ Ⓒ
6. Ⓐ Ⓑ Ⓒ
7. Ⓐ Ⓑ Ⓒ
8. Ⓐ Ⓑ Ⓒ
9. Ⓐ Ⓑ Ⓒ
10. Ⓐ Ⓑ Ⓒ

IDENTIFYING PEOPLE

You will hear questions or statements about people. Some questions will begin with *Who* or *Whose.* Others will be *yes/no* questions. The answer to a *yes/no* question is sometimes a statement without *yes* or *no.*

Example 1

Who's responsible for making the bank deposits?
(A) Ms. Rotelli always makes the deposits.
(B) We'll send our response soon.
(C) We use the National Bank.

The correct answer is (A). Choice (B) tries to confuse you with the similar-sounding word *response* for *responsible.* Choice (C) tries to confuse you by repeating the word *bank.*

Example 2

Are you in charge of this project?
(A) No, they only charged us 100 dollars.
(B) No, Mrs. Ono is the supervisor.
(C) No, it's not very large.

The correct answer is (B). Choice (A) tries to confuse you by using *charged* but with a different meaning. Choice (C) tries to confuse you with the similar-sounding word *large* for *charge.*

Example 3

I called the contractor to repair the leak.
(A) You should have called a plumber.
(B) His contract is due next week.
(C) The telephone repair person contacted me.

The correct answer is (A). A plumber can repair a leaking pipe. Choice (B) tries to confuse you by using the word *contract* with a different meaning and using the similar-sounding word *week* for *leak.* Choice (C) tries to confuse you by using the associated word *telephone* for *called* and the similar-sounding word *contacted* for *contractor.* The word *repair* is repeated.

These are some words you might hear in questions about people:

who
whose
who's
name
an occupation title *(barber, plumber, teacher)*

Practice: Identifying People

DIRECTIONS: Listen to the questions and statements, which are followed by three responses. They will not be written out for you. Choose the best response to each one.

1. Ⓐ Ⓑ Ⓒ
2. Ⓐ Ⓑ Ⓒ
3. Ⓐ Ⓑ Ⓒ
4. Ⓐ Ⓑ Ⓒ
5. Ⓐ Ⓑ Ⓒ
6. Ⓐ Ⓑ Ⓒ
7. Ⓐ Ⓑ Ⓒ
8. Ⓐ Ⓑ Ⓒ
9. Ⓐ Ⓑ Ⓒ
10. Ⓐ Ⓑ Ⓒ

IDENTIFYING AN OPINION

You will hear questions or statements about someone's opinion. Some questions will begin with *What* or *How*. Others will be *yes/no* questions. The answer to a *yes/no* question is sometimes a statement without *yes* or *no*.

Example 1

What did you think of the movie?
(A) I liked it a lot.
(B) I saw it yesterday.
(C) I moved the furniture myself.

The correct answer is (A). Choice (B) tries to confuse you by giving an inappropriate response to an opinion question. Choice (C) tries to confuse you with the similar-sounding word *moved* for *movie*.

Example 2

Do you think we need to hire more people?
(A) Yes, I'd like to hear more about it.
(B) Yes, we need a few more employees.
(C) Yes, prices are getting higher.

The correct answer is (B). Choice (A) tries to confuse you with the similar-sounding word *hear* for *hire*. Choice (C) tries to confuse you with *higher*, which sounds the same as *hire*.

Example 3

I loved this book.
(A) I like to cook, too.
(B) Book me a ticket, please.
(C) I didn't think it was so great.

The correct answer is (C). The listener does not agree with the speaker. Choice (A) uses the associated word *like* for *love* and the similar-sounding word *cook* for *book*. Choice (B) repeats the word *book* but with a different meaning and as a verb, not a noun.

These are some words you might hear in questions about an opinion:

what	believe
how	your opinion
why	like/didn't like
because	love
think	

Practice: Identifying an Opinion

DIRECTIONS: Listen to the questions and statements, which are followed by three responses. They will not be written out for you. Choose the best response to each one.

1. (A) (B) (C)
2. (A) (B) (C)
3. (A) (B) (C)
4. (A) (B) (C)
5. (A) (B) (C)
6. (A) (B) (C)
7. (A) (B) (C)
8. (A) (B) (C)
9. (A) (B) (C)
10. (A) (B) (C)

IDENTIFYING A CHOICE

You will hear questions or statements that give someone a choice. Some questions will begin with *What* or other *wh*-question words. Others will be *yes/no* questions. The answer to a *yes/no* question is sometimes a statement without *yes* or *no.* These questions usually will have two choices joined by *or.*

Example 1

Which does that author write more of, poems or essays?
(A) She almost always writes poems.
(B) I read those poems yesterday.
(C) She owns two homes.

The correct answer is (A). Choice (B) tries to confuse you by repeating the word *poems.* Choice (C) tries to confuse you with the similar-sounding word *homes* for *poems.*

Example 2

Do you prefer yellow or blue?
(A) Yes, I do.
(B) He's a very nice fellow.
(C) Blue's my favorite color.

The correct answer is (C). Choice (A) tries to confuse you by giving an inappropriate response to a choice question. Choice (C) tries to confuse you with the similar-sounding word *fellow* for *yellow.*

Example 3

I can't decide between the morning flight or the afternoon one.
(A) We took a ride yesterday afternoon.
(B) Go before noon. It's less crowded.
(C) There are more flies at noon.

The correct answer is (B). The listener gives the speaker a reason to choose the morning flight. Choice (A) tries to confuse you by using the similar-sounding word *ride* for *decide.* Choice (C) uses the similar-sounding words *more* for *morning, flies* for *flight,* and *noon* for *afternoon.*

These are some words you might hear in questions that give someone a choice:

what
which
or
prefer
rather

Practice: Identifying a Choice

DIRECTIONS: Listen to the questions and statements, which are followed by three responses. They will not be written out for you. Choose the best response to each one.

1. (A) (B) (C)
2. (A) (B) (C)
3. (A) (B) (C)
4. (A) (B) (C)
5. (A) (B) (C)
6. (A) (B) (C)
7. (A) (B) (C)
8. (A) (B) (C)
9. (A) (B) (C)
10. (A) (B) (C)

IDENTIFYING A SUGGESTION

You will hear questions or statements that give a suggestion. Some questions will begin with *Why* or *Let's.* Others will be *yes/no* questions. The answer to a *yes/no* question is sometimes a statement without *yes* or *no.* Most of the questions that give a suggestion are *yes/no* questions.

Example 1

Why don't we take a break?
(A) That sounds like a good idea.
(B) It didn't break.
(C) This is very good cake.

The correct answer is (A). Choice (B) tries to confuse you by using the word *break* with a different meaning. Choice (C) tries to confuse you by using the similar-sounding word *cake* for *break.*

Example 2

Can I get you something to eat?
(A) Yes, I picked up something.
(B) Thank you. That's very kind of you.
(C) We ate everything on the table.

The correct answer is (B). Choices (A) and (C) try to confuse you by incorrectly answering a present tense question with a past tense answer.

Example 3

Let's not take a taxi.
(A) Yes, I'd rather walk.
(B) The tax is included.
(C) I wrote a note to Tashi.

The correct answer is (A). The speaker made the suggestion not to take a taxi and the listener agreed. Choice (B) tries to confuse you by using the similar-sounding word *tax* for *taxi.* Choice (C) tries to confuse you by using the similar-sounding phrase *note to* with *not take* and *taxi* with *Tashi.*

These are some words you might hear in questions giving a suggestion:

why don't we	how about
why don't you	should
let's	ought to
what about	

Practice: Identifying a Suggestion

DIRECTIONS: Listen to the questions and statements, which are followed by three responses. They will not be written out for you. Choose the best response to each one.

1. (A) (B) (C)
2. (A) (B) (C)
3. (A) (B) (C)
4. (A) (B) (C)
5. (A) (B) (C)
6. (A) (B) (C)
7. (A) (B) (C)
8. (A) (B) (C)
9. (A) (B) (C)
10. (A) (B) (C)

IDENTIFYING A REASON

You will hear questions that ask for a reason or statements that give a reason. Some questions will begin with *Why.* Others will be *yes/no* questions. The answer to a *yes/no* question is sometimes a statement without *yes* or *no.*

Example 1

Why didn't you make the dinner reservation?
(A) I reserved my hotel room.
(B) I eat dinner at six.
(C) I forgot the name of the restaurant.

The correct answer is (C). Choice (A) tries to confuse you by using the word *reserved* in a different context. Choice (B) tries to confuse you by repeating the word *dinner.*

Example 2

Aren't you working late again tonight?
(A) No, I have to go home early.
(B) I left at eight o'clock.
(C) Wait until tomorrow night.

The correct answer is (A). Choice (B) tries to confuse you by answering incorrectly with the past tense. Choice (C) tries to confuse you by using the similar-sounding words *wait* for *late* and *night* for *tonight.*

Example 3

I can't drive without my glasses.
(A) Can you dive, but not swim?
(B) The glasses are full of water.
(C) And I don't have a license.

The correct answer is (C). The reason the speaker can't drive is he doesn't have his eyeglasses. The listener can't drive because he doesn't have a driver's license. Choice (A) uses the similar-sounding word *dive* for *drive.* Choice (B) uses *water glasses* instead of *eyeglasses.*

These are some words you might hear in questions asking for a reason:

why
why didn't
excuse
reason

Practice: Identifying a Reason

DIRECTIONS: Listen to the questions and statements, which are followed by three responses. They will not be written out for you. Choose the best response to each one.

1. Ⓐ Ⓑ Ⓒ
2. Ⓐ Ⓑ Ⓒ
3. Ⓐ Ⓑ Ⓒ
4. Ⓐ Ⓑ Ⓒ
5. Ⓐ Ⓑ Ⓒ
6. Ⓐ Ⓑ Ⓒ
7. Ⓐ Ⓑ Ⓒ
8. Ⓐ Ⓑ Ⓒ
9. Ⓐ Ⓑ Ⓒ
10. Ⓐ Ⓑ Ⓒ

IDENTIFYING A LOCATION

You will hear questions or statements about a location. Some questions will begin with *What* or *Where.* Others will be *yes/no* questions. The answer to a *yes/no* question is sometimes a statement without *yes* or *no.*

Example 1

What about moving the desk next to the door?

(A) There isn't enough room.
(B) I didn't open the door.
(C) He's next in line.

The correct answer is (A). Choices (B) and (C) try to confuse you by repeating the words *door* and *next.*

Example 2

Can you tell me how to get to the post office?

(A) OK, I'll wait in your office.
(B) Yes, get me some stamps.
(C) Sure. Go to the corner and take a right.

The correct answer is (C). Choice (A) tries to confuse you by repeating the word *office.* Choice (B) tries to confuse you by using the word *get* but with a different meaning.

Example 3

I left my pen on your desk.

(A) My dogs are in the pen.
(B) I put it in the drawer.
(C) No, I left at eleven.

The correct answer is (B). The location of the pen moved from the desk to the desk drawer. Choice (A) repeats *pen* but with a different meaning. Choice (C) repeats the word *left* with a different meaning and uses the similar-sounding word *eleven* for *pen.*

These are some words you might hear in questions asking about a location.

what	near
where	far
how far	by
next to	behind
beside	right
under	left
over	names of places
at	

Practice: Identifying a Location

DIRECTIONS: Listen to the questions and statements, which are followed by three responses. They will not be written out for you. Choose the best response to each one.

1. Ⓐ Ⓑ Ⓒ
2. Ⓐ Ⓑ Ⓒ
3. Ⓐ Ⓑ Ⓒ
4. Ⓐ Ⓑ Ⓒ
5. Ⓐ Ⓑ Ⓒ
6. Ⓐ Ⓑ Ⓒ
7. Ⓐ Ⓑ Ⓒ
8. Ⓐ Ⓑ Ⓒ
9. Ⓐ Ⓑ Ⓒ
10. Ⓐ Ⓑ Ⓒ

GRAMMAR TIP

Whose* vs. *Who

In Part 2, you may hear questions with *whose* or *who*. These questions require different types of answers.

Whose is a question about possession. It asks about the owner of something. It requires a possessive word in the answer. The possessive can be a pronoun or a noun with *'s/s'*.

Who is a question about a person's identity. It requires a person's name or occupation in the answer.

Question: *Whose* office is this?
Answer: It's *John's* office.
Question: *Who* is that woman?
Answer: She's the new *accountant*.

VOCABULARY TIP

Expressions with *Make*

Expressions with *make* are common in conversation. Here are some that you may hear:

- make an appointment
- make a phone call
- make money
- make noise
- make friends
- make a suggestion
- make an effort
- make a complaint
- make a mistake

I'd like to *make an appointment* to see the doctor.
Please don't *make noise*. We're trying to work.
He's looking for a new job because he wants to *make more money*.

STRATEGY REVIEW

Language Strategies

In the exercises for Part 2, you learned how certain words would help you identify the purpose of a question. Knowing these words will help you choose the right answer. Listen for words that identify:

- time, such as *when, how long, what time,* etc.
- people, such as *who, whose, who's,* etc.
- an opinion, such as *what, how, why,* etc.
- a choice, such as *what, which, or,* etc.
- a suggestion, such as *why don't we, let's, what about,* etc.
- a reason, such as *why don't we, excuse, reason,* etc.
- a location, such as *what, where, how far,* etc.

Test Strategies

In the exercises for Part 2, you saw how certain answer choices try to confuse you. Here are the ways that choices may seem correct to you.

- Some choices have words that sound similar to the correct answer.
- Some choices have words related to the correct answer.
- Some choices have words used in a different context.
- Some choices use an incorrect verb tense or person.
- Some choices are an inappropriate response to the type of question.

STRATEGY PRACTICE

DIRECTIONS: Listen to the questions and statements, which are followed by three responses. They will not be written out for you. Choose the best response to each one. Listen again and see if you can recognize how a choice tries to confuse you.

1. (A) (B) (C)
2. (A) (B) (C)
3. (A) (B) (C)
4. (A) (B) (C)
5. (A) (B) (C)
6. (A) (B) (C)
7. (A) (B) (C)
8. (A) (B) (C)
9. (A) (B) (C)
10. (A) (B) (C)
11. (A) (B) (C)
12. (A) (B) (C)
13. (A) (B) (C)
14. (A) (B) (C)
15. (A) (B) (C)
16. (A) (B) (C)
17. (A) (B) (C)
18. (A) (B) (C)
19. (A) (B) (C)
20. (A) (B) (C)

Part 3: Conversations

These are the directions for Part 3 of the TOEIC® test. Study them now. If you understand these directions now, you will not have to read them during the test.

PART 3

Directions: You will hear some conversations between two people. You will be asked to answer three questions about what the speakers say in each conversation. Select the best response to each question and mark the letter (A), (B), (C), or (D) on your answer sheet. The conversations will not be printed in your test book and will be spoken only one time.

STRATEGY OVERVIEW

LANGUAGE STRATEGIES

In this chapter, you will learn how certain words will help you identify the purpose of a question. These are the purposes you will learn about:

- identifying time
- identifying people
- identifying intent
- identifying the topic
- identifying a reason
- identifying a location
- identifying an opinion
- identifying stress and tone

The words you will learn in this chapter will help you develop strategies to choose the correct answer.

TEST STRATEGIES

In Part 3, like in Parts 1 and 2, some answer choices are designed to trick you. They are written to seem like the correct answer. You must learn to recognize the way the answer choices may seem correct:

- Some choices have words that sound similar to the correct answer.
- Some choices have words like the correct answer, but with a different meaning.
- Some choices have words used in a different context.

- Some choices have incorrect details.
- Some choices make incorrect inferences.
- Some choices have irrelevant details.

Look at these examples:

Example 1

SPEAKER A: The prices at this restaurant are low, but the food's always cold.
SPEAKER B: I know, and the people who work here aren't very friendly.
SPEAKER A: Let's eat somewhere else.

What do they say about the restaurant?

(A)	The people are friendly.	(incorrect detail)
(B)	The prices are low.	(correct answer)
(C)	The food is old.	(sounds like correct answer)
(D)	The service is slow.	(sounds like correct answer)

Example 2

SPEAKER A: I'd like to book a flight to Santiago.
SPEAKER B: Certainly. When would you like to fly?
SPEAKER A: Next Monday. Can you make a hotel reservation for me, also?

What is Speaker B's occupation?

(A)	Travel agent.	(correct answer)
(B)	Pilot.	(incorrect inference)
(C)	Hotel manager.	(incorrect detail)
(D)	Librarian.	(incorrect inference)

Example 3

SPEAKER A: How's your accounting class, Marvin?
SPEAKER B: The teacher's interesting, but the work is really hard.
SPEAKER A: Well, at least you're not bored.

What does Marvin say about his class?

(A)	It's boring.	(incorrect detail)
(B)	The chairs are hard.	(word used in a different context)
(C)	There's too much work.	(incorrect detail)
(D)	The teacher is interesting.	(correct answer)

IMPORTANT NOTE:

This chapter focuses on learning strategies for Part 3 of the TOEIC. In this chapter there is only one question for each conversation. This one question focuses on a particular strategy. The Strategy Review at the end of this chapter has three questions for each conversation just like the TOEIC.

IDENTIFYING TIME

On the TOEIC test, one of the three questions for a conversation may ask about time. For example:

When will he go?
How often does she come?
How long will they stay?

> **TIP**
>
> Read the questions and the answer choices quickly ***before*** you listen to the conversation. When you listen to the conversation, listen for answers to the questions about time.

Example 1

SPEAKER A: You're expecting Jeff Tuesday morning, right?
SPEAKER B: No, he won't be here tomorrow. Not until the day after.
SPEAKER A: At least he'll be here for Wednesday night's reception.

When is Jeff coming to visit? Ⓐ Ⓑ Ⓒ Ⓓ
(A) Today.
(B) Tomorrow.
(C) Tuesday.
(D) Wednesday.

The correct answer is (D). Tomorrow is Tuesday, and he is coming the day after on Wednesday. Choice (A) tries to confuse you with the similar sounding word *today* for *day*. Choice (B) is mentioned as the day he is NOT coming. Choice (C) is the original day he was to have come, but he is not coming on Tuesday.

Example 2

SPEAKER A: Is this a daily or a weekly newsletter?
SPEAKER B: Neither. It's a monthly.
SPEAKER A: Once every four weeks. That's enough time to read it.

How often does the newsletter come out? Ⓐ Ⓑ Ⓒ Ⓓ
(A) Every day.
(B) Once a week.
(C) Once every other week.
(D) Once a month.

The correct answer is (D). The newsletter is a monthly. It is delivered once a month. Choice (A) means *daily*, which is mentioned, but Speaker B says it's not a daily. Choice

(B) means *weekly*, which is mentioned, but Speaker B says it is not a weekly. Choice (C) is incorrect because it says *every other week.*

Look for these words in a question that asks about time:

when
how often
how soon
how long ago
what time

Practice: Identifying Time

DIRECTIONS: Listen to the conversation and then choose the statement that best answers the question.

1. When did the package arrive? (A) (B) (C) (D)
(A) This morning.
(B) Two days ago.
(C) Last Tuesday.
(D) On Friday.

2. How long ago did the speakers visit Paris? (A) (B) (C) (D)
(A) A month ago.
(B) Two months ago.
(C) A year ago.
(D) Eight years ago.

3. When will Mark start his new job? (A) (B) (C) (D)
(A) This afternoon.
(B) On Monday.
(C) In eight days.
(D) In two weeks.

4. How often does the woman travel to Tokyo? (A) (B) (C) (D)
(A) Once a month.
(B) Four times a month.
(C) Once a year.
(D) Four times a year.

5. How soon will the contract be ready? (A) (B) (C) (D)
(A) By morning.
(B) By this afternoon.
(C) In three days.
(D) In nine days.

6. How long ago did the man buy the cell phone? Ⓐ Ⓑ Ⓒ Ⓓ
   (A) A week ago.
   (B) Three weeks ago.
   (C) A year ago.
   (D) Five years ago.

7. When will the conference take place? Ⓐ Ⓑ Ⓒ Ⓓ
   (A) This afternoon.
   (B) Tomorrow.
   (C) On Friday.
   (D) Next month.

8. How often does Tim order office supplies? Ⓐ Ⓑ Ⓒ Ⓓ
   (A) Every two days.
   (B) Once a week.
   (C) Every ten days.
   (D) Once a month.

9. How soon will the car be ready? Ⓐ Ⓑ Ⓒ Ⓓ
   (A) This afternoon.
   (B) Tomorrow.
   (C) The day after tomorrow.
   (D) On Friday.

10. How long has the woman been waiting? Ⓐ Ⓑ Ⓒ Ⓓ
   (A) Ten minutes.
   (B) Fifteen minutes.
   (C) Thirty minutes.
   (D) Forty minutes.

IDENTIFYING PEOPLE

On the TOEIC test, one of the three questions for a conversation may ask about people and their occupations. For example:

Who are the speakers?
What is his job?

> **TIP**
>
> Read the questions and the answer choices quickly ***before*** you listen to the conversation. When you listen to the conversation, listen for answers to the questions about people.

Example 1

SPEAKER A: I've made your hotel reservations and reconfirmed your flights.
SPEAKER B: What about transfers from the airport to the hotel?
SPEAKER A: I can get you a car and driver, or you could take a taxi.

What is the first speaker's occupation? Ⓐ Ⓑ Ⓒ Ⓓ
(A) A chauffeur.
(B) A hotel clerk.
(C) A flight attendant.
(D) A travel agent.

The correct answer is (D). Choice (A) is associated with *car and driver,* which is mentioned in a different context in the conversation. Choice (B) is associated with *hotel reservations.* Choice (C) is associated with *flights.*

Example 2

SPEAKER A: Laura, can you help me figure out how many chairs we need for the seminar?
SPEAKER B: You should direct all your questions to John. He's the one in charge of this event.
SPEAKER A: Sorry. I just thought since you're the office manager, you would know.

Who is responsible for organizing the event? Ⓐ Ⓑ Ⓒ Ⓓ
(A) Laura.
(B) The director.
(C) John.
(D) The office manager.

The correct answer is (C). Choice (A) mentions *Laura,* but she says she is not in charge. Choice (B) tries to confuse you with the similar-sounding word *director* for *direct.* Choice (D) is Laura's occupation, and she has said she is not in charge.

Look for these words in a question that asks about people:

who
whom*
whose
job
name

*rarely used on the TOEIC test

Practice: Identifying People

DIRECTIONS: Listen to the conversation and then choose the statement that best answers the question.

1. Who received a promotion? Ⓐ Ⓑ Ⓒ Ⓓ
(A) Only Pat.
(B) Only Sam.
(C) Both Sam and Jim.
(D) Sam, Jim, and Pat.

2. What is Ms. Fujita's job? Ⓐ Ⓑ Ⓒ Ⓓ
(A) She's the director.
(B) She's the accountant.
(C) She's the director's assistant.
(D) She's the accountant's assistant.

3. Who is the man talking to? Ⓐ Ⓑ Ⓒ Ⓓ
(A) A waitress.
(B) A grocery store clerk.
(C) A friend.
(D) A specialist.

4. Who left the telephone message? Ⓐ Ⓑ Ⓒ Ⓓ
(A) An accountant.
(B) A painter.
(C) A telephone operator.
(D) An office manager.

5. Whose office is at the end of the hall? Ⓐ Ⓑ Ⓒ Ⓓ
(A) Cindy's boss's office.
(B) Cindy's office.
(C) John's boss's office.
(D) John's office.

6. What is the new accountant's name? (A) (B) (C) (D)

(A) Bill.

(B) Bob.

(C) Mr. Wilson.

(D) Mrs. Ortega.

7. What is Frank's profession? (A) (B) (C) (D)

(A) He's a lawyer.

(B) He's an economist.

(C) He's a student.

(D) He's a professor.

8. Who is in the hospital? (A) (B) (C) (D)

(A) Marsha.

(B) Jim.

(C) Linda.

(D) Jim's wife.

9. Whose car is parked by the front door? (A) (B) (C) (D)

(A) Martin's car.

(B) Sandy's car.

(C) The secretary's car.

(D) The director's car.

10. What is the woman's job? (A) (B) (C) (D)

(A) She's a bank teller.

(B) She's a police officer.

(C) She's a bus driver.

(D) She's a mail carrier.

IDENTIFYING INTENT

On the TOEIC test, one of the three questions for a conversation may ask about a person's intent to do something. For example:

What will she do?
What does she plan on buying?

> **TIP**
>
> Read the questions and the answer choices quickly ***before*** you listen to the conversation. When you listen to the conversation, listen for answers to the questions about intent.

Example 1

SPEAKER A: I'm going to the electronics store after lunch. Do you want to go?
SPEAKER B: Sure. Are you getting something for your computer?
SPEAKER A: No, I just need to pick up a new battery for my phone.

What does Speaker A want to purchase? Ⓐ Ⓑ Ⓒ Ⓓ
(A) Food.
(B) A computer.
(C) A battery.
(D) A phone.

The correct answer is (C). Choice (A) uses the word *food,* which is associated with *lunch* but isn't what she's going to buy. Choice (B), *computer,* is mentioned in *something for your computer,* but she says that's not what she will buy. Choice (D), *phone,* is mentioned, but it is the battery, not the phone itself, that she will buy.

Example 2

SPEAKER A: Could you answer the phone for me this afternoon?
SPEAKER B: Of course. Are you going to be in a meeting?
SPEAKER A: No, I have to leave a little early to get to the bank before it closes.

What does she want to do? Ⓐ Ⓑ Ⓒ Ⓓ
(A) Buy clothes.
(B) Go to the bank.
(C) Go to a meeting.
(D) Answer the phones.

The correct answer is (B). Choice (A) tries to confuse you with the similar-sounding word *clothes* for *closes.* Choice (C), *go to a meeting,* is mentioned, but she says that she isn't going to do that. Choice (D) is what she asks her colleague to do.

Look for these words in a question that asks about intent:

plan
going to
will
probably

Practice: Identifying Intent

DIRECTIONS: Listen to the conversation and then choose the statement that best answers the question.

1. What do the speakers plan to do this Sunday? Ⓐ Ⓑ Ⓒ Ⓓ
(A) Watch a baseball game.
(B) See a movie.
(C) Go to a concert.
(D) Visit the capital.

2. What will the man probably do? Ⓐ Ⓑ Ⓒ Ⓓ
(A) Buy a new rug.
(B) Buy new furniture.
(C) Paint the old furniture.
(D) Get another office.

3. What is the woman going to do? Ⓐ Ⓑ Ⓒ Ⓓ
(A) Eat a pizza.
(B) Pick up her office.
(C) Put things in order.
(D) Make a delivery.

4. What will the man probably have? Ⓐ Ⓑ Ⓒ Ⓓ
(A) Some ice cream.
(B) Some hot tea.
(C) Some cold cuts.
(D) Some iced tea.

5. What form of transportation will the speakers use? Ⓐ Ⓑ Ⓒ Ⓓ
(A) Train.
(B) Walking.
(C) Bus.
(D) Cab.

6. How will the woman pay? Ⓐ Ⓑ Ⓒ Ⓓ
(A) With a money order.
(B) With a credit card.
(C) With cash.
(D) With a check.

7. What will the woman probably do? Ⓐ Ⓑ Ⓒ Ⓓ
   (A) Turn off the air-conditioning.
   (B) Open the window.
   (C) Turn on the air-conditioning.
   (D) Close the window.

8. What will the man do? Ⓐ Ⓑ Ⓒ Ⓓ
   (A) Buy a new machine.
   (B) Fix the old machine.
   (C) Plug the machine in.
   (D) Use his coworker's machine.

9. What does the woman want to do? Ⓐ Ⓑ Ⓒ Ⓓ
   (A) Look at the movie schedule.
   (B) Borrow some paper.
   (C) Read the news.
   (D) Buy a newspaper.

10. What will the woman probably buy? Ⓐ Ⓑ Ⓒ Ⓓ
   (A) A sweater.
   (B) A skirt.
   (C) A suit.
   (D) A dress.

IDENTIFYING THE TOPIC

On the TOEIC test, one of the three questions for a conversation may ask about the topic. For example:

What are they talking about?
What is the problem?

TIP

Read the questions and the answer choices quickly ***before*** you listen to the conversation. When you listen to the conversation, listen for answers to the questions about the topic.

Example 1

SPEAKER A: Would you like more coffee?
SPEAKER B: No! This coffee tastes terrible. Is the machine broken again?
SPEAKER A: No, I think it's just dirty. No one ever cleans it.

What is the problem? Ⓐ Ⓑ Ⓒ Ⓓ

(A) The coffee is cold.
(B) The machine is dirty.
(C) The machine is broken.
(D) There isn't any more coffee.

The correct answer is (B). Choice (A) repeats the word *coffee,* but the problem with the coffee is its taste, not its temperature. Choice (C) is mentioned as a possibility but is not the problem. Choice (D) tries to confuse you by repeating the word *more.*

Example 2

SPEAKER A: Give me your number and I'll call you later.
Speaker B: OK. It's 555-1331.
Speaker A: Is that home or office?

What are they discussing? Ⓐ Ⓑ Ⓒ Ⓓ

(A) A telephone number.
(B) An address.
(C) A letter.
(D) An office.

The correct answer is (A). Choice (B) uses *address,* which is associated with *home.* Choice (C) tries to confuse you with the similar-sounding word *letter* for *later.* Choice (D) tries to confuse you by repeating the word *office.*

Look for these words in a question that asks about the topic:

talking about
discussing
about

Practice: Identifying the Topic

DIRECTIONS: Listen to the conversation and then choose the statement that best answers the question.

1. What is wrong with the car? Ⓐ Ⓑ Ⓒ Ⓓ

(A) It has broken glass.
(B) It has a flat tire.
(C) It doesn't run fast.
(D) It's out of gas.

2. What are the speakers talking about? Ⓐ Ⓑ Ⓒ Ⓓ
   (A) A cake.
   (B) Some steak.
   (C) A diet.
   (D) The cook.

3. What is the problem with the restaurant? Ⓐ Ⓑ Ⓒ Ⓓ
   (A) It doesn't look nice.
   (B) It's too far away.
   (C) The service isn't good.
   (D) The food is bad.

4. What are the speakers discussing? Ⓐ Ⓑ Ⓒ Ⓓ
   (A) Airplane tickets.
   (B) Movie tickets.
   (C) A hotel reservation.
   (D) Books.

5. What is the lecture about? Ⓐ Ⓑ Ⓒ Ⓓ
   (A) How to speak in public.
   (B) How to save money.
   (C) How to buy a house.
   (D) How to live without a lot of money.

6. What are the speakers talking about? Ⓐ Ⓑ Ⓒ Ⓓ
   (A) Going to the movies.
   (B) A TV show.
   (C) Eating dinner.
   (D) A snowstorm.

7. What is the problem with the hamburger? Ⓐ Ⓑ Ⓒ Ⓓ
   (A) It doesn't taste good.
   (B) It's still in the kitchen.
   (C) It's undercooked.
   (D) It's burnt.

8. What are the speakers talking about? Ⓐ Ⓑ Ⓒ Ⓓ
   (A) Photocopy paper.
   (B) Money.
   (C) The newspaper.
   (D) Furniture.

9. What is the book about? (A) (B) (C) (D)

(A) Earning money.
(B) Managing your finances.
(C) Finding a job.
(D) Organizing your time.

10. What are the speakers discussing? (A) (B) (C) (D)

(A) Going to work.
(B) Going to a party.
(C) Going out for dinner.
(D) Going out for a drink.

IDENTIFYING A REASON

On the TOEIC test, one of the three questions for a conversation may ask about a reason for doing something. For example:

Why is he going?
Why is she speaking softly?

> **TIP**
>
> Read the questions and the answer choices quickly ***before*** you listen to the conversation. When you listen to the conversation, listen for answers to the questions about the reason.

Example 1

SPEAKER A: Maria, I hear you're moving away. Did you get a new job?
SPEAKER B: No, I'm going back to school. I'm going to get a degree in economics.
SPEAKER A: Oh, yes. I hear the university in that city is very good.

Why is Maria moving to a new city? (A) (B)  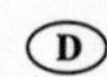

(A) Because she got a new job.
(B) Because she wants to study at the university.
(C) Because the economy is bad.
(D) Because her old city isn't very good.

The correct answer is (B). Choice (A) repeats the words *a new job,* but Maria says that is not the reason she is moving. Choice (C) tries to confuse you by using the word *economy,* which is similar to *economics.* Choice (D) tries to confuse you by repeating the words *very good* in a different context.

Example 2

SPEAKER A: Look how late it is. I'll never get to the meeting on time.
SPEAKER B: Well, here comes the bus now, so you're on your way.
SPEAKER A: I'm still going to be late.

Why is Speaker A upset? Ⓐ Ⓑ Ⓒ Ⓓ
(A) It's time to go home.
(B) He forgot to eat.
(C) He has to take the bus.
(D) He's going to arrive late.

The correct answer is (D). Choice (A) tries to confuse you by using the word *time* in a different context. Choice (B) tries to confuse you by using the similar-sounding word *eat* for *meeting*. Choice (C), *take the bus,* is mentioned, but it is not the reason that Speaker A is upset.

Look for this word in a question that asks about a reason:

why

Practice: Identifying a Reason

DIRECTIONS: Listen to the conversation and then choose the statement that best answers the question.

1. Why are there no chairs? Ⓐ Ⓑ Ⓒ Ⓓ
(A) The chairs haven't been ordered yet.
(B) Nobody wants to sit down.
(C) The chairs haven't arrived yet.
(D) People prefer to sit on the floor.

2. Why will the man call the woman? Ⓐ Ⓑ Ⓒ Ⓓ
(A) Because he needs some help.
(B) To invite her to dinner.
(C) Because he's bored.
(D) To arrange a meeting.

3. Why is the woman going to Hawaii? Ⓐ Ⓑ Ⓒ Ⓓ
(A) To spend her vacation.
(B) To buy new clothes.
(C) To attend a conference.
(D) To visit friends.

4. Why did the woman arrive late? Ⓐ Ⓑ Ⓒ Ⓓ
   (A) She was in an accident.
   (B) She had a flat tire.
   (C) She felt tired.
   (D) She was waiting for someone.

5. Why is the window closed? Ⓐ Ⓑ Ⓒ Ⓓ
   (A) It's cool outside.
   (B) The air-conditioning is on.
   (C) The room isn't warm enough.
   (D) The street is very noisy.

6. Why doesn't the man want to take the elevator? Ⓐ Ⓑ Ⓒ Ⓓ
   (A) The elevator is slow.
   (B) They're going down.
   (C) It's late.
   (D) He likes to walk.

7. Why is the man staying late at the office? Ⓐ Ⓑ Ⓒ Ⓓ
   (A) He has to finish his work.
   (B) He's expecting a phone call.
   (C) He has a day off tomorrow.
   (D) He isn't tired.

8. Why isn't the meeting in the conference room? Ⓐ Ⓑ Ⓒ Ⓓ
   (A) There aren't enough chairs.
   (B) It isn't big enough.
   (C) The office is more comfortable.
   (D) It's being painted.

9. Why does the woman suggest taking the subway? Ⓐ Ⓑ Ⓒ Ⓓ
   (A) The office is close.
   (B) A car is too fast.
   (C) Traffic is heavy.
   (D) It's late.

10. Why didn't the man eat lunch? Ⓐ Ⓑ Ⓒ Ⓓ
    (A) He forgot to eat.
    (B) He wasn't hungry.
    (C) He got to the cafeteria too late.
    (D) He didn't have time.

IDENTIFYING A LOCATION

On the TOEIC test, one of the three questions for a conversation may ask about the location. For example:

Where are the speakers?
Where is the hotel?

> **TIP**
>
> Read the questions and the answer choices quickly ***before*** you listen to the conversation. When you listen to the conversation, listen for answers to the questions about the location.

Example 1

SPEAKER A: Are you going up?
SPEAKER B: Yes. Which floor do you want?
SPEAKER A: The fourth floor, please. I'm going to Dr. Roberts' office.

Where does this conversation take place? Ⓐ Ⓑ Ⓒ Ⓓ
(A) In an airplane.
(B) In an elevator.
(C) In a flower shop.
(D) In a doctor's office.

The correct answer is (B). Choice (A), *in an airplane,* is associated with *going up.* Choice (C) tries to confuse you by using the similar-sounding word *flower* for *floor.* Choice (D) repeats the words *doctor's office,* but that is where the speaker is going.

Example 2

SPEAKER A: Do you still have those books about art museums that I lent you?
SPEAKER B: Yes, but not here in the office. They're at home.
SPEAKER A: I really need them back soon. I have to return them to the library.

Where are the books now? Ⓐ Ⓑ Ⓒ Ⓓ
(A) At an art museum.
(B) In the office.
(C) At home.
(D) In the library.

The correct answer is (C). Choice (A) is mentioned as the topic of the books, not their location. Choice (B) is mentioned as a place where the books are not. Choice (C) is the place where the speaker will take the books.

Look for this word in a question that asks about location:

where

Practice: Identifying a Location

DIRECTIONS: Listen to the conversation and then choose the statement that best answers the question.

1. Where will the speakers get together? (A) (B) (C) (D)

(A) Downstairs.
(B) At the park.
(C) At the office.
(D) At a café.

2. Where are the speakers? (A) (B) (C) (D)

(A) At a train station.
(B) At a bus stop.
(C) At a swimming pool.
(D) At an airport.

3. Where does the conversation take place? (A) (B) (C) (D)

(A) In a hotel.
(B) At an airport.
(C) In a parking garage.
(D) At a store.

4. Where did the man leave his phone? (A) (B) (C) (D)

(A) In the office.
(B) At a restaurant.
(C) In a cab.
(D) On a bus.

5. Where will the man wait? (A) (B) (C) (D)

(A) Upstairs.
(B) By the front door.
(C) Outside.
(D) Near the elevator.

6. Where does this conversation take place? (A) (B) (C) (D)

(A) On a bus.
(B) In a cab.
(C) At a fair.
(D) In a store.

7. Where are the speakers? (A) (B) (C) (D)
   (A) In a grocery store.
   (B) In a restaurant.
   (C) In a kitchen.
   (D) On an airplane.

8. Where are the speakers going? (A) (B) (C) (D)
   (A) To a bookstore.
   (B) To the library.
   (C) To school.
   (D) To the police station.

9. Where does this conversation take place? (A) (B) (C) (D)
   (A) In Los Angeles.
   (B) At an airport.
   (C) At a travel agency.
   (D) On an airplane.

10. Where are the speakers? (A) (B) (C) (D)
   (A) In an office.
   (B) In a gym.
   (C) In a garage.
   (D) In a park.

IDENTIFYING AN OPINION

On the TOEIC test, one of the three questions for a conversation may ask about a speaker's opinion. For example:

What is her opinion about cooking?
What does the speaker think about soccer?

TIP

Read the questions and the answer choices quickly ***before*** you listen to the conversation. When you listen to the conversation, listen for answers to the questions about an opinion.

Example 1

SPEAKER A: I think I'll like working with the new manager. He's very efficient.
SPEAKER B: I agree with you, Max. And he's friendly, too.
SPEAKER A: I'm sure he's the most experienced person in this office.

What is Max's opinion of the manager? 

(A) He's agreeable.
(B) He's friendly.
(C) He's efficient.
(D) He's inexperienced.

The correct answer is (C). Choice (A) tries to confuse you by using *agreeable,* related to but different in meaning from *agree.* Choice (B) is the opinion of Max's friend. Choice (D) sounds similar to what Max said but actually has the opposite meaning.

Example 2

SPEAKER A: What a movie. I've never laughed so hard.
SPEAKER B: It really was awfully funny.
SPEAKER A: I just love movies like that.

What is said about the movie?  

(A) It was hard to understand.
(B) It was funny.
(C) It was awful.
(D) It was about love.

The correct answer is (B). Choices (A), (C), and (D) try to confuse you by using the words *hard, awful,* and *love* but with different meanings.

Look for these words in a question that asks about an opinion:

think of
opinion
say about
believe

Practice: Identifying an Opinion

DIRECTIONS: Listen to the conversation and then choose the statement that best answers the question.

1. What does the man think of the bus?  
   (A) It's inconvenient.
   (B) It's relaxing.
   (C) It's too expensive.
   (D) It's fast.

2. What do the speakers say about Bob? (A) (B) (C) (D)
   (A) His work is good.
   (B) He's improving.
   (C) He talks too much.
   (D) He isn't doing a good job.

3. What is the speakers' opinion of the hotel? (A) (B) (C) (D)
   (A) It's nice.
   (B) It isn't comfortable.
   (C) It's too big.
   (D) Its service could be better.

4. What do the speakers think of the weather? (A) (B) (C) (D)
   (A) It's too warm.
   (B) There's too much snow.
   (C) It rains a lot.
   (D) It's too cold.

5. What do the speakers say about TV? (A) (B) (C) (D)
   (A) It's boring.
   (B) There aren't many programs.
   (C) It's funny.
   (D) The programs are good.

6. What is the woman's opinion of the lecture? (A) (B) (C) (D)
   (A) It wasn't enjoyable.
   (B) It was terrible.
   (C) It was interesting.
   (D) It wasn't long enough.

7. What does José say about his job? (A) (B) (C) (D)
   (A) It's important.
   (B) It's too far away.
   (C) It's difficult.
   (D) It's like his old job.

8. What does Sally think of her Spanish class? (A) (B) (C) (D)
   (A) She thinks it's too hard.
   (B) She likes it.
   (C) She thinks it's very easy.
   (D) She's having fun.

9. What do the speakers say about Bill? (A) (B) (C) (D)
   (A) He's lazy.
   (B) He's sick today.
   (C) He's usually late.
   (D) He's usually right.

10. What does the man think of the pizza? (A) (B) (C) (D)

(A) It's not very good.
(B) It's delicious.
(C) It's terrible.
(D) It's too greasy.

IDENTIFYING STRESS AND TONE

On the TOEIC test you will hear conversations where the speakers use tone or stress to indicate what they mean.

A statement can become a question if it is said with rising intonation.

Statement You're going to work early.

Question You're going to work early?

A statement spoken with rising intonation can mean (1) *Are you going to work early?* or (2) *Why are you going to work early?*

Intonation can be used to convey the speaker's feeling about something. *I love pizza* said with sarcastic intonation means *I hate pizza.*

Stress is used to emphasize the important part of a statement. In a sentence emphasized as: *I ate <u>ten</u> cookies,* the important information is the amount of cookies eaten (ten cookies, not five cookies). If the noun is emphasized as: *I ate ten <u>cookies</u>,* the important information is what was eaten (cookies, rather than sandwiches).

Example 1

> **TIP**
>
> Read the questions and the answer choices quickly ***before*** you listen to the conversation. When you listen to the conversation, listen for the meaning conveyed by the intonation and stress.

SPEAKER A: You didn't like this movie?
SPEAKER B: I really like war movies. (said with intonation of disgust)
SPEAKER A: I always thought you preferred them over comedies.

What does the second speaker think about war movies? (A) (B) (C) (D)

(A) She hasn't seen one.
(B) She likes them a lot.
(C) She prefers comedies.
(D) She hates them.

The correct answer is (D). *I really like war movies* said with an intonation of disgust really means that the speaker does not like war movies.

Example 2

SPEAKER A: While you're out, will you get me a ten-cent stamp?
SPEAKER B: Ten stamps. Sure. What denomination?
SPEAKER A: No, <u>one</u> stamp, worth ten cents.

What does the first speaker want? Ⓐ Ⓑ Ⓒ Ⓓ

(A) Ten cents.
(B) Ten stamps.
(C) One ten-cent stamp.
(D) A one-cent stamp.

The correct answer is (C). The stress on the word *one* in the last line makes it clear that that is the number of stamps she wants.

Practice: Identifying Stress and Tone

DIRECTIONS: Listen to the conversation and then choose the statement that best answers the question.

1. What is the problem? Ⓐ Ⓑ Ⓒ Ⓓ
   (A) The repair person is tired.
   (B) The machine is broken.
   (C) They can't turn the machine on.
   (D) The machine is downstairs.

2. Why is the woman surprised? Ⓐ Ⓑ Ⓒ Ⓓ
   (A) She's paying for dinner.
   (B) The man is offering to treat.
   (C) They're going out to eat.
   (D) The man is picking up the food.

3. What did the woman do last night? Ⓐ Ⓑ Ⓒ Ⓓ
   (A) She went home.
   (B) She slept.
   (C) She stayed at the office.
   (D) She went to a restaurant.

4. What does the woman like to eat? Ⓐ Ⓑ Ⓒ Ⓓ
   (A) Chicken.
   (B) Ham.
   (C) Fish.
   (D) Hamburgers.

5. What did the man think of the meeting? (A) (B) (C) (D)
   (A) It was informative.
   (B) It was a waste of time.
   (C) It was interesting.
   (D) It was useful.

6. What is the man going to do? (A) (B) (C) (D)
   (A) Cash a check.
   (B) Call the bank.
   (C) Count his money.
   (D) Go to the bank.

7. What does the man want to do? (A) (B) (C) (D)
   (A) Cook.
   (B) Stay inside.
   (C) Watch TV.
   (D) Go to a soccer game.

8. What does the woman think of the restaurant? (A) (B) (C) (D)
   (A) The food is delicious.
   (B) It's a popular place.
   (C) The food isn't good.
   (D) The prices aren't high.

9. What does the man think of the job? (A) (B) (C) (D)
   (A) It's a bad job.
   (B) It could be better.
   (C) It's a great job.
   (D) It could be more interesting.

10. What did the man do? (A) (B) (C) (D)
   (A) He left the office.
   (B) He finished his work.
   (C) He had some coffee.
   (D) He continued working.

GRAMMAR TIP

Talking About the Future

Listen for time expressions. Sometimes the simple present tense is used to express future ideas, especially when talking about a schedule.

Our flight *leaves* at noon tomorrow.
The conference *takes* place next July.
The movie *starts* at 6:30 tonight.

VOCABULARY TIP

Two-word Verbs with *Back*

Two-word verbs with *back* are quite common in conversation. They usually mean *return*.

Verb	Meaning
be back	return to a place
call back	return a phone call
pay back	return money
fly back	return to a place by plane

I'm going to London tomorrow, but I'll *be back* next week.
Tell Mr. Kim that I'm going to *call back* later.
I can *pay* you *back* the $100 that you lent me next month.
They *flew back* to Tokyo last night.

STRATEGY REVIEW

Language Strategies

In the exercises for Part 3, you learned how certain words would help you identify the purpose of a question. Knowing these words will help you choose the right answer. Listen for words that identify:

- time, such as *when, how long, what time,* etc.
- people, such as *who, whose,* etc.
- intent, such as *plan, going to, will,* etc.
- the topic, such as *talking about, discussing, about,* etc.
- a reason, such as *why*
- a location, such as *where*
- an opinion, such as *think of, opinion, say about, believe,* etc.

Remember to listen for tone and stress to identify meaning.

Test Strategies

In the exercises for Part 3, you saw how certain answer choices try to confuse you. Here are the ways that choices may seem correct to you.

- Some choices have words that sound similar to the correct answer.
- Some choices have words like the correct answer, but with a different meaning.
- Some choices have words used in a different context.
- Some choices have incorrect details.
- Some choices make incorrect inferences.
- Some choices have irrelevant details.

STRATEGY PRACTICE

DIRECTIONS: Listen to the conversations. You will answer three questions about each conversation. Choose the best answer to each question. Listen again and see if you can recognize how a choice tries to confuse you.

1. How long have the speakers been waiting? Ⓐ Ⓑ Ⓒ Ⓓ
(A) Two minutes.
(B) Fifteen minutes.
(C) Fifty minutes.
(D) Sixty minutes.

2. What are they buying? Ⓐ Ⓑ Ⓒ Ⓓ
(A) Shirts.
(B) Skirts.
(C) Shorts.
(D) Wallets.

3. What will they use to pay for their purchases? Ⓐ Ⓑ Ⓒ Ⓓ
(A) Money order.
(B) Credit card.
(C) Check.
(D) Cash.

4. According to the man, where will the speakers spend their vacation? Ⓐ Ⓑ Ⓒ Ⓓ
   (A) At a friend's house.
   (B) At a beach.
   (C) At a lake.
   (D) At a club.

5. What does the man want to do during his vacation? Ⓐ Ⓑ Ⓒ Ⓓ
   (A) Visit a club.
   (B) Go fishing.
   (C) Swim.
   (D) Rest.

6. How will they get there? Ⓐ Ⓑ Ⓒ Ⓓ
   (A) By car.
   (B) By bus.
   (C) By train.
   (D) By plane.

---

7. Why did Tina miss the meeting? Ⓐ Ⓑ Ⓒ Ⓓ
   (A) She was sick.
   (B) She arrived too late.
   (C) She had an accident.
   (D) Her car wouldn't start.

8. What does the woman want to discuss with Tina? Ⓐ Ⓑ Ⓒ Ⓓ
   (A) A news report.
   (B) A budget report.
   (C) A traffic report.
   (D) A weather report.

9. What time does the woman want to see Tina? Ⓐ Ⓑ Ⓒ Ⓓ
   (A) 2:00.
   (B) 7:00.
   (C) 8:00.
   (D) 11:00.

---

10. Where is the woman's new job? Ⓐ Ⓑ Ⓒ Ⓓ
   (A) At a pool.
   (B) At a school.
   (C) At an office.
   (D) At a hospital.

11. How does the woman feel about her new job? Ⓐ Ⓑ Ⓒ Ⓓ
   (A) She likes it.
   (B) She's bored.
   (C) She feels terrible.
   (D) She's uncomfortable.

12. How often does the woman get a paycheck? Ⓐ Ⓑ Ⓒ Ⓓ
   (A) Once a week.
   (B) Once a month.
   (C) Every two weeks.
   (D) Every two months.

---

13. What color is the jacket? Ⓐ Ⓑ Ⓒ Ⓓ
   (A) White.
   (B) Green.
   (C) Blue.
   (D) Red.

14. Why is the man returning it to the store? Ⓐ Ⓑ Ⓒ Ⓓ
   (A) The woman dislikes it.
   (B) It doesn't look good.
   (C) It doesn't fit right.
   (D) It lost a button.

15. How much did the man pay for it? Ⓐ Ⓑ Ⓒ Ⓓ
   (A) $70.
   (B) $300.
   (C) $317.
   (D) $370.

Part 4: Talks

These are the directions for Part 4 of the TOEIC® test. Study them now. If you understand these directions now, you will not have to read them during the test.

PART 4

Directions: You will hear some talks given by a single speaker. You will be asked to answer three questions about what the speaker says in each talk. Select the best response to each question and mark the letter (A), (B), (C), or (D) on your answer sheet. The talks will not be printed in your test book and will be spoken only one time.

STRATEGY OVERVIEW

LANGUAGE STRATEGIES

In this chapter, you will learn how certain words will help you identify the purpose of a question. These are the purposes you will learn about.

- identifying the sequence
- identifying the audience
- identifying a location
- identifying the topic
- identifying a request

The words you will learn in this chapter will help you develop strategies to choose the correct answer.

TEST STRATEGIES

In Part 4, like in Parts 1, 2, and 3, some answer choices are designed to trick you. They are written to seem like the correct answer. You must learn to recognize the way the answer choices may seem correct:

- Some choices have words that sound similar to the correct answer.
- Some choices use words related to the correct answer.
- Some choices use words like the correct answer, but with a different meaning.
- Some choices have words used in a different context.
- Some choices have incorrect details.
- Some choices make incorrect inferences.

Look at these examples:

Example 1

You will hear:

"Bilbo's Department Store has openings for cashiers, management trainees, and buyer's assistants. Call 555-2121 to apply or send your résumé to 152 South State Street."

For one of the three questions, you might hear:

Who is this advertisement for?

(A)	Job seekers.	(correct answer)
(B)	Shoppers.	(incorrect inference)
(C)	Train passengers.	(word used with a different meaning)
(D)	Employers.	(word related to correct answer)

Example 2

You will hear:

"Next Tuesday is Library Forgiveness Day. All overdue books and late fines are forgiven. Return your overdue books to the library on Tuesday and you won't be charged a late fine."

For one of the three questions, you might hear:

What are library users asked to do next Tuesday?

(A)	Pay a fine.	(incorrect detail)
(B)	Return overdue books.	(correct answer)
(C)	Give new books to the library.	(sounds like correct answer)
(D)	Charge their fines to their credit card.	(incorrect detail)

IDENTIFYING THE SEQUENCE

You will read questions that ask about sequence. A sequence is the order in which events occur: *First*, one thing happens. *Then*, something else happens. *Finally*, another thing happens.

> **TIP**
>
> Read the questions and the answer choices quickly ***before*** you listen to the talk. When you listen to the talk, listen for answers to the questions about sequence.

Example

We have arrived at our final destination. Please wait for the plane to come to a complete stop and the doors to open before leaving your seat. On entering the airport, you will go through Immigration. Please have your passport ready to show to the Immigration officer.

When can you leave your seat? Ⓐ Ⓑ Ⓒ Ⓓ

(A) After the doors are opened.
(B) After you complete some forms.
(C) After your passport is ready.
(D) After you enter the airport.

The correct answer is (A). Choice (B) tries to confuse you by repeating the word *complete* in a different context. Choices (C) and (D) repeat details of the talk that are not related to the question.

Look for these words in a question that asks about sequence:

when
before
after
first
last

Practice: Identifying the Sequence

DIRECTIONS: Listen to the talk and then choose the statement that best answers the question.

1. What should you do before answering the questions? (A) (B) (C) (D)
   (A) Write carefully.
   (B) Check the answer sheet.
   (C) Turn the test over.
   (D) Read the directions.

2. What will happen after the concert? (A) (B) (C) (D)
   (A) Refreshments will be served.
   (B) A professor will give a talk.
   (C) The director will introduce someone.
   (D) People will discuss their hobbies.

3. What should you do when entering the building? (A) (B) (C) (D)
   (A) Read the signs.
   (B) Get a pass.
   (C) Go immediately to your destination.
   (D) Contact your company.

4. What should you do before you pay? (A) (B) (C) (D)
   (A) Check the size of your items.
   (B) Write a check.
   (C) Show your receipt.
   (D) Talk to a guard.

5. Which show will be first? (A) (B) (C) (D)
   (A) The stock market report.
   (B) The weather report.
   (C) The news.
   (D) The interview.

6. Which event will take place first? (A) (B) (C) (D)
   (A) A parade.
   (B) Speeches.
   (C) Fireworks.
   (D) A soccer game.

7. What will happen after lunch? (A) (B) (C) (D)
   (A) Coffee will be served.
   (B) Professor Jamison will speak.
   (C) Schedule changes will be made.
   (D) Ms. Carter will give a talk.

8. Which country will the president visit first? (A) (B) (C) (D)
   (A) Colombia.
   (B) Mexico.
   (C) Peru.
   (D) Ecuador.

9. What is the first step when using the bread machine? (A) (B) (C) (D)
   (A) Assemble the machine.
   (B) Choose a recipe.
   (C) Measure the ingredients.
   (D) Taste the bread.

10. What is the last piece of information you should enter? (A) (B) (C) (D)
   (A) A credit card number.
   (B) The name of the class.
   (C) Your address.
   (D) Your Social Security number.

IDENTIFYING THE AUDIENCE

You will read questions that ask about audience. The audience is the person or persons listening to the talk.

> **TIP**
>
> Read the questions and the answer choices quickly *before* you listen to the talk. When you listen to the talk, listen for answers to the questions about audience.

Example

Good service is the basis of good business and will earn you good tips. Make sure the food you serve is prepared just as the customer requested it. Keep water glasses filled and remove dirty dishes as soon as the customer has finished eating.

Who is this talk directed to?   

(A) Restaurant customers.
(B) Waiters.
(C) Business owners.
(D) Dishwashers.

The correct answer is (B). Choice (A) repeats a detail of the talk that is not related to the answer. Choices (C) and (D) make incorrect inferences about details of the talk.

Look for these words in a question that asks about audience:

who
directed to
talking to

Practice: Identifying the Audience

DIRECTIONS: Listen to the talk and then choose the statement that best answers the question.

1. Who is this talk directed to? Ⓐ Ⓑ Ⓒ Ⓓ
(A) Bookstore owners.
(B) Professors.
(C) Students.
(D) Economists.

2. Who is the speaker talking to? Ⓐ Ⓑ Ⓒ Ⓓ
(A) Store employees.
(B) Customers.
(C) Police officers.
(D) Bank tellers.

3. Who is this message for? Ⓐ Ⓑ Ⓒ Ⓓ
(A) Ambulance drivers.
(B) Patients.
(C) Medical advisors.
(D) Office workers.

4. Who is the speaker talking to? Ⓐ Ⓑ Ⓒ Ⓓ
(A) Airline pilots.
(B) Flight attendants.
(C) Airplane passengers.
(D) People with small children.

5. Who is this talk directed to? Ⓐ Ⓑ Ⓒ Ⓓ
(A) Radio station employees.
(B) Public servants.
(C) Government officials.
(D) All city residents.

6. Who would call this telephone number? Ⓐ Ⓑ Ⓒ Ⓓ
(A) People who want information about entertainment.
(B) People who want to hear a weather report.
(C) People who need jobs.
(D) People who need bus and train schedules.

7. Who is the speaker talking to? Ⓐ Ⓑ Ⓒ Ⓓ
(A) Museum guards.
(B) Bus drivers.
(C) City bus passengers.
(D) Tourists.

8. Who is this announcement for? (A) (B) (C) (D)
   (A) Auto mechanics.
   (B) Construction workers.
   (C) Commuters.
   (D) Airplane passengers.

9. Who is this advertisement directed to? (A) (B) (C) (D)
   (A) Employers.
   (B) Computer technicians.
   (C) Trainers.
   (D) Job seekers.

10. Who is this talk directed to? (A) (B) (C) (D)
   (A) People who want to become bankers.
   (B) People who want to buy a house.
   (C) People who want to work in an office.
   (D) People who want to go to the supermarket.

IDENTIFYING A LOCATION

You will read questions that ask about location. A location is the place where an announcement is made.

> **TIP**
>
> Read the questions and the answer choices quickly ***before*** you listen to the talk. When you listen to the talk, listen for answers to the questions about location.

Example

Thank you for calling Island Travel. If you'd like to book a place on our Hawaii tour, press 1. To make hotel or airplane reservations, press 2.

Where would you hear this message? Ⓐ Ⓑ Ⓒ Ⓓ
(A) At a bookstore.
(B) At a hotel.
(C) On an airplane.
(D) At a travel agency.

The correct answer is (D). Choice (A) uses the word *book* with a different meaning. Choices (B) and (C) repeat details of the message that are not related to the correct answer.

Look for this word in a question that asks about a location:

where

Practice: Identifying a Location

DIRECTIONS: Listen to the talk and then choose the statement that best answers the question.

1. Where would you hear this announcement? Ⓐ Ⓑ Ⓒ Ⓓ
(A) At a coffee shop.
(B) At a grocery store.
(C) At an airport.
(D) At a factory.

2. Where is this announcement being made? Ⓐ Ⓑ Ⓒ Ⓓ
(A) On a subway.
(B) At the airport.
(C) On a bus.
(D) In a taxi.

3. Where would you hear this announcement? (A) (B) (C) (D)
   (A) At a bus station.
   (B) At a school.
   (C) At a nightclub.
   (D) At a soccer stadium.

4. Where is Martha going? (A) (B) (C) (D)
   (A) To the park.
   (B) To the gym.
   (C) Home.
   (D) To a restaurant.

5. Where would you hear this announcement? (A) (B) (C) (D)
   (A) On an elevator.
   (B) At a theater.
   (C) In a store.
   (D) On a bus.

6. Where can this talk be heard? (A) (B) (C) (D)
   (A) In a restaurant.
   (B) In a private home.
   (C) At a museum.
   (D) At a university.

7. Where is the speaker? (A) (B) (C) (D)
   (A) At a restaurant.
   (B) At a party.
   (C) At a theater.
   (D) At a hotel.

8. Where is this announcement being made? (A) (B) (C) (D)
   (A) At a school.
   (B) In a garden.
   (C) At a swimming pool.
   (D) On a farm.

9. Where can this announcement be heard? (A) (B) (C) (D)
   (A) At a bookstore.
   (B) At a hotel.
   (C) At a library.
   (D) At an accountant's office.

10. Where is Donna now? (A) (B) (C) (D)
   (A) At the office.
   (B) On the way to the office.
   (C) At the airport.
   (D) On the way to the airport.

IDENTIFYING THE TOPIC

You will read questions that ask about topics. A topic is the main subject of the talk.

> **TIP**
>
> Read the questions and the answer choices quickly ***before*** you listen to the talk. When you listen to the talk, listen for answers to the questions about the topic.

Example

Umbrella sales are sure to go up with all this rain we've been having. Rain continues all week. Saturday will be cloudy and breezy, and the rain returns on Sunday. This is the time to invest in an umbrella company!

What is this announcement about?   (C) 

(A) A sale on umbrellas.
(B) The weather.
(C) Train schedules.
(D) Stock market investments.

The correct answer is (B). Choices (A) and (D) try to confuse you by repeating details that are not related to the question. Choice (C) uses the similar-sounding word *train* for *rain.*

Look for these words in a question that asks about the topic:

- topic
- purpose
- about
- talk about
- discussing
- kind

Practice: Identifying the Topic

DIRECTIONS: Listen to the talk and then choose the statement that best answers the question.

1. What will Mr. Kim talk about? Ⓐ Ⓑ Ⓒ Ⓓ
(A) Law.
(B) Retirement.
(C) Photography.
(D) Traveling.

2. What is the topic of the meeting? Ⓐ Ⓑ Ⓒ Ⓓ
(A) Office expenses.
(B) Going out for lunch.
(C) Riding in taxis.
(D) Changes in the office.

3. What is the purpose of this announcement? Ⓐ Ⓑ Ⓒ Ⓓ
(A) To give the weather report.
(B) To talk about traffic problems.
(C) To announce that schools are closed.
(D) To report the news.

4. What is the magazine about? Ⓐ Ⓑ Ⓒ Ⓓ
(A) Commercials.
(B) Sports.
(C) Television.
(D) News.

5. What kind of business is advertised? Ⓐ Ⓑ Ⓒ Ⓓ
(A) A conference planning service.
(B) A hotel.
(C) A catering service.
(D) An entertainment business.

6. What is this announcement about? Ⓐ Ⓑ Ⓒ Ⓓ
(A) Weather.
(B) Vacations.
(C) Books.
(D) Mail.

7. What is the purpose of this talk? Ⓐ Ⓑ Ⓒ Ⓓ
(A) To explain why eating breakfast is important.
(B) To explain what to eat for breakfast.
(C) To explain when to eat breakfast.
(D) To explain who should eat breakfast.

8. What kind of insurance is advertised? Ⓐ Ⓑ Ⓒ Ⓓ
   (A) Health insurance.
   (B) Life insurance.
   (C) Car insurance.
   (D) Fire insurance.

9. What is the purpose of this announcement? Ⓐ Ⓑ Ⓒ Ⓓ
   (A) To report the news.
   (B) To explain the new schedule.
   (C) To introduce musicians.
   (D) To discuss rock music.

10. What is the topic of this report? Ⓐ Ⓑ Ⓒ Ⓓ
   (A) Business sales.
   (B) Taxi fares.
   (C) Elections.
   (D) A tax increase.

IDENTIFYING A REQUEST

You will read questions that ask about requests. A request is what the speaker wants the audience to do.

> **TIP**
>
> Read the questions and the answer choices quickly ***before*** you listen to the talk. When you listen to the talk, listen for answers to the questions about the request.

Example

The ABC Supermarket has openings for managers. Interested applicants should apply in person at 24 Riverdale Avenue on Saturday at 9:00 A.M. Bring three copies of your résumé. Phone calls will not be accepted.

How can you apply for this job? Ⓐ Ⓑ Ⓒ Ⓓ
(A) Call the supermarket.
(B) Send in a résumé.
(C) Go to 24 Riverdale Avenue.
(D) Fill out an application.

The correct answer is (C). Choices (A) and (B) repeat details of the announcement that are not correct. Choice (D) tries to confuse you by using the similar-sounding and related word *application* for *applicant*.

Look for these words in a question that asks about a request:

request
ask
how can

Practice: Identifying a Request

DIRECTIONS: Listen to the talk and then choose the statement that best answers the question.

1. What are passengers asked to do? Ⓐ Ⓑ Ⓒ  Ⓓ
(A) Stand up.
(B) Stay seated.
(C) Make a complete stop.
(D) Remain on the train.

2. What are the members of the audience asked to do? Ⓐ Ⓑ Ⓒ Ⓓ
   (A) Record the show.
   (B) Take pictures of the actors.
   (C) Turn off their cell phones.
   (D) Wait in the lobby.

3. How can you make an appointment with Mr. Schwartz? Ⓐ Ⓑ Ⓒ Ⓓ
   (A) Wait for the beep.
   (B) Return the call.
   (C) Press 1.
   (D) Send an e-mail message.

4. What are the passengers asked to do? Ⓐ Ⓑ Ⓒ Ⓓ
   (A) Stand in line.
   (B) Pay by check.
   (C) Show their passports.
   (D) Carry their own bags.

5. What are drivers asked to do? Ⓐ Ⓑ Ⓒ Ⓓ
   (A) Go downtown.
   (B) Drive north on State Street.
   (C) Use Constitution Avenue.
   (D) Avoid accidents.

6. How can callers speak to a customer service representative? Ⓐ Ⓑ Ⓒ Ⓓ
   (A) Call the business line.
   (B) Turn off the phone.
   (C) Leave a message on the answering machine.
   (D) Stay on the line.

7. What are people asked to do? Ⓐ Ⓑ Ⓒ Ⓓ
   (A) Send food and clothing.
   (B) Leave their homes.
   (C) Donate money.
   (D) Go to Springfield.

8. What are staff members asked to do? Ⓐ Ⓑ Ⓒ Ⓓ
   (A) Give Mrs. Jackson some help.
   (B) Ask the manager for assistance.
   (C) Introduce themselves to Mrs. Jackson.
   (D) Learn the office routine.

9. What are staff members asked to do? Ⓐ Ⓑ Ⓒ Ⓓ
   (A) Test the alarm.
   (B) Continue with their usual routine.
   (C) Leave the building.
   (D) Avoid the elevator.

10. What is the driver of the white car asked to do? Ⓐ Ⓑ Ⓒ Ⓓ
(A) Make a delivery.
(B) Visit the building.
(C) Use the back entrance.
(D) Move the car.

GRAMMAR TIP

Imperative Sentences

In the talks in Part 4, you may hear imperative sentences. Imperative sentences tell someone to do something. The verb in an imperative is in the base form. The subject *you* is not mentioned, so the verb is usually the first word of the sentence.

Come back later.
Line up at the door.
Show your ticket to the agent.
Take a seat in the waiting room.

VOCABULARY TIP

Adjectives with *-ing*

In the listening sections, you will hear many words that end with *-ing*. They are not always verbs. Often they are adjectives.

Some common adjectives with *-ing*
amazing
annoying
boring
confusing
exciting
frightening
interesting
surprising

They showed a *boring* movie on the airplane.
I read the financial report, but it was *confusing*.
We had a very *exciting* trip.
The conference was *interesting*, and I really enjoyed it.

STRATEGY REVIEW

Language Strategies

In the exercises for Part 4, you learned how certain words would help you identify the purpose of a question. Knowing these words will help you choose the right answer. Listen for words that identify:

- a sequence, such as *when, before, first,* etc.
- the audience, such as *who, directed to, talking to,* etc.
- the location, such as *where*
- the topic, such as *talk about, discussing, about,* etc.
- a request, such as *request, ask, how can,* etc.

Test Strategies

In the exercises for Part 4, you saw how certain answer choices try to confuse you. Here are the ways that choices may seem correct to you.

- Some choices have words that sound similar to the correct answer.
- Some choices use words related to the correct answer.
- Some choices use words like the correct answer, but with a different meaning.
- Some choices have words used in a different context.
- Some choices have incorrect details.
- Some choices make incorrect inferences.

STRATEGY PRACTICE

DIRECTIONS: Listen to the talks and choose the best response to the questions. There are three questions for each talk. Listen again and see if you can recognize how an answer choice tries to confuse you.

1. What will happen next? Ⓐ Ⓑ Ⓒ Ⓓ
(A) Mr. Howard will give a talk.
(B) Mr. Howard will sign books.
(C) Mr. Howard will ask questions.
(D) Mr. Howard will make some copies.

2. When will there be an interview with Mr. Howard? Ⓐ Ⓑ Ⓒ Ⓓ
(A) This evening at 7:30.
(B) This evening at 11:30.
(C) Tomorrow morning at 7:30.
(D) Tomorrow morning at 11:30.

3. What is Mr. Howard's job? Ⓐ Ⓑ Ⓒ Ⓓ
(A) He's an author.
(B) He's a teacher.
(C) He's a bookseller.
(D) He's a radio show host.

---

4. How is the weather this morning? Ⓐ Ⓑ Ⓒ Ⓓ
(A) Rainy.
(B) Icy.
(C) Windy.
(D) Warm.

5. When will it start to snow? Ⓐ Ⓑ Ⓒ Ⓓ
(A) This morning.
(B) This afternoon.
(C) This evening.
(D) Tomorrow.

6. Why will schools be closed tomorrow? Ⓐ Ⓑ Ⓒ Ⓓ
(A) Because of traffic delays.
(B) Because of bad weather.
(C) Because of the weekend.
(D) Because of a holiday.

---

7. What does Mary ask Charles to do? Ⓐ Ⓑ Ⓒ Ⓓ
(A) Make dinner reservations.
(B) Wait for her at the airport.
(C) Meet her at the hotel.
(D) Call her tomorrow.

8. How will Mary get to the hotel? (A) (B) (C) (D)
(A) By car.
(B) By taxi.
(C) By train.
(D) By walking.

9. What does Mary want to do after dinner? (A) (B) (C) (D)
(A) Go to the movies.
(B) Sit and talk.
(C) Take a walk.
(D) Have a rest.

---

10. What will be the first item in the program? (A) (B) (C) (D)
(A) A question and answer session.
(B) A musical performance.
(C) A slide show.
(D) A lecture.

11. Who will play music? (A) (B) (C) (D)
(A) An Italian artist.
(B) Matilda Wimple.
(C) Dr. James.
(D) Students.

12. What refreshments will be served? (A) (B) (C) (D)
(A) Coffee.
(B) Dinner.
(C) Breakfast.
(D) Wine and cheese.

---

13. What can be seen from the guest's room? (A) (B) (C) (D)
(A) The ocean.
(B) The pool.
(C) The park.
(D) The parking lot.

14. Where does the speaker ask the guest to park? (A) (B) (C) (D)
(A) On the other side of the pool.
(B) By the side of the building.
(C) By the front door.
(D) In the garage.

15. What is free for hotel guests? (A) (B) (C) (D)
(A) The fitness room.
(B) The sauna.
(C) Breakfast.
(D) Dinner.

Listening Comprehension Review

Do this Listening Comprehension Review as if you were taking Parts 1, 2, 3, and 4 of the TOEIC® test. You should take no more than 45 minutes to do this review. Use the Listening Comprehension Review Answer Sheet on page 344.

LISTENING TEST

In the Listening test, you will be asked to demonstrate how well you understand spoken English. The entire Listening test will last approximately 45 minutes. There are four parts, and directions are given for each part. You must mark your answers on the separate answer sheet. Do not write your answers in the test book.

PART 1

Directions: For each question in this part, you will hear four statements about a picture in your test book. When you hear the statements, you must select the one statement that best describes what you see in the picture. Then find the number of the question on your answer sheet and mark your answer. The statements will not be printed in your test book and will be spoken only one time.

Example

Sample Answer

Statement (C), "They're standing near the table," is the best description of the picture, so you should select answer (C) and mark it on your answer sheet.

1.

2.

3.

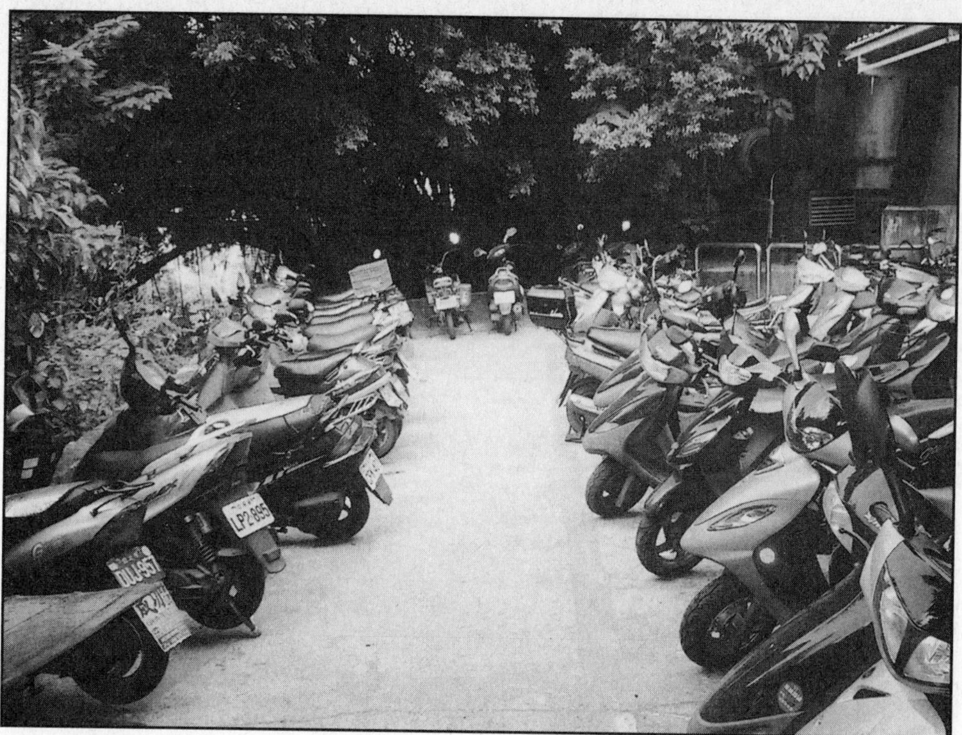

4.

GO ON TO THE NEXT PAGE

5. 

6.

7.

8.

GO ON TO THE NEXT PAGE

9.

10.

PART 2

Directions: You will hear a question or statement and three responses spoken in English. They will not be printed in your test book and will be spoken only one time. Select the best response to the question or statement and mark the letter (A), (B), or (C) on your answer sheet.

Sample Answer

Example

You will hear: Where is the meeting room?

You will also hear: (A) To meet the new director.
(B) It's the first room on the right.
(C) Yes, at two o'clock.

Your best response to the question "Where is the meeting room?" is choice (B), "It's the first room on the right," so (B) is the correct answer. You should mark answer (B) on your answer sheet.

11. Mark your answer on your answer sheet.

12. Mark your answer on your answer sheet.

13. Mark your answer on your answer sheet.

14. Mark your answer on your answer sheet.

15. Mark your answer on your answer sheet.

16. Mark your answer on your answer sheet.

17. Mark your answer on your answer sheet.

18. Mark your answer on your answer sheet.

19. Mark your answer on your answer sheet.

20. Mark your answer on your answer sheet.

21. Mark your answer on your answer sheet.

22. Mark your answer on your answer sheet.

23. Mark your answer on your answer sheet.

24. Mark your answer on your answer sheet.

25. Mark your answer on your answer sheet.

26. Mark your answer on your answer sheet.

27. Mark your answer on your answer sheet.

28. Mark your answer on your answer sheet.

29. Mark your answer on your answer sheet.

30. Mark your answer on your answer sheet.

31. Mark your answer on your answer sheet.

32. Mark your answer on your answer sheet.

33. Mark your answer on your answer sheet.

34. Mark your answer on your answer sheet.

35. Mark your answer on your answer sheet.

36. Mark your answer on your answer sheet.

37. Mark your answer on your answer sheet.

38. Mark your answer on your answer sheet.

39. Mark your answer on your answer sheet.

40. Mark your answer on your answer sheet.

GO ON TO THE NEXT PAGE

PART 3

Directions: You will hear some conversations between two people. You will be asked to answer three questions about what the speakers say in each conversation. Select the best response to each question and mark the letter (A), (B), (C), or (D) on your answer sheet. The conversations will not be printed in your test book and will be spoken only one time.

41. What is the man doing?
(A) Mailing a letter.
(B) Replying to e-mail.
(C) Answering the phone.
(D) Repairing the computer.

42. What does the woman want to do?
(A) Have lunch.
(B) Drink coffee.
(C) Go to bed.
(D) Take a seat.

43. When will the man meet the woman?
(A) At noon.
(B) In ten minutes.
(C) At 5:00.
(D) In fifteen minutes.

---

44. Where does this conversation take place?
(A) In an apartment.
(B) In an office.
(C) On a plane.
(D) At a hotel.

45. What will the woman do?
(A) Sleep.
(B) Work.
(C) Cook.
(D) Read.

46. How does the man feel?
(A) Bored.
(B) Tired.
(C) Angry.
(D) Hungry.

---

47. What is the man's job?
(A) Clock repair person.
(B) Receptionist.
(C) Telemarketer.
(D) Usher.

48. What time is the woman's appointment?
(A) 1:00.
(B) 4:00.
(C) 8:00.
(D) 9:00.

49. What will the woman do?
(A) Make a call.
(B) Sit down.
(C) Play ball.
(D) Make a new appointment.

---

50. When does the woman plan to invite people for dinner?
(A) Tuesday.
(B) Thursday.
(C) Friday.
(D) Saturday.

51. Who will she invite?
(A) Business associates.
(B) School friends.
(C) Neighbors.
(D) Her sisters.

52. How many guests does she plan to have?
(A) Two.
(B) Four.
(C) Six.
(D) Ten.

---

53. When will they go to the presentation?
(A) 9:00.
(B) 11:00.
(C) 1:00.
(D) 2:00.

54. What is the presentation about?
(A) Cooking.
(B) Books.
(C) Trains.
(D) Games.

55. What does the man want to do after the presentation?
(A) Go home.
(B) Have lunch.
(C) Buy a watch.
(D) Look around.

---

56. When is the report due?
(A) Monday.
(B) Tuesday.
(C) Wednesday.
(D) Thursday.

57. What kind of report is it?
(A) A news report.
(B) A management report.
(C) An expense report.
(D) A meeting report.

58. How does the man feel about the situation?
(A) Sad.
(B) Frightened.
(C) Ill.
(D) Mad.

---

59. Where does this conversation take place?
(A) In a hotel.
(B) At a restaurant.
(C) At the beach.
(D) In an apartment building.

60. What is the woman's favorite thing about the place?
(A) The restaurants.
(B) The pool.
(C) The beds.
(D) The fitness room.

61. What will the man do all day?
(A) Sleep.
(B) Eat.
(C) Swim.
(D) Exercise.

---

62. Where does the conversation take place?
(A) In a waiting room.
(B) In a store.
(C) In a post office.
(D) In a library.

63. What does the woman want?
(A) A book.
(B) Adhesive tape.
(C) Envelopes.
(D) Letter paper.

64. What does the man suggest doing?
(A) Placing an order.
(B) Using the smaller size.
(C) Looking somewhere else.
(D) Getting a bigger box.

GO ON TO THE NEXT PAGE

65. How many phone calls did they answer?
(A) Two.
(B) Four.
(C) Nine.
(D) Ten.

66. What is the woman waiting for?
(A) An e-mail message.
(B) A phone call.
(C) A package.
(D) A letter.

67. What does the man want help with?
(A) Writing a report.
(B) Sending mail.
(C) Cleaning his office.
(D) Fixing his computer.

68. How will the woman pay?
(A) By check.
(B) With a credit card.
(C) In cash.
(D) With a money order.

69. What is the woman buying?
(A) Cards.
(B) Shoes.
(C) A book.
(D) A purse.

70. How much does her purchase cost?
(A) $17.50.
(B) $25.
(C) $75.
(D) $100.

PART 4

Directions: You will hear some talks given by a single speaker. You will be asked to answer three questions about what the speaker says in each talk. Select the best response to each question and mark the letter (A), (B), (C), or (D) on your answer sheet. The talks will not be printed in your test book and will be spoken only one time.

71. Where would this announcement be heard?
(A) On a train.
(B) At an airport.
(C) In an airplane.
(D) On a bus.

72. Who is speaking?
(A) A pilot.
(B) A tour guide.
(C) A weather forecaster.
(D) A passenger.

73. What can be seen from the window?
(A) A cemetery.
(B) Radar screens.
(C) Some woods.
(D) A mountain.

---

74. Where is the tour?
(A) In a garden.
(B) In a forest.
(C) In a museum.
(D) In a flower shop.

75. What does the tour guide ask the participants to do?
(A) Pick some flowers.
(B) Wear warm clothes.
(C) Stay in their seats.
(D) Clean the windows.

76. Where is the first stop?
(A) Under the trees.
(B) On the left.
(C) By a river branch.
(D) To the rear.

---

77. Who is the message intended for?
(A) City garbage collectors.
(B) Community bus drivers.
(C) Kids with school on Saturdays.
(D) Members of the community.

78. What was the clean-up drive like last year?
(A) There were free refreshments.
(B) Fifty people showed up.
(C) It wasn't successful.
(D) There were no participants.

79. What time will the clean-up drive begin?
(A) 10:00 A.M.
(B) 1:00 P.M.
(C) 3:00 P.M.
(D) 3:15 P.M.

---

80. What is Dr. Quimby Jones's profession?
(A) Radio show host.
(B) Medical doctor.
(C) Professor.
(D) Farmer.

81. What is the last item on the radio program?
(A) A talk about economics.
(B) Reading letters and e-mails from listeners.
(C) A discussion about agriculture.
(D) Answering telephone calls.

82. How long does the entire radio show last?
(A) Ten minutes.
(B) Thirty minutes.
(C) One hour.
(D) One hour and ten minutes.

GO ON TO THE NEXT PAGE

83. Who is the speaker?
(A) A university president.
(B) A special guest.
(C) A professor.
(D) A student.

84. What is the subject of the class?
(A) Chinese history.
(B) Art history.
(C) Writing.
(D) Travel.

85. What will the class do today?
(A) Read books.
(B) Look at slides.
(C) Watch a video.
(D) Visit an art museum.

---

86. According to the weather report, what is the weather like now?
(A) There are floods.
(B) There is heavy rain.
(C) There is a hailstorm.
(D) There are strong winds.

87. How long will this weather condition last?
(A) Two to four hours.
(B) Four more hours.
(C) Twenty-four hours.
(D) Thirty-four hours.

88. What should people near the Green River listen for tomorrow?
(A) Vacation orders.
(B) The train schedule.
(C) Orders to evacuate.
(D) A new weather report.

---

89. What helped pay for the food at the luncheon?
(A) Employee contributions.
(B) Last year's revenue.
(C) The generosity of the speaker.
(D) Donations from local restaurants.

90. What is the main purpose of the speech?
(A) To discuss future sales plans.
(B) To analyze last year's meeting.
(C) To improve customer service.
(D) To describe the luncheon.

91. What will the meeting participants do this afternoon?
(A) Write new ads.
(B) Meet in groups.
(C) Visit customers' homes.
(D) Plan next year's luncheon.

---

92. What has been the major complaint about the parking lot?
(A) There hasn't been enough security.
(B) There are never enough parking spaces.
(C) Cars get too hot or people get too wet.
(D) People are charged too much to park there.

93. When will the parking garage probably be finished?
(A) In December.
(B) In January.
(C) In six months.
(D) In one year.

94. Where should people park until the garage is completed?
(A) On the street.
(B) Around the corner.
(C) In another parking garage.
(D) In a shopping center parking lot.

---

95. What is the telephone number that people should call?
(A) 703-555-8000.
(B) 603-555-6069.
(C) 603-555-9000.
(D) 212-555-5394.

96. Who created this advertisement?
(A) Investment bankers.
(B) A real estate company.
(C) A group of realtors.
(D) Real estate investors.

97. Who is likely to call the phone number?
(A) A person who wants to get rid of a house.
(B) A person who would rather rent a house.
(C) A person who needs a house immediately.
(D) A person who is thinking about buying a house.

98. Where would this announcement be heard?
(A) At a farm.
(B) At a theater.
(C) At a grocery store.
(D) At a cell phone store.

99. Where can the lost cell phone be claimed?
(A) In aisle 10.
(B) In the produce section.
(C) In the frozen food section.
(D) In the customer service office.

100. Who can take advantage of the sale?
(A) People with a Shoppers' Club card.
(B) All customers.
(C) Children.
(D) Parents.

READING

In the second section of the TOEIC® test, you will be tested on how well you understand written English. There are three parts to this section with special directions for each part:

Part 5	Incomplete Sentences
Part 6	Text Completion
Part 7	Reading Comprehension

Each part contains activities to help you practice these strategies. Each part ends with a Strategy Review consisting of questions similar to those on the TOEIC test. In this part of the Introductory Course for the TOEIC test, you will learn strategies to help you on the Reading section.

Part 5: Incomplete Sentences

These are the directions for Part 5 of the TOEIC® test. Study them now. If you understand these directions now, you will not have to read them during the test.

READING TEST

In the Reading test, you will read a variety of texts and answer several different types of reading comprehension questions. The entire Reading test will last 75 minutes. There are three parts, and directions are given for each part. You are encouraged to answer as many questions as possible within the time allowed.

You must mark your answers on the separate answer sheet. Do not write your answers in the test book.

PART 5

Directions: A word or phrase is missing in each of the sentences below. Four answer choices are given below each sentence. Select the best answer to complete the sentence. Then mark the letter (A), (B), (C), or (D) on your answer sheet.

STRATEGY OVERVIEW

LANGUAGE STRATEGIES

You will learn the most common types of grammar items found in Part 5.

Word families

Similar words

Pronouns

Prepositions

Coordinate conjunctions

Subordinate conjunctions

Verb tense

Phrasal verbs

TEST STRATEGIES

- Use grammar clues to figure out the part of speech needed to complete the statement.
- Read to find the context of the statement. Decide which vocabulary word best fits the context.
- Find the noun that a pronoun refers to. Is it the subject or object of the sentence?
- Identify the position of an item to choose the correct preposition.

- Choose the best conjunction to join two parts of a statement by deciding whether the two parts (1) are choices, (2) contradict each other, (3) give similar information, (4) describe a reason, or (5) give information about time.
- Look for a time expression to choose the verb tense needed.
- Eliminate answer choices that you know are incorrect.
- Move on to the next question if you don't immediately know the answer.

WORD FAMILIES

Word families are words that have the same root but different endings. The ending shows the part of speech of the word. The ending tells you how a word is used in a sentence. The root word is often a noun or verb, but it can be any part of speech.

Look at the roots and endings in the chart.

	Part of Speech			
Root	**Noun**	**Verb**	**Adjective**	**Adverb**
public	publicity (public)	publicize	(public)	publicly
nation	nationality (nation)	nationalize	national	nationally
care	(care)	(care)	careful / careless	carefully / carelessly
wide	width	widen	(wide)	widely
accept	acceptance	(accept)	acceptable	acceptably
agree	agreement	(agree)	agreeable	agreeably

Sentences

Noun	The new product needs a lot of *publicity*.
	The *public* responded well to the new product.
Verb	Companies *publicize* products on the Internet, on TV, and in magazines.
Adjective	The company made a *public* announcement about the new product.
Adverb	Company representatives announced the new product *publicly*.

Strategies

1. Try to answer the question on your own without reading all the choices. One or two answers may obviously be incorrect. Look for grammar clues that will help you choose the correct word.

   We need to ________ the language in this report; it is too complex. (A) (B) (C) (D)

   (A) simplify (C) simply
   (B) simple (D) simplicity

   Looking quickly at the answer choices, you see that the choices are the same word family (*simple*). In the statement, you see the verb phrase *need to*. You know that this phrase is part of an infinitive (*verb*). The only verb among the answer choices is *simplify*.

2. If you do not immediately know the answer to a question, move on. Do not waste time on one question. Allow yourself a few minutes at the end of a section. Come back to the question after you finish the section.

   When you come back to a question about word families, figure out what part of speech is required (noun, verb, adjective, or adverb). Then decide which answer choice fits that part of speech. Eliminate options that you know are not correct.

3. If you still do not know the answer, guess.

Practice

DIRECTIONS: Mark the choice that best completes the sentence.

1. We will ______ our decision when we sign the papers. (A) (B) (C) (D)
   (A) formalize (C) formally
   (B) formal (D) formality

2. The ______ of your speech cannot be more than 30 minutes. (A) (B) (C) (D)
   (A) long (C) lengthen
   (B) length (D) lengthened

3. The ______ location for our new office is downtown. (A) (B) (C) (D)
   (A) preference (C) preferable
   (B) preferably (D) prefer

4. As soon as everybody is happy with the ______, we will sign the papers. (A) (B) (C) (D)
   (A) agree (C) agreement
   (B) agreeable (D) agreeably

5. It was very ______ of the boss to buy us those nice gifts. (A) (B) (C) (D)
(A) thoughtfully (C) thoughts
(B) thoughtful (D) thought

6. Our company believes it is the best ______ to handle the account. (A) (B) (C) (D)
(A) organize (C) organizationally
(B) organizational (D) organization

7. We need to ______ sales of the new product. (A) (B) (C) (D)
(A) strong (C) strengthen
(B) strongly (D) strenuous

8. This new software is ______ easy to use. (A) (B) (C) (D)
(A) wonderful (C) wondering
(B) wonderfully (D) wonder

9. He was very happy about his ______ into the university graduate program. (A) (B) (C) (D)
(A) acceptance (C) acceptably
(B) acceptable (D) accept

10. They hired her because her ______ is international finance. (A) (B) (C) (D)
(A) special (C) specialty
(B) specially (D) specialize

SIMILAR WORDS

Words may look similar, but they may have very different meanings. Sentence context and grammar will help you decide which is the correct word.

These are some examples of words that look similar:

object	liver	omit	contract
reject	liven	admit	contrast
project	livid	remit	control
deject	lively	permit	contrive

Strategies

1. Always look at the context. When the answer choices are words that look similar and are the same part of speech, the context will help you choose.

Mr. Kim stayed at the office all night to work on his ________. Ⓐ Ⓑ Ⓒ Ⓓ

(A) object (C) project
(B) reject (D) eject

All of these answer choices can be nouns or verbs, so part of speech will not help you decide. Look at the context. Mr. Kim is at the office, and he is working on something. *Project* means *an assigned piece of work*, so it fits the context.

2. Figure out what part of speech is required.

We wanted to ________ the office, so we painted the walls yellow. Ⓐ Ⓑ Ⓒ Ⓓ

(A) liver (C) livid
(B) liven (D) lively

The verb *want to* is always followed by a verb. *Liven* is the only choice that is a verb. Even if you do not know what *liven* means, you can see that *–en* is a verb ending. *Liver* is a noun, and *livid* and *lively* are adjectives, so none of these choices would fit the sentence correctly.

3. If you do not immediately know the answer, move on to the next question. Come back to the ones you are unsure about if you have time at the end.

Practice

DIRECTIONS: Mark the choice that best completes the sentence.

1. Everyone was ______ with the high quality of Mr. Clark's work. Ⓐ Ⓑ Ⓒ Ⓓ
   (A) compressed (C) impressed
   (B) oppressed (D) repressed

2. We will hire a legal ______ to prepare the documents. Ⓐ Ⓑ Ⓒ Ⓓ
   (A) expect (C) export
   (B) exploit (D) expert

3. Your ______ during our visit was greatly appreciated. Ⓐ Ⓑ Ⓒ Ⓓ
   (A) hospice (C) hospitality
   (B) hospital (D) hospitalize

4. You will need to ______ the check before we can cash it. Ⓐ Ⓑ Ⓒ Ⓓ
   (A) sing (C) sigh
   (B) sign (D) sight

5. The new employee ______ to us that he didn't have much experience. Ⓐ Ⓑ Ⓒ Ⓓ
   (A) omitted (C) permitted
   (B) remitted (D) admitted

6. I enjoyed listening to her ______ and learned a lot from it. Ⓐ Ⓑ Ⓒ Ⓓ
   (A) spare (C) spend
   (B) sparse (D) speech

7. The restaurant doesn't ______ to deliver meals to the office; it's a free service. Ⓐ Ⓑ Ⓒ Ⓓ
   (A) change (C) chance
   (B) charge (D) chase

8. Ms. Patel started working here last month, so she is our newest ______. Ⓐ Ⓑ Ⓒ Ⓓ
   (A) employee (C) empower
   (B) emptied (D) empire

9. They offered her a job and she signed the ______ right away. Ⓐ Ⓑ Ⓒ Ⓓ
   (A) contract (C) contrast
   (B) contrive (D) control

10. Your supervisor will need to ______ your request for time off. Ⓐ Ⓑ Ⓒ Ⓓ
    (A) reprove (C) disprove
    (B) improve (D) approve

PRONOUNS

Pronouns take the place of nouns. Subject pronouns take the place of the noun subject of a sentence or clause. Subjects come ***before*** a verb. Object pronouns come ***after*** a verb or preposition.

Subject Pronouns	
Singular	**Plural**
I	we
you	you
he, she, it	they

Object Pronouns	
Singular	**Plural**
me	us
you	you
him, her, it	them

Sentences

Mr. and Mrs. Brown are at the hotel now. *They* arrived by plane last night.
We bought a *new computer*. It is on the desk in my office.
George and I are going to the conference tomorrow. My boss will wait for *us* at 6:00.
Mr. Lang knows the answer. You should ask *him*.

Strategies

1. Find the noun the pronoun refers to. Is it singular or plural? Is it a man, a woman, or a thing?

   The consultants are ready, and ______ will present the results. (A) (B) (C) (D)

   (A) she (C) his
   (B) they (D) it

   The pronoun refers to *consultants*, a plural noun. Even if you do not know the meaning of *consultants*, you know that –*s* is the plural ending. Therefore, the correct answer is *they*, the plural subject pronoun.

2. Determine whether the pronoun is in the position of subject (before the main verb) or object (after a verb or preposition).

   When Mary arrived, I told ______ the news. (A) (B) (C) (D)

   (A) her (C) him
   (B) she (D) he

   The pronoun refers to *Mary*, a woman's name. It follows the verb, *told*, so it is in the position of object. Therefore, the correct answer is *her*, an object pronoun that refers to a woman.

3. If you do not immediately know the answer, move on to the next question. Come back to the ones you are unsure about if you have time at the end.

Practice

DIRECTIONS: Mark the choice that best completes the sentence.

1. The door is open. Shut ______ if you want.
   (A) them (C) her
   (B) him (D) it

   Ⓐ Ⓑ Ⓒ Ⓓ

2. I'll finish this job faster if I can find someone to work with ______.
   (A) you (C) him
   (B) we (D) me

   Ⓐ Ⓑ Ⓒ Ⓓ

3. Mr. Yeoh is our computer expert. ______ will help you with that problem.
   (A) He (C) Him
   (B) She (D) Her

   Ⓐ Ⓑ Ⓒ Ⓓ

4. The manager gave us a day off because ______ worked extra hours last week.
   (A) he (C) us
   (B) we (D) him

   Ⓐ Ⓑ Ⓒ Ⓓ

5. My brother's wife is an architect. ______ designed my house.
   (A) He (C) You
   (B) She (D) It

   Ⓐ Ⓑ Ⓒ Ⓓ

6. My mother talked to me yesterday, but I didn't tell ______ I was sick.
   (A) him (C) her
   (B) she (D) it

   Ⓐ Ⓑ Ⓒ Ⓓ

7. I get too many e-mails. I can't read ______ all.
   (A) them (C) him
   (B) they (D) us

   Ⓐ Ⓑ Ⓒ Ⓓ

8. You know a lot about the account, so Ms. Wing might ask ______ for some help.
   (A) her (C) you
   (B) she (D) me

   Ⓐ Ⓑ Ⓒ Ⓓ

9. Tom needs to see the document. Please make an extra copy for ______.
   (A) he (C) her
   (B) it (D) him

   Ⓐ Ⓑ Ⓒ Ⓓ

10. Mary gave me a glass of water because ______ was very thirsty.
    (A) she (C) I
    (B) me (D) her

    Ⓐ Ⓑ Ⓒ Ⓓ

PREPOSITIONS

Prepositions come ***before*** nouns. Prepositions can show the location of an object. Often this is in relation to another object. Prepositions can also show the direction of a moving object.

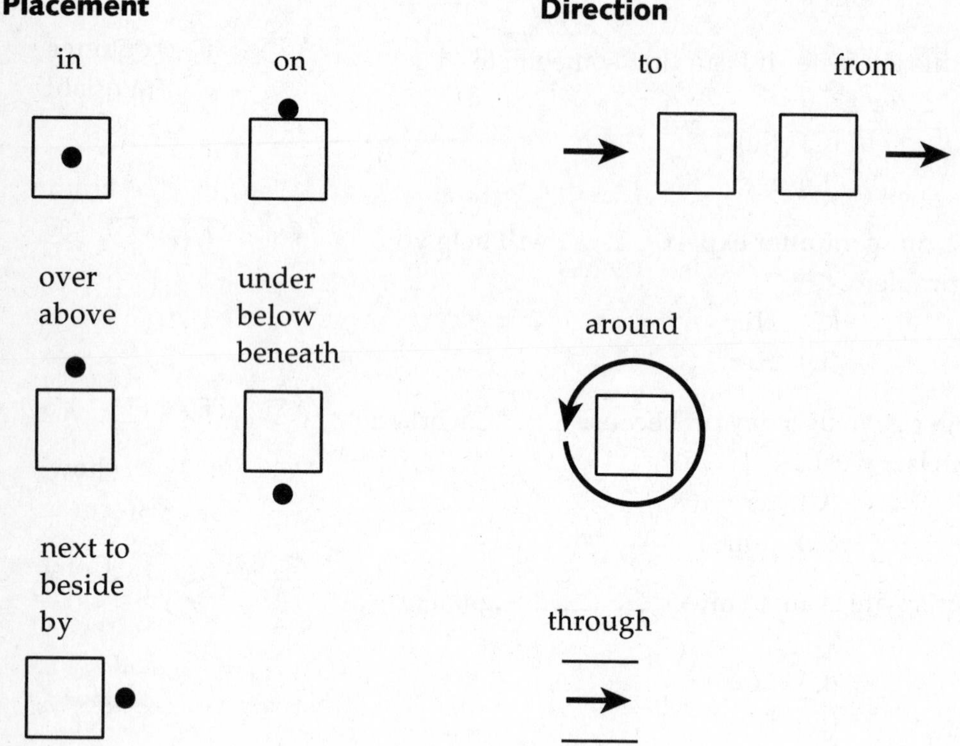

Sentences

You'll find pens *in* the top drawer.
I don't like to sit *beside* the door.
We had to drive *around* the block to find a parking space.
We will get there more quickly if we walk *through* the park.

Strategies

1. Look at the noun that follows the preposition. Use logic. Where can an object logically be placed in relation to it?

   We keep a supply of pens ______ that closet. (A) (B) (C) (D)

   (A) in (C) over
   (B) under (D) from

   A closet is in the wall, has a door, and is for storing things. We can't place things *under* or *over* a closet. The sentence is not about movement, so *from* is not possible. We put things *in* a closet.

2. Look at the main verb of the sentence. If it is about movement—*carry, take, bring, walk, travel, drive, fly,* for example—then choose a preposition that shows direction.

   The plane flew ______ a terrible storm. (A) (B) (C) (D)

   (A) on (C) through
   (B) at (D) from

   The sentence is about movement, so *on* and *at* are not likely answers. *From* shows direction, but it would be used with a place. A plane might fly *through* a storm.

3. If you do not immediately know the answer, move on to the next question. Come back to the ones you are unsure about if you have time at the end.

Practice

DIRECTIONS: Mark the choice that best completes the sentence.

1. He carried all those heavy packages ______ the store to the office. (A) (B) (C) (D)

   (A) to (C) under
   (B) from (D) in

2. The mail carrier left the mail ______ your desk. (A) (B) (C) (D)

   (A) at (C) to
   (B) above (D) on

3. You have to walk ______ the lobby in order to get to the elevators. (A) (B) (C) (D)

   (A) over (C) through
   (B) in (D) on

4. They decided to rent an office ______ a large building downtown. (A) (B) (C) (D)

   (A) in (C) to
   (B) above (D) on

5. We will have better light if we sit ______ the window. (A) (B) (C) (D)
   (A) from (C) around
   (B) to (D) beside

6. I walked all the way ______ the building, but I couldn't find the back entrance. (A) (B) (C) (D)
   (A) from (C) around
   (B) above (D) on

7. There are extra chairs ______ the conference room. (A) (B) (C) (D)
   (A) through (C) in
   (B) beneath (D) to

8. They hung the notice ______ the office wall. (A) (B) (C) (D)
   (A) on (C) below
   (B) in (D) through

9. She held the umbrella ______ her head as she walked in the rain. (A) (B) (C) (D)
   (A) under (C) between
   (B) over (D) from

10. Our office is on the top floor of the building, and on the floor right ______ us there is a great restaurant. (A) (B) (C) (D)
    (A) on (C) below
    (B) through (D) above

COORDINATE CONJUNCTIONS

Conjunctions join words, phrases, and clauses. Coordinate conjunctions join two or more equal grammar structures: two nouns (N), two verbs (V), two verb phrases (VP), two independent clauses (IC), etc.

Conjunction	Use
and	adds similar information
but	shows a contradiction
or	shows a choice
nor	shows a negative choice

Sentences

N+N	Neither my boss *nor* I will be at the office next week.
V+V	We can stay for the lecture *or* leave now.
VP + VP	I will finish the report *and* submit it before Friday.
IC+IC	He works long hours, *but* he doesn't make much money.

- *Or* is often paired with *either*:

  We can *either* wait for him now *or* come back later.

- *Nor* is often paired with *neither*:

  I will finish the project *neither* tonight *nor* tomorrow.

Strategies

1. When the answer choices include coordinate conjunctions, ask yourself these questions: Are the two parts of the sentence choices? (Choose *or* or *nor*.) Do the two parts contradict each other? (Choose *but*.) Are the two parts similar to each other? (Choose *and*.)

   The office is large ______ in a good location. (A) (B) (C) (D)

   (A) or (C) and
   (B) nor (D) but

   The two parts of the sentence, *large* and *in a good location*, both describe something good about an office. They are similar to each other, so the correct answer is *and*.

2. Look for the word *either* in the sentence. *Either* tells you that the correct answer may be *or*. *Neither* tells you that the correct answer may be *nor*. Remember *either . . . or* and *neither . . . nor* as paired conjunctions.

3. If you do not immediately know the answer, move on to the next question. Come back to the ones you are unsure about if you have time at the end.

Practice

DIRECTIONS: Mark the choice that best completes the sentence.

1. We need to order some computer paper ______ several boxes of envelopes. (A) (B) (C) (D)

   (A) or (C) either
   (B) but (D) and

2. Neither Ms. Chen ______ Mr. Martinez was able to attend the seminar. (A) (B) (C) (D)

   (A) nor (C) neither
   (B) and (D) or

3. We can sit either by the window ______ next to the door.

(A) or (C) nor
(B) and (D) but

Ⓐ Ⓑ Ⓒ Ⓓ

4. He went to the train station ______ bought a ticket to New York.

(A) but (C) nor
(B) and (D) or

Ⓐ Ⓑ Ⓒ Ⓓ

5. You can look at the clothes in the shop windows, ______ you can't buy any of them.

(A) but (C) nor
(B) or (D) neither

Ⓐ Ⓑ Ⓒ Ⓓ

6. They're interested in buying a computer ______ not a printer.

(A) and (C) or
(B) but (D) nor

Ⓐ Ⓑ Ⓒ Ⓓ

7. You can carry your coat with you ______ I can hang it in the closet for you.

(A) or (C) nor
(B) either (D) neither

Ⓐ Ⓑ Ⓒ Ⓓ

8. Mr. Lopez ______ showed up for the meeting nor called to give his excuses.

(A) nor (C) neither
(B) or (D) either

Ⓐ Ⓑ Ⓒ Ⓓ

9. Martha typed the documents ______ Tom signed them.

(A) or (C) nor
(B) and (D) either

Ⓐ Ⓑ Ⓒ Ⓓ

10. Mr. Ling buys the newspaper every morning ______ he never reads it.

(A) but (C) and
(B) or (D) nor

Ⓐ Ⓑ Ⓒ Ⓓ

SUBORDINATE CONJUNCTIONS

Subordinate conjunctions join two clauses: an independent clause (IC) and a dependent clause (DC). An independent clause can stand alone; a dependent clause cannot. The conjunction introduces the dependent clause. The dependent clause can come before the independent clause or after it.

Conjunction	Use
because since	introduces a reason
although though even though	introduces a contradiction
before after when whenever while as soon as	introduces a time clause

Sentences

IC+DC The office closed early *because* the weather was so bad.
DC+IC *Even though* they worked all night, they weren't able to meet the deadline.
IC+DC He checked his messages *as soon as* he arrived at the office.

Strategies

1. When the answer choices include subordinate conjunctions, ask yourself these questions: Does the dependent clause describe a reason? (Choose *because* or *since*.) Does the dependent clause contradict the main clause? (Choose *though, even though*, or *although*.) Is the dependent clause an action that occurred before, after, or at the same time as the action in the main clause? (Choose *before, after*, or a similar time expression.)

   ______ he was a hard worker, they did not give him a salary raise. (A) (B) (C) (D)
   (A) Because (C) Since
   (B) Whenever (D) Although

   In this example, the dependent clause contradicts the main clause: a hard worker can expect to get a salary raise. The correct choice is *Although*.

2. If you do not immediately know the answer, move on to the next question. Come back to the ones you are unsure about if you have time at the end.

Practice

DIRECTIONS: Mark the choice that best completes the sentence.

1. ______ they were tired, they worked overtime. (A) (B) (C) (D)
   (A) Because (C) Since
   (B) Whenever (D) Although

2. Mr. Kim visits our office ______ he is in the neighborhood. (A) (B) (C) (D)
   (A) before (C) whenever
   (B) but (D) even though

3. ______ Mr. Park worked for us, he had received training abroad. (A) (B) (C) (D)
   (A) Before (C) Either
   (B) As soon as (D) Whenever

4. Please answer the phone ______ it rings. (A) (B) (C) (D)
   (A) even though (C) and
   (B) when (D) before

5. He took a second job ______ he needed extra money. (A) (B) (C) (D)
   (A) because (D) before
   (B) though (D) but

6. The soccer game won't be postponed ______ it looks like rain. (A) (B) (C) (D)
   (A) because (C) since
   (B) although (D) when

7. ______ profits have improved, we're all getting bonuses. (A) (B) (C) (D)
   (A) Since (C) Even though
   (B) Before (D) By

8. Ms. Adams refused the promotion ______ it meant she would get a big raise. (A) (B) (C) (D)
   (A) because (C) though
   (B) and (D) when

9. The hotel will accept no guests ______ it's being renovated. (A) (B) (C) (D)
   (A) and (C) before
   (B) while (D) although

10. Restaurant food handlers must wear latex gloves ______ they are required by health regulations. (A) (B) (C) (D)
    (A) because (C) though
    (B) before (D) and

VERB TENSES

The main verb tells you when the action in the sentence occurs. Look for time expressions. Certain time expressions indicate certain verb tenses. The verb tense and the time expressions often appear together.

Verb Tense	Use	Time Expressions
Simple Present	Habit	*every:* every day, every week, every month *adverbs of frequency:* always, usually, often, sometimes, never, rarely
Present Continuous	An action occurring now	now at this moment at this time currently
Simple Past	An action completed in the past	*last:* last night, last weekend, last June, last year *ago:* an hour ago, two weeks ago
Present Perfect Present Perfect Continuous	An action started in the past and continuing to the present	*since:* since 1991, since last night *for:* for two months, for a long time
Future	An action occurring in the future	*next:* next Monday, next summer, next May *tomorrow:* tomorrow morning, tomorrow evening

Sentences

Simple Present	We *meet* in the conference room every Friday morning.
Present Continuous	They *are* currently *working* on an agreement.
Simple Past	We *finished* the project last night.
Present Perfect	She *has been* the company director for close to three years.
Future	He *will take* his vacation next August.

Strategies

1. Look for a time expression that tells you when the action occurs.

   We ______ for a new office assistant since the beginning of the year. (A) (B) (C) (D)

   (A) are looking (C) will look
   (B) looked (D) have been looking

   A time expression with *since* can indicate the present perfect or the present perfect continuous. *Have been looking* is present perfect continuous, so that is the correct choice.

2. If you do not immediately know the answer, move on to the next question. Come back to the ones you are unsure about if you have time at the end.

Practice

DIRECTIONS: Mark the choice that best completes the sentence.

1. A messenger ______ the package tomorrow afternoon. Ⓐ Ⓑ Ⓒ Ⓓ
   (A) delivers (C) has delivered
   (B) will deliver (D) delivered

2. Ms. Brigham's assistant ______ here for quite a while. Ⓐ Ⓑ Ⓒ Ⓓ
   (A) works (C) has been working
   (B) is working (D) will work

3. The Paris branch of our bank ______ five years ago today. Ⓐ Ⓑ Ⓒ Ⓓ
   (A) opens (C) opened
   (B) has opened (D) was opening

4. My assistant usually ______ my messages early in the morning. Ⓐ Ⓑ Ⓒ Ⓓ
   (A) is checking (C) will check
   (B) has been checking (D) checks

5. My supervisor promises that I ______ a raise next year. Ⓐ Ⓑ Ⓒ Ⓓ
   (A) have gotten (C) will get
   (B) am getting (D) get

6. I ______ lunch at my desk almost every day. Ⓐ Ⓑ Ⓒ Ⓓ
   (A) eat (C) ate
   (B) am eating (D) eaten

7. The boss ______ for those reports since this morning. Ⓐ Ⓑ Ⓒ Ⓓ
   (A) is waiting (C) has been waiting
   (B) waits (D) waited

8. We ______ each other at the conference next month. Ⓐ Ⓑ Ⓒ Ⓓ
   (A) see (C) saw
   (B) will see (D) have seen

9. Currently, our company ______ for a larger office space. Ⓐ Ⓑ Ⓒ Ⓓ
   (A) is looking (C) looks
   (B) has been looking (D) looked

10. I ______ that workshop three months ago. Ⓐ Ⓑ Ⓒ Ⓓ
    (A) attend (C) have attended
    (B) will attend (D) attended

PHRASAL VERBS

Phrasal verbs usually have two parts: a verb and a particle (*give back*). Some phrasal verbs have two particles (*give up on*). The particles look like prepositions, but they are part of the verb. The meaning of a phrasal verb is not usually related to the meaning of the parts. There are no rules to help you predict the meaning. You have to learn what each one means. Some have more than one meaning.

Verb	Meaning
turn on	start a machine
turn off	stop a machine
turn in	submit
turn up	appear

Sentences

We *turned on* the radio and listened to the news report.
I always *turn off* the computer before I leave the office.
We have to *turn in* our timesheets at the end of the month.
Only five people *turned up* at the meeting.

Strategies

1. See if you can eliminate any of the choices.

   They ______ the meeting because of the bad weather. Ⓐ Ⓑ Ⓒ Ⓓ
   (A) called up
   (B) called off
   (C) called back
   (D) called on

   You may know that *call up* means *make a phone call* and *call back* means *return a phone call*. You can eliminate these two choices. Even if you are now guessing, you have a 50 percent chance. If you know that *call on* means *visit* or *choose someone in class*, that leaves only *call off*. *Call off* means *cancel*, the correct answer.

2. If you do not immediately know the answer, move on to the next question. Come back to the ones you are unsure about if you have time at the end.

Practice

DIRECTIONS: Mark the choice that best completes the sentence.

1. I would like to call this client, so please ______ his phone number in the directory for me. Ⓐ Ⓑ Ⓒ Ⓓ
   (A) look to (C) look on
   (B) look up (D) look out

2. Who will ______ the manager's projects while she is on vacation? Ⓐ Ⓑ Ⓒ Ⓓ
   (A) take away (C) take over
   (B) take up (D) take off

3. The personnel officer believes that we can ______ with our present staff. Ⓐ Ⓑ Ⓒ Ⓓ
   (A) get off (C) get up
   (B) get on (D) get by

4. Don't forget to ______ the photocopier after you have made your copies. Ⓐ Ⓑ Ⓒ Ⓓ
   (A) turn on (C) turn up
   (B) turn in (D) turn off

5. If I don't answer the phone, leave a message and I will ______ right away. Ⓐ Ⓑ Ⓒ Ⓓ
   (A) call up (C) call on
   (B) call back (D) call off

6. They ______ working until they finished the project. Ⓐ Ⓑ Ⓒ Ⓓ
   (A) kept off (C) kept on
   (B) kept to (D) kept down

7. Did I tell you? I ______ Ms. Flynn at the conference. Ⓐ Ⓑ Ⓒ Ⓓ
   (A) ran over (C) ran out
   (B) ran into (D) ran along

8. I can't find the document anywhere. I ______! Ⓐ Ⓑ Ⓒ Ⓓ
   (A) give up (C) give over
   (B) give out (D) give back

9. You don't need to tell me your decision right now. Take some time to ______. Ⓐ Ⓑ Ⓒ Ⓓ
   (A) check it over (C) think it over
   (B) look it over (D) give it over

10. We need to clean up the room and ______ the chairs after the meeting is over. Ⓐ Ⓑ Ⓒ Ⓓ
    (A) put away (C) put off
    (B) put on (D) put down

GRAMMAR TIP

Prepositions of Time

The prepositions *at, on,* and *in* indicate an exact time.

Time	Preposition	Examples
hour	at	at 10:00 at 5:30 at noon
day/date	on	on Monday on Independence Day on May 15
month/year	in	in May in 1995

The work day begins *at* 9:00.
They will be here *on* Wednesday.
The annual report is due *in* February.

VOCABULARY TIP

Adjectives with *-ly*

Many adverbs end in *-ly*. However, not all words that end in *-ly* are adverbs. Some are adjectives.

Adjectives ending in *-ly*
costly
friendly
kindly
lively
lonely
lovely

We took the train because plane tickets are so *costly*.
The new office assistant is a very *friendly* person.
This is a very busy office, and you'll never feel *lonely*.
There is a *lovely* view of the city from the hotel room.

STRATEGY REVIEW

- Use grammar clues to figure out the part of speech needed to complete the statement.
- Read to find the context of the statement. Decide which vocabulary word best fits the context.
- Find the noun that a pronoun refers to and whether it is the subject or object of the sentence.
- Identify the position of an item to choose the correct preposition.
- Choose the best conjunction to join two parts of a statement by deciding whether the two parts (1) are choices, (2) contradict each other, (3) give similar information, (4) describe a reason, or (5) give information about time.
- Look for a time expression to figure out the verb tense needed.
- Eliminate answer choices that you know are incorrect.
- Move on to the next question if you don't immediately know the answer.

STRATEGY PRACTICE

DIRECTIONS: Read the following statements and choose the word or phrase that best completes the sentence. Use the strategies you have learned.

1. The office manager prefers her coffee with cream _____ sugar. (A) (B) (C) (D)
   (A) but (C) and
   (B) nor (D) plus

2. Office hours will be from 8:30 _____ 5:00. (A) (B) (C) (D)
   (A) at (C) by
   (B) to (D) toward

3. If the secretary _____ where the missing files are, we can stop looking for them. (A) (B) (C) (D)
   (A) knew (C) had known
   (B) would know (D) knows

4. The cashier has to turn the key _____ to open the safe. (A) (B) (C) (D)
   (A) clocked (C) clockwise
   (B) clock (D) clocking

5. The chairman of the board is not _____; he has been married for two years. (A) (B) (C) (D)
   (A) singular (C) only
   (B) single (D) sole

6. When the president arrived, everyone _____. (A) (B) (C) (D)
   (A) has left already (C) already left
   (B) had already left (D) left already

7. Mr. Hao was able to get the envelopes _____ before the mail carrier arrived. (A) (B) (C) (D)
   (A) addressed (C) were addressing
   (B) were addressed (D) being addressed

8. Since many of our clients insist on French food, we _____ make reservations for lunch at the restaurant Lion d'Or. (A) (B) (C) (D)
   (A) often have (C) have often to
   (B) have to often (D) often have to

9. _____ you finish typing that report, make five copies of it and give it to all of the officers. (A) (B) (C) (D)
   (A) While (C) But
   (B) When (D) Although

10. Let's have this letter ______ by express mail.

(A) sends (C) sent
(B) send (D) being sent

Ⓐ Ⓑ Ⓒ Ⓓ

11. Since we need to know who belongs to this organization, could you have the computer do a printout of the entire ______?

(A) membership (C) members
(B) remembrances (D) memories

Ⓐ Ⓑ Ⓒ Ⓓ

12. Ms. Parker was very ______ with the answers the job applicant gave during the interview.

(A) impress (C) impression
(B) impressionable (D) impressed

Ⓐ Ⓑ Ⓒ Ⓓ

13. I'll stay late tonight if we ______ by 5:00.

(A) did not finish (C) had not finished
(B) do not finish (D) will not finish

Ⓐ Ⓑ Ⓒ Ⓓ

14. The final draft will be completed ______ Wednesday.

(A) to (C) on
(B) at (D) from

Ⓐ Ⓑ Ⓒ Ⓓ

15. The benefits program ______ in the next few months.

(A) had changed (C) changed
(B) were changed (D) will be changed

Ⓐ Ⓑ Ⓒ Ⓓ

16. Mr. Honda is a terrific worker. He ______ two promotions this year.

(A) has been giving (C) was given
(B) gave (D) giving

Ⓐ Ⓑ Ⓒ Ⓓ

17. If we keep ______ like this, we should be done before the deadline.

(A) working (C) to work
(B) worked (D) work

Ⓐ Ⓑ Ⓒ Ⓓ

18. I don't need those statistics right now, but please have them ready ______ five o'clock.

(A) on (C) in
(B) by (D) since

Ⓐ Ⓑ Ⓒ Ⓓ

19. I'll be home for dinner unless the boss ______ me to work overtime.

(A) will ask (C) asks
(B) is asking (D) asked

Ⓐ Ⓑ Ⓒ Ⓓ

20. Make sure you get these contracts ______ before you meet with the lawyer.

(A) signed (C) signing
(B) to sign (D) sign

Ⓐ Ⓑ Ⓒ Ⓓ

PART 6: TEXT COMPLETION

These are the directions for Part 6 of the TOEIC® test. Study them now. If you understand these directions now, you will not have to read them during the test.

PART 6

Directions: Read the texts that follow. A word or phrase is missing in some of the sentences. Four answer choices are given below each of the sentences. Select the best answer to complete the text. Then mark the letter (A), (B), (C), or (D) on your answer sheet.

STRATEGY OVERVIEW

LANGUAGE STRATEGIES

You will learn the most common types of grammar items in the text completion passages in Part 6.

Words in context

Pronouns

Prepositions

Time clauses

Adjective comparisons

Gerunds or infinitives

A text completion passage is a passage with words deleted. You will need to understand the whole passage to choose the correct word to complete each blank.

You will find the grammar topics you studied in Part 5 useful for Part 6. Similarly, the grammar topics in Part 6 will help you in Part 5.

TEST STRATEGIES

- Read the sentences before and after the blank to figure out the context.
- Look for a noun after the blank to tell you whether you need an adjective or a pronoun.
- Read the sentences before and after the blank to figure out when the action occurs.
- Look at the verb tense in one part of the sentence to figure out what tense is needed in the other part of the sentence.
- Look for *the* and *than* in comparisons to determine the correct adjective form.
- Figure out whether the main verb is followed by a gerund or an infinitive.
- Move on to the next question if you don't immediately know the answer.

WORDS IN CONTEXT

In Part 6, you complete a sentence with a word that fits the context of the passage. Read the sentences before and after the sentence with the blank to understand the context and choose the correct answer.

Sentences

Mr. Jones no longer works for this company. He ______ after working here for 35 years. His colleagues gave him a party and a gold watch to help him celebrate.

Context: Did Mr. Jones retire, quit, or was he fired? His colleagues helped him celebrate, so it was something positive. Therefore, he didn't quit and he wasn't fired, which are both negative. In addition, he worked for the company for 35 years, there was a party and the gift of a gold watch, all things which indicate that he retired.

Strategies

1. Read the sentence before the incomplete sentence and the sentence after it. Quickly determine the context. Is it about money, getting or losing a job, renting an office, etc.?

   John is looking for employment. He has already sent his ______ to several companies.

   Ⓐ Ⓑ Ⓒ Ⓓ

   (A) order (C) check
   (B) résumé (D) package

   In this example, all four choices are things that someone might send to a company. By reading the sentence before the blank, we see *looking for employment*. This is the context. Therefore, we know that John sent his *résumé*.

2. If you do not immediately know the answer, move on to the next question. Come back to the ones you are unsure about if you have time at the end.

Practice

DIRECTIONS: Mark the choice that best completes the sentence.

1. You have not paid your invoices in three months. Interest of 16.8% is being applied to your ______ balance.

   Ⓐ Ⓑ Ⓒ Ⓓ

   (A) upstanding (C) remainder
   (B) remunerated (D) overdue

2. Members must be single and earn at least $2 million a year. If you meet these qualifications, you are ______ for membership.

   Ⓐ Ⓑ Ⓒ Ⓓ

   (A) eligible (C) inadequate
   (B) titled (D) financed

3. Ms. Jones worked for the company for just two weeks before she unexpectedly left. We will never know whether she was terminated or whether she ______.

(A) fired
(B) resigned
(C) hired
(D) applied

Ⓐ Ⓑ Ⓒ Ⓓ

4. Some people don't know how to eat properly. Their table manners are ______.

(A) attractive
(B) shameful
(C) appealing
(D) edifying

Ⓐ Ⓑ Ⓒ Ⓓ

5. We are unable to respond to your request at this time. We will try to ______ you within the week.

(A) ignore
(B) get back to
(C) delay
(D) turn around

Ⓐ Ⓑ Ⓒ Ⓓ

6. If you have any suggestions, do not hesitate to let us know. We look forward to hearing your ______.

(A) feedback
(B) talk
(C) complaints
(D) problems

Ⓐ Ⓑ Ⓒ Ⓓ

7. The highway is under repair, and traffic is often at a standstill. You might find it ______ to take the subway.

(A) inconvenient
(B) faster
(C) inadvisable
(D) idle

Ⓐ Ⓑ Ⓒ Ⓓ

8. We never thought the meeting would be so long and boring. Next time let's make it shorter and more ______.

(A) dull
(B) interesting
(C) curious
(D) lengthy

Ⓐ Ⓑ Ⓒ Ⓓ

9. At our new headquarters, we finally have more than enough room for everyone. Our offices are modern and ______.

(A) traditional
(B) undersized
(C) overcrowded
(D) spacious

Ⓐ Ⓑ Ⓒ Ⓓ

10. The way you do business is hardly effective or efficient. In fact, you are the most ______ manager in our company.

(A) capable
(B) talented
(C) incompetent
(D) accomplished

Ⓐ Ⓑ Ⓒ Ⓓ

POSSESSIVE ADJECTIVES AND PRONOUNS

Possessive adjectives and pronouns show ownership. The owner is someone or something mentioned earlier in the passage. A possessive adjective is followed by a noun. A possessive pronoun is not.

Possessive Adjectives	
Singular	**Plural**
my	our
your	your
his, her, its	their

Possessive Pronouns	
Singular	**Plural**
mine	ours
yours	yours
his, her, its	theirs

Sentences

Mrs. Kim is out of the office today. Please leave the message on *her* desk.
You can hang *your* coat in this closet.
Their office is by the elevators, and *ours* is at the end of the hall.
Have you found your keys? *Mine* are in my pocket.

Strategies

1. If the blank is followed by a noun, choose an adjective. If it is not followed by a noun, choose a pronoun.

2. You may have to read a sentence or two back to determine who the owner is.

   Lisa and I share this workspace. That desk is Lisa's, and this one is ______. (A) (B) (C) (D)

   (A) hers (C) her
   (B) mine (D) my

   In this example, the blank is not followed by a noun, so a possessive pronoun is needed. The word refers to *I* in the first sentence, so the correct answer is *mine.*

3. If you do not immediately know the answer, move on to the next question. Come back to the ones you are unsure about if you have time at the end.

Practice

DIRECTIONS: Mark the choice that best completes the sentence.

1. We take turns leading the weekly staff meeting. ______ turn will be the first week of next month. (A) (B) (C) (D)

   (A) My (C) Ours
   (B) Theirs (D) Mine

2. Mr. Chang is not available at the moment, but I am sure _______ assistant will be able to help you. Ⓐ Ⓑ Ⓒ Ⓓ
(A) he (C) him
(B) his (D) your

3. These are my books here. I put _______ over there. Ⓐ Ⓑ Ⓒ Ⓓ
(A) your (C) yours
(B) mine (D) my

4. I have received all the reports except Maria's. As soon as I receive _______, I can start the evaluation. Ⓐ Ⓑ Ⓒ Ⓓ
(A) her (C) hers
(B) my (D) its

5. The representatives from the Tokyo office won't be on time for the meeting. Unfortunately, _______ flight was delayed. Ⓐ Ⓑ Ⓒ Ⓓ
(A) they (C) its
(B) it (D) their

6. I read Mr. Long's application last night. I think _______ was the best of them all. Ⓐ Ⓑ Ⓒ Ⓓ
(A) him (C) its
(B) his (D) hers

7. I borrowed _______ book. I will return it to you as soon as I finish reading it. Ⓐ Ⓑ Ⓒ Ⓓ
(A) your (C) yours
(B) my (D) mine

8. A lot of companies have advertisements in that magazine. _______ usually appears on the back page. Ⓐ Ⓑ Ⓒ Ⓓ
(A) My (C) Her
(B) Ours (D) Your

9. Always have _______ lawyer review documents before you sign them. Ⓐ Ⓑ Ⓒ Ⓓ
(A) hers (C) theirs
(B) mine (D) your

10. If Ms. Lane is interested in working here, she should send _______ résumé to the personnel manager. Ⓐ Ⓑ Ⓒ Ⓓ
(A) her (C) hers
(B) it (D) his

PREPOSITIONS: TIME

Some prepositions tell you about time. They indicate when an action occurs relative to a point in time.

Prepositions of Time	Use
at, on, in	occurring at an exact point in time
before, by, after	occurring before or after a point in time
around	occurring near a point in time
from . . . to, from . . . until, between	occurring between two points in time

Sentences

The package arrived *on* Monday.
We hope to finish the project *before* the weekend.
They should be here *around* 3:00.
He left his job *in* May.
We worked *from* noon *until* 6:00.

Strategies

1. Read the sentences before and after the blank. This will help you determine when the action occurs relative to the time mentioned.

   Mr. Wilson will be in a meeting all morning. He will be available ______ 12:00. Ⓐ Ⓑ Ⓒ Ⓓ

   (A) before (C) after
   (B) on (D) until

   Mr. Wilson will be in a meeting in the morning, so he will not be available before 12:00, he will be available *after* 12:00.

2. If you do not immediately know the answer, move on to the next question. Come back to the ones you are unsure about if you have time at the end.

Practice

DIRECTIONS: Mark the choice that best completes the sentence.

1. The director wants this work finished as soon as possible. If we finish ______ Friday, he will give us a bonus. Ⓐ Ⓑ Ⓒ Ⓓ

   (A) after (C) from
   (B) by (D) at

2. The personnel manager has announced the date for the workshop. It will take place ______ July 15. Ⓐ Ⓑ Ⓒ Ⓓ

   (A) in (C) to
   (B) on (D) at

3. We can't say exactly when the report will be ready, but it will be ______ October 1. Ⓐ Ⓑ Ⓒ Ⓓ

(A) on (C) around
(B) at (D) until

4. This project will require a lot of work. If we work from Monday ______ Friday, we still won't get it done. Ⓐ Ⓑ Ⓒ Ⓓ

(A) to (C) on
(B) from (D) at

5. The meeting begins ______ 11:30. We expect everyone to be on time. Ⓐ Ⓑ Ⓒ Ⓓ

(A) on (C) in
(B) to (D) at

6. Ms. Kovacs has owned this business for several years now. She bought it ______ 2008. Ⓐ Ⓑ Ⓒ Ⓓ

(A) on (C) from
(B) in (D) until

7. I will be very busy at work all week. ______ Friday I will have more free time. Ⓐ Ⓑ Ⓒ Ⓓ

(A) After (C) Before
(B) In (D) Between

8. We have found a new office to rent. We will move into it ______ September. Ⓐ Ⓑ Ⓒ Ⓓ

(A) on (C) to
(B) at (D) in

9. Most of our employees take their vacations in the summer. ______ June and August, things are very quiet around here. Ⓐ Ⓑ Ⓒ Ⓓ

(A) From (C) Between
(B) After (D) Before

10. We take inventory twice a year. We do it ______ June and December. Ⓐ Ⓑ Ⓒ Ⓓ

(A) from (C) on
(B) in (D) after

VERB TENSE: TIME CLAUSES

A time clause shows the time of the action of the verb in the main clause. A time clause begins with a word or phrase such as *before, after, until, when, while, as soon as, by the time*. The verb tense in one clause gives you a clue about the correct tense for the other clause.

Sentences

I call the maintenance office when the photocopier needs a repair.
simple present *simple present*

We finished the report before the meeting started.
simple past *simple past*

BUT:

We will return to the office as soon as the meeting is over.
future *simple present*

A time clause about the future uses a present tense verb. The future tense verb is in the main clause. The verb in the time clause is in the present tense even though the action will occur in the future.

Strategies

1. When you need to choose a verb to complete a clause, look at the tense of the main verb in the other clause.

   We ______ lunch after we got off the plane. (A) (B) (C) (D)

   (A) had (C) have had
   (B) have (D) will have

   The verb in the time clause, *got*, is in the past tense, and past tense is the only logical choice for the verb in the main clause. The correct answer is *had*.

2. If you do not immediately know the answer, move on to the next question. Come back to the ones you are unsure about if you have time at the end.

Practice

DIRECTIONS: Mark the choice that best completes the sentence.

1. When the messenger ______, will you please give him this package? (A) (B) (C) (D)

   (A) will arrive (C) arriving
   (B) arrives (D) arrived

2. Ms. Brigham had very little office experience when we ______ her. (A) (B) (C) (D)

   (A) hire (C) have hired
   (B) will hire (D) hired

3. When there are long lines at the cafeteria, I ______ my lunch at the sandwich shop across the street.
(A) buy (C) have bought
(B) bought (D) buying

Ⓐ Ⓑ Ⓒ Ⓓ

4. As soon as the rain stops, we ______ to the bank.
(A) walk (C) will walk
(B) walked (D) have walked

Ⓐ Ⓑ Ⓒ Ⓓ

5. As soon as the ad appeared in the newspaper, several people ______ to find out about the office for rent.
(A) called (C) call
(B) will call (D) calls

Ⓐ Ⓑ Ⓒ Ⓓ

6. He will call you before he ______ for the airport.
(A) left (C) leaves
(B) leave (D) will leave

Ⓐ Ⓑ Ⓒ Ⓓ

7. Ms. Kim always ______ notes while Mr. Lee talks with the client.
(A) will take (C) took
(B) has taken (D) takes

Ⓐ Ⓑ Ⓒ Ⓓ

8. We stayed at the office until we ______ the work.
(A) finish (C) will finish
(B) finished (D) are finishing

Ⓐ Ⓑ Ⓒ Ⓓ

9. I usually ______ my phone messages before I look at my e-mail.
(A) check (C) checked
(B) checks (D) will check

Ⓐ Ⓑ Ⓒ Ⓓ

10. We will call you when we ______ our decision.
(A) will make (C) make
(B) making (D) made

Ⓐ Ⓑ Ⓒ Ⓓ

ADJECTIVE COMPARISONS

Comparative adjectives are used to compare one thing to another thing. Superlative adjectives are used to compare one thing to a group of things.

For comparisons, one-syllable and some two-syllable adjectives add *-er* at the end of the word. Longer adjectives have *more* in front.

high higher   easy easier   careless more careless

A comparative sentence uses *than* if it mentions both of the things that are being compared. It does not use *than* if it only mentions one thing.

I am taller.   I am taller *than* my sister.

For superlatives, one-syllable and some two-syllable adjectives add *-est* at the end of the word. Longer adjectives have *most* in front. Superlative adjectives also have *the* before the adjective.

high highest   easy easiest   careless most careless

Some comparative and superlative forms are irregular.

Adjective	Comparative	Superlative
good	better	the best
bad	worse	the worst
far	farther	the farthest

Sentences

This room is *better*.
This report is *longer than* last year's report.
That is *the most expensive* hotel in the city.
It's *the fastest* computer that we have.

Strategies

1. If a comparative sentence has *the* before the blank, choose the superlative. If the blank is followed by *than*, choose the comparative.

   Read the book. It's ______ than the movie.   (A) (B) (C) (D)
   (A) interest   (C) more interesting
   (B) interesting   (D) the most interesting

   This sentence uses the word *than*, so the missing word is the comparative adjective *more interesting*.

2. If you do not immediately know the answer, move on to the next question. Come back to the ones you are unsure about if you have time at the end.

Practice

DIRECTIONS: Mark the choice that best completes the sentence.

1. He was the ______ of all the applicants. Ⓐ Ⓑ Ⓒ Ⓓ
   (A) qualified (C) most qualified
   (B) more qualified (D) more qualified than

2. Stock prices are ______ than they were last week. Ⓐ Ⓑ Ⓒ Ⓓ
   (A) high (C) highly
   (B) higher (D) the highest

3. ______ person in our community is the mayor. Ⓐ Ⓑ Ⓒ Ⓓ
   (A) The most famous (C) Famously
   (B) More famous (D) Famous

4. Company benefits are ______ now than last year. Ⓐ Ⓑ Ⓒ Ⓓ
   (A) good (C) the best
   (B) best (D) better

5. I don't recommend that restaurant. It serves the ______ food that I have ever eaten. Ⓐ Ⓑ Ⓒ Ⓓ
   (A) bad (C) worse than
   (B) worse (D) worst

6. You should speak with my colleague. He is ______ than I am about this matter. Ⓐ Ⓑ Ⓒ Ⓓ
   (A) knowledge (C) more knowledgeable
   (B) knowledgeable (D) the most knowledgeable

7. When she was ______ than I am now, she started her own company. Ⓐ Ⓑ Ⓒ Ⓓ
   (A) young (C) youngest
   (B) younger (D) the youngest

8. Mr. Nakamura was ______ arrival at the meeting. Ⓐ Ⓑ Ⓒ Ⓓ
   (A) early (C) earliest
   (B) earlier (D) the earliest

9. I never take the bus. The subway is ______. Ⓐ Ⓑ Ⓒ Ⓓ
   (A) quicker (C) quicken
   (B) quickly (D) quicker than

10. Let's go to the bank first. It's ______ the post office. Ⓐ Ⓑ Ⓒ Ⓓ
    (A) close (C) closer than
    (B) closer (D) the closest

GERUNDS OR INFINITIVES

Gerunds (verb + *-ing*) and infinitives (*to* + verb) can be used as nouns. They can follow the main verb of the sentence. The choice between the gerund or the infinitive depends on the main verb. Some verbs are followed by gerunds and some are followed by infinitives. Here are some of the most common verbs.

Followed by Gerunds	Followed by Infinitives
enjoy	offer
consider	want
discuss	forget
suggest	have
delay	promise
avoid	hope
admit	need
stop	hurry

Some verbs can be used both ways.

love
hate

You can find lists of these verbs in most grammar reference books.

Sentences

They *promised to bring* the check before the end of the day.
Everybody *enjoyed hearing* about the new director's plans.
We will *discuss hiring* more staff.
They *need to make* a decision before the end of the week.

Strategies

1. Look at the main verb. Is that verb followed by a gerund or an infinitive? Don't be confused by the tense of the main verb. That has no effect on the verb that follows it.

   He hurried ______ to the airport on time. (A) (B) (C) (D)
   (A) get
   (B) gets
   (C) to get
   (D) getting

   The main verb is *hurry*, which is followed by an infinitive. It doesn't matter that the verb is in the past tense or that the subject of the sentence is *He*. A verb following the main verb *hurry* is always an infinitive.

2. If you do not immediately know the answer, move on to the next question. Come back to the ones you are unsure about if you have time at the end.

Practice

DIRECTIONS: Mark the choice that best completes the sentence.

1. The new accountant is considering ______ to another department. Ⓐ Ⓑ Ⓒ Ⓓ
   (A) to transfer (C) transferred
   (B) transferring (D) transfer

2. Mr. Smith wanted ______ his coworkers. Ⓐ Ⓑ Ⓒ Ⓓ
   (A) to meet (C) met
   (B) meeting (D) meet

3. We forgot ______ the door when we left. Ⓐ Ⓑ Ⓒ Ⓓ
   (A) locked (C) lock
   (B) locking (D) to lock

4. They had ______ lunch until tomorrow. Ⓐ Ⓑ Ⓒ Ⓓ
   (A) postpone (C) postponing
   (B) to postpone (D) to be postponed

5. The doctor told him to avoid ______ meat. Ⓐ Ⓑ Ⓒ Ⓓ
   (A) eating (C) eaten
   (B) eat (D) to eat

6. We offered ______ for coffee during the break. Ⓐ Ⓑ Ⓒ Ⓓ
   (A) to go (C) gone
   (B) going (D) went

7. Jack admitted ______ home office equipment for his personal use. Ⓐ Ⓑ Ⓒ Ⓓ
   (A) to take (C) take
   (B) taking (D) took

8. The new employee promised not ______ late again. Ⓐ Ⓑ Ⓒ Ⓓ
   (A) to be (C) be
   (B) being (D) been

9. I hope ______ the MBA program at Harvard. Ⓐ Ⓑ Ⓒ Ⓓ
   (A) entered (C) entering
   (B) enter (D) to enter

10. Stop ______ your money. Ⓐ Ⓑ Ⓒ Ⓓ
    (A) to waste (C) wasting
    (B) wasted (D) waste

GRAMMAR TIP

Prepositions of Location

The prepositions *at, on,* and *in* indicate location. Use *at* with an address, *on* with a street name, and *in* with a town, city, state/province, or country.

Location	Preposition	Examples
address	at	at 125 Main Street
street	on	on Main Street
town / city / state / province / country	in	in Tokyo in California in Quebec in Brazil

The new office is *at* 2396 Oakland Avenue.
There is a post office *on* Maple Street.
The conference will take place *in* Paris.

VOCABULARY TIP

Word Choice

Some words may be used in a similar context but have a different meaning or a different grammatical function.

Borrow* or *Lend

Borrow and *lend* are often confused. Both are used to talk about using something that belongs to another person. *Lend* is what the owner of the object does. *Borrow* is what the user of the object does.

I forgot my dictionary. Can I *borrow* yours?
I don't have enough money for lunch. Can you *lend* me five dollars?

Clothes* or *Cloth

Clothes are the things we wear. Shirts and pants are examples of clothes. The word *clothes* is always plural. It is pronounced /klõz/. *Cloth* is pronounced /kloth/. *Cloth* is the material used to make clothes and other things. For example, cloth can be cotton or wool. A *cloth* is a piece of fabric that is used for cleaning things.

Nice *clothes* are often expensive.
These *clothes* are made of good, strong *cloth*.
I need a *cloth* to wipe off the table.

STRATEGY REVIEW

- Read the sentences before and after the blank to figure out the context.
- Look for a noun after the blank to tell you whether you need an adjective or a pronoun.
- Read the sentences before and after the blank to figure out when the action occurs.
- Look at the verb tense in one part of the sentence to figure out what tense is needed in the other part of the sentence.
- Look for *the* and *than* in comparisons to determine the correct adjective form.
- Figure out whether the main verb is followed by a gerund or an infinitive.
- Move on to the next question if you don't immediately know the answer.

STRATEGY PRACTICE

DIRECTIONS: Read the following passages and choose the word or phrase that best completes the blanks. Use the strategies you have learned.

Questions 1–3 refer to the following letter.

624 South Wells Street
Reno, Nevada 89400

Mr. Norm Thompson
97 Vine Circle
Reno, Nevada 89400

Dear Mr. Thompson:

I want to rent an apartment. My friend says that you are a good ____________

1. (A) landlord
(B) occupant
(C) tenant
(D) painter

and that you own apartments in different parts of the city. Can I rent an apartment from you? My family needs a new place to live. We love our ____________. It's

2. (A) neighbor
(B) neighborly
(C) neighboring
(D) neighborhood

quiet, and it's close to my job. However, our apartment is ____________ small

3. (A) too
(B) a lot
(C) some
(D) enough

for us. There are four of us: my wife, our two children, and me. We need a larger apartment. We are looking for one with three bedrooms and a large kitchen.

We live near Plumas Pass, and we would like to stay in this area. If you have an apartment in Plumas Pass that is available now, please let me know. Thank you for your help.

Sincerely,

Fabian Ricardo

Fabian Ricardo

Questions 4–6 refer to the following article.

Montalvo Industries announced Friday that it will take on 100 new ____________ over the next 6 months.

4. (A) employees
(B) merchants
(C) customers
(D) products

"Our market is expanding," said company CEO Shirley Henrico, "so we need to ____________ our production. That's why we need to hire more workers." The

5. (A) grow
(B) more
(C) bigger
(D) increase

company plans to build a new, larger factory on the outskirts of the city, which will be equipped with all the latest technology. "We are building a very modern factory," said Ms. Henrico. "We are very proud of ____________."

6. (A) us
(B) it
(C) me
(D) him

Questions 7–9 refer to the following advertisement.

The Stardust Cinema announces the third annual

Festival of ________ Films

7. (A) Classic
(B) National
(C) Cartoon
(D) International

September 20–27

We will show the best films of this year from all around the world. See your favorite foreign actors perform in our comfortable, modern theater. ________ will be four different shows every day.

8. (A) There
(B) They
(C) We
(D) It

Tickets are $10 a show, or $35 for four shows. Children 12–17 years old must be accompanied by an adult. Children under 12 will not be ________.

9. (A) treated
(B) educated
(C) admitted
(D) employed

Questions 10–12 refer to the following advertisement.

Tropical Tours Ltd., the nation's leading tour company, has an opening for an experienced ________ to lead our tours in South America.

10. (A) tourist
(B) guide
(C) driver
(D) helper

We are looking for somebody who has traveled in South America and has experience working in the tourist industry. If you enjoy ________,

11. (A) will travel
(B) traveled
(C) traveling
(D) to travel

are a good organizer, and like people, this is the job for you. To apply for the position, please send your resume to Tropical Tours Ltd., PO Box 49603, Pleasantville, NY. Resumes must be received ________

12. (A) after
(B) before
(C) during
(D) while

June 10. Any resumes received later than that date will not be read.

PART 7: READING COMPREHENSION

These are the general directions for Part 7 of the TOEIC® test. Study them now. If you understand these general directions now, you will not have to read them during the test.

> **PART 7**
>
> **Directions:** In this part you will read a selection of texts, such as magazine and newspaper articles, letters, and advertisements. Each text is followed by several questions. Select the best answer for each question and mark the letter (A), (B), (C), or (D) on your answer sheet.

There are also specific directions that precede each passage, and it is important to read them carefully. These specific directions give you information about the passage and the number of questions.

In the first section of Part 7, the single-passage section, there are 28 questions. You will read seven to ten reading passages and you will answer two to four questions for each passage. You will see directions like this:

Questions 153–155 refer to the following e-mail.
Questions 162–163 refer to the following announcement.

In the second section of Part 7, the double-passage section, there are 20 questions. You will read four pairs of reading passages and you will answer five questions for each pair of passages. You will see directions like this:

Questions 181–185 refer to the following invoice and letter.
Questions 186–190 refer to the following advertisement and e-mail.

Part 7 Sections	Number of Questions	Number of Passages	Questions	Question Numbers
Single passages	28	7 to 10	2 to 4 per passage	153–180
Double passages	20	4 pairs	5 per pair of passages	181–200

In this section, you will read the most common types of passages found on the TOEIC test:

- advertisements
- business correspondence
- forms, charts, and graphs
- articles and reports
- announcements and paragraphs

STRATEGY OVERVIEW

LANGUAGE STRATEGIES

Be prepared for four question types on the TOEIC test:

Main Idea

Detail

Inference

Vocabulary

You will find these questions in both the single passage and double passage section of Part 7. Look at the samples of each question type.

- MAIN IDEA QUESTIONS

  What is being advertised?

  What is the purpose of the letter?

  What is the main idea of this article?

  What is this announcement about?

  What is the purpose of this graph?

  What is the reason for this correspondence?

  What is the topic of the meeting?

  What is being discussed?

- DETAIL QUESTIONS

  How much is a (product)?

  When was the e-mail sent?

  What percentage of users are over 30?

  Who is (name or title)?

  What dates are critical?

  Who has to attend the meeting?

  How much time does the graph cover?

  Where is Mr. Brown working now?

- INFERENCE QUESTIONS

  Who might use (the product)?

  What is the tone of the memo?

  Who would use the information?

  Who would most likely read this report?

  What is the writer's opinion?

Where would you find these instructions?

Why did Ms. Jones write this letter?

What will the employee do next?

- VOCABULARY QUESTIONS

  The word "promotion" in paragraph 1, line 3, is closest in meaning to . . .

  The word "competent" in line 2 is closest in meaning to . . .

  The word "produce" in line 1 of the ad is closest in meaning to . . .

  The word "data" below the graph is closest in meaning to . . .

Some double-passage questions will require you to understand information from both passages. These questions are usually detail questions. They will ask for specific information about time and reason.

- DETAIL QUESTIONS: TIME

  When will the meeting take place?

  How long will the conference last?

- DETAIL QUESTIONS: REASON

  Why will Mr. Wilson have to call the travel agent?

  Why does Ms. Craft believe Mr. Jones will be hired?

- DETAIL QUESTIONS: QUANTITY

  How many mobile phones were purchased?

  How much did the consumer pay for the product?

TEST STRATEGIES

In Part 7, you must read as quickly as you can. You must also read efficiently. These strategies will help you read more efficiently and answer the questions on Part 7 correctly.

- Read quickly and efficiently.
- Read the questions BEFORE you read the passage.

  If you know what a question asks, you will have a specific purpose when you read. Look for the answer to the question as you read.

Read these sample questions and note the information wanted.

Advertisement

How much is (a product)?	detail
What is being advertised?	main idea
Who might use the product?	inference

Business correspondence

When was the fax sent?	detail
What is the purpose of the letter?	main idea
What is the tone of the memo?	inference

Forms, charts, and graphs

What percentage of users are over 30?	detail
What is the purpose of the circle graph?	main idea
Who could use this information?	inference

Articles and reports

What dates are critical?	detail
What is the main idea of this article?	main idea
Who would most likely read this report?	inference

Announcements and paragraphs

Who is (name or title)?	detail
What is the announcement about?	main idea
What is the writer's opinion?	inference

- Do NOT read the answers before you read the passage.

  Save yourself some time. You will probably find the answer to the question yourself and you will not be confused by the answer options. Some answer options may look correct.

- If you cannot answer a question, read the four answer options. Scan the passage (look over the passage very quickly) and look for these four options. The option may be a synonym or paraphrase of the correct answer.

- The questions follow the sequence of the passage. The answer to the first question is found in the first part of the passage. The answer to the second question is found after that.

  In double passages, however, you need information in both texts to answer one or more of the questions. In double passages, the answer might not follow the sequence of the text.

- For double-passage questions, check both passages for similar information. The information may be contradictory or more information might be added.

Example 1 **Time**

Question: When will the meeting begin?

Passage 1 Information on agenda

8:30 Breakfast
9:00 Meeting in Room 304
10:00 Break

Passage 2 Information in e-mail

Writer: "Unfortunately, two participants will be late so the meeting will have to start an hour later."

Question:	When will the meeting begin? (A) 8:30 A.M. (B) 9:00 A.M. (C) 10:00 A.M. (D) 10:00 P.M.
Answer:	(C) 10:00 A.M. According to Passage 1, the meeting was originally scheduled for 9:00 in the morning. (Clue: Breakfast is served in the morning. The agenda listed 9:00 as the start time.) However, according to passage 2, the participants would be one hour late, which is 10:00 A.M. The correct answer is (C).

Example 2 **Reason**

Question:	Which copier model will they buy?
Passage 1	Information on advertisement
Model X01	The fastest photocopier on the market
Model XX23	Our most energy-efficient model
Model 7Y66	Can fax and scan all size documents.
Model 3544	One toner cartridge can last for 10,000 pages.
Passage 2	Information in e-mail

Writer: "When you shop online for a new copier, make sure that the copier is quick, energy efficient and doesn't use a lot of toner. But most importantly the copier has to be able to copy books, letters, and extra long sheets of paper."

Question:	Which copier model will they buy? (A) X01 (B) XX23 (C) 7Y66 (D) 3544
Answer:	(C) 7Y66. According to Passage 1, this model can fax and scan all size documents. According to passage 2, the writer believes the most important feature is the ability to copy different documents (books, letters, and extra long sheets of paper). The correct answer is (C).

Example 3 **Quantity**

Question:	What was the total number of units shipped?
Passage 1	Information on invoice

QTY	Unit Price	Total
100	$2.00	$200.00

Passage 2 Information in letter

Writer: "Enclosed please find check number 3434 for $400. We had ordered only 50 units, but you sent four times as many. We can use the extra 100 units so we will keep them and pay an additional $200 for the extra 100 units. Thanks for doubling our order."

Question: What was the total number of units shipped?
(A) 50
(B) 100
(C) 200
(D) 400

Answer: (C) 200. According to Passage 1, 100 units were shipped. According to passage 2, the shipping department made a mistake and sent 200 units. The customer had ordered 50, but four times as many units were shipped (200 units). The correct answer is (C).

This looks like a lot of mathematics, but it's not. The invoice says 100 units were shipped. The writer of the letter says an additional 100 units were shipped. 100+100 = 200.

The TOEIC test does not require you to do math. But you need to know the meaning of words like "double." One hundred units doubled equals 200 units.

PRACTICE: READING COMPREHENSION

Single Passage: Advertisement 1

Small computer software company is looking for an office manager. College degree not required, but applicant must have at least two years experience at a similar job. Call Ms. Chang (director) at 348-555-0987.

1. What kind of job is advertised?
   (A) Director of a computer company
   (B) Office manager
   (C) Computer programmer
   (D) College professor

   Ⓐ Ⓑ Ⓒ Ⓓ

2. What is a requirement for this job?
   (A) A college degree
   (B) Less than two years experience
   (C) Telephone skills
   (D) Two or more years experience

   Ⓐ Ⓑ Ⓒ Ⓓ

READING FAST

Read the passage as fast as you can. How long did it take?

_______ minutes _______ seconds

OFFICE SUPPLY SALE

This week only

- Computer paper (white only) 25% off
- Envelopes (all colors, including pink, purple, and gold) 50% off
- Notebooks—buy five, get one free
- Pens (blue, black, and red ink) 12 for $1

Sale ends Saturday

3. What kind of computer paper is on sale? Ⓐ Ⓑ Ⓒ Ⓓ
(A) White
(B) All colors
(C) Pink, purple, and gold
(D) Red, blue, and black

4. How can you get a free notebook? Ⓐ Ⓑ Ⓒ Ⓓ
(A) Pay one dollar
(B) Spend $25 on computer paper
(C) Buy colored envelopes
(D) Buy five notebooks

5. When is the sale? Ⓐ Ⓑ Ⓒ Ⓓ
(A) All weekend
(B) On Sunday only
(C) All week
(D) On Saturday only

READING FAST

Read the passage as fast as you can. How long did it take?

_______ minutes _______ seconds

Sea Island Resort

Spend your next vacation with us.

Enjoy our:

- private beach
- two swimming pools
- four tennis courts
- five restaurants
- beautiful weather all year

It's easy to get here.
We're just eight kilometers from the airport.

Call your travel agent to make reservations.

6. What is this ad for? Ⓐ Ⓑ Ⓒ Ⓓ
   (A) An airline
   (B) A travel agency
   (C) A vacation place
   (D) A sports club

7. What is one thing you cannot do at Sea Island Resort? Ⓐ Ⓑ Ⓒ Ⓓ
   (A) Swim
   (B) Play tennis
   (C) Eat
   (D) Play golf

8. The word "private" in line 5 is closest in meaning to Ⓐ Ⓑ Ⓒ Ⓓ
   (A) not public
   (B) large
   (C) sandy
   (D) personal

9. How can you make reservations for Sea Island Resort? Ⓐ Ⓑ Ⓒ Ⓓ
   (A) Call a travel agent
   (B) Write a letter to the resort owner
   (C) Call the airport
   (D) Send an e-mail

READING FAST

Read the passage as fast as you can. How long did it take?

_______ minutes _______ seconds

Market Products, Inc.
830 2nd Ave. Suite 20B
New York, NY 10015

June 7, 20__

Ms. Lucy Harper
2091 W 4th Avenue
Apartment 101
Buffalo, NY 12345

Dear Ms. Harper:

Thank you for your letter of April 15 looking for a job at Market Products. You have good experience and an excellent education. I am sorry to tell you, however, that we don't have any job openings at this time. We will keep your résumé and contact you if we have any job openings in the future. Good luck.

Best regards,

Joan Rogers

Joan Rogers
Human Resources Director

10. Why did Joan Rogers write this letter? (A) (B) (C) (D)
- (A) To offer Ms. Harper a job
- (B) To sell products to Ms. Harper
- (C) To reply to Ms. Harper's letter
- (D) To explain the work of Market Products

11. When did she write the letter? (A) (B) (C) (D)
- (A) On April 5
- (B) On April 15
- (C) On June 7
- (D) On June 17

READING FAST

Read the passage as fast as you can. How long did it take?

_______ minutes _______ seconds

From: DIGICAM
Sent: Monday, April 9, 20__ 11:32 A.M.
To: Gavin Realtor
Subject: Your pictures are ready!

Dear Customer,

Thank you for using DIGICAM. Your digital photos are ready. Please pick them up at Cherry Mall. The total cost is $28.92. If you are unhappy with your pictures, please call us at 354-555-4756. Enjoy your photos.

Sincerely,

The DIGICAM photo team

12. What type of correspondence is this? (A) (B) (C) (D)

(A) A cover letter
(B) An e-mail
(C) A memo
(D) A fax

13. What is the reason for this correspondence? (A) (B) (C) (D)

(A) There is a job opening at Digicam.
(B) Some photos are ready.
(C) The client forgot to pay.
(D) The customer was unhappy.

14. What should customers who do not like their photos do? (A) (B) (C) (D)

(A) Call Cherry Mall
(B) Return their photos
(C) Ask for a refund
(D) Call Digicam

READING FAST

Read the passage as fast as you can. How long did it take?

_______ minutes _______ seconds

Memorandum

The XYZ Company

From: Brianna Herbert
Date: Friday, May 17
To: Accounting Department staff
Re: Next week

I will be out of the office at an accountants' conference next week, May 20–24. If you need help during that time, please contact my assistant, Sherry Noyes.

Thank you.

15. Where will Brianna Herbert be next week? Ⓐ Ⓑ Ⓒ Ⓓ
(A) In the office
(B) At a conference
(C) On vacation
(D) At the XYZ Company

16. Who is Sherry Noyes? Ⓐ Ⓑ Ⓒ Ⓓ
(A) An accountant
(B) The writer of the memo
(C) The owner of the XYZ Company
(D) Brianna Herbert's assistant

17. The word "contact" in line 8 is closest in meaning to Ⓐ Ⓑ Ⓒ Ⓓ
(A) work with
(B) call
(C) touch
(D) look at

18. Who should read the memo? Ⓐ Ⓑ Ⓒ Ⓓ
(A) All staff at the XYZ company
(B) Brianna Herbert
(C) People who work in the accounting department
(D) Conference planners

READING FAST

Read the passage as fast as you can. How long did it take?

______ minutes ______ seconds

ROSIE'S STEAKHOUSE
We care about your service.

Date: *Feb 17, 20__*
Server's Name: *Julie*
Number of guests: *2*

The server was:	(Excellent)	Good	Fair	Poor
The food was:	Excellent	Good	Fair	(Poor)

Other comments: *Our server was very friendly and polite. She brought our drinks on time. However, we waited a long time for our food. Also, my husband was angry because his fish was not well-cooked. We will not return.*

19. How did the customers rate the food? Ⓐ Ⓑ Ⓒ Ⓓ
- (A) Excellent
- (B) Good
- (C) Fair
- (D) Poor

20. Which of the following describes Julie? Ⓐ Ⓑ Ⓒ Ⓓ
- (A) Slow
- (B) Friendly
- (C) Fair
- (D) Angry

READING FAST

Read the passage as fast as you can. How long did it take?

_______ minutes _______ seconds

CITY ZOO

Month	Number of visitors
January	5,000
February	4,500
March	4,675
April	4,980
May	5,950
June	5,897

21. How many people visited the zoo in February? Ⓐ Ⓑ Ⓒ Ⓓ
(A) 4,000
(B) 4,500
(C) 4,675
(D) 5,000

22. When did 4,980 people visit the zoo? Ⓐ Ⓑ Ⓒ Ⓓ
(A) March
(B) April
(C) May
(D) June

23. Which was the most popular month to visit the zoo? Ⓐ Ⓑ Ⓒ Ⓓ
(A) March
(B) April
(C) May
(D) June

READING FAST

Read the passage as fast as you can. How long did it take?

_______ minutes _______ seconds

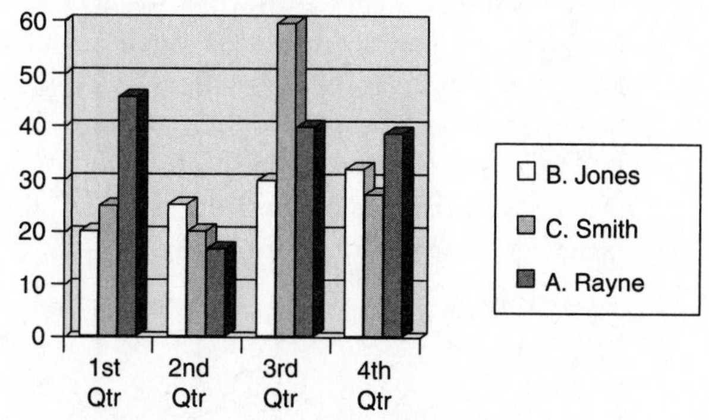

(Each quarter represents 3 months in the year)

24. The word "represents" is closest in meaning to (A) (B) (C) (D)
(A) costs
(B) stands for
(C) means
(D) takes on

25. Who had the highest sales in the first quarter? (A) (B) (C) (D)
(A) B. Jones
(B) C. Smith
(C) A. Rayne
(D) There was a tie.

26. How much money in sales did C. Smith have in the third quarter? (A) (B) (C) (D)
(A) $60
(B) $30,000
(C) $40,000
(D) $60,000

27. How many months does this graph represent? (A) (B) (C) (D)
(A) 1
(B) 3
(C) 4
(D) 12

READING FAST

Read the passage as fast as you can. How long did it take?

______ minutes ______ seconds

Maple Plaza, our city's newest mall, will open on October 25. The new mall will have 31 stores and 8 restaurants. It will also have a movie theater, which will open in November. The biggest store at the mall will be McGruder's Department Store. There will be a party to celebrate the new mall on October 26 from noon to 5:00 PM. All members of the public are invited.

28. What will happen on October 25? Ⓐ Ⓑ Ⓒ Ⓓ

(A) A movie theater will open.
(B) McGruder's will have a sale.
(C) There will be a party.
(D) A new mall will open.

29. How many stores will Maple Plaza have? Ⓐ Ⓑ Ⓒ Ⓓ

(A) 8
(B) 26
(C) 31
(D) 34

READING FAST

Read the passage as fast as you can. How long did it take?

_______ minutes _______ seconds

Do you know that computers can cause headaches? According to a recent report, many computer workers have this problem. If you work at a computer more than six hours a day, you might get headaches. To avoid this problem, take a break once every hour. Get up and walk around for a few minutes. Let your eyes and mind rest. This is a good way to stop headaches without taking aspirin.

30. What type of reading is this? Ⓐ Ⓑ Ⓒ Ⓓ
(A) A memo
(B) An article
(C) An advertisement
(D) An e-mail

31. According to the report, who gets headaches? Ⓐ Ⓑ Ⓒ Ⓓ
(A) People who use computers more than six hours a day
(B) All computer workers
(C) Everybody who works more than six hours a day
(D) Computer programmers

32. How can you avoid headaches? Ⓐ Ⓑ Ⓒ Ⓓ
(A) Walk every six hours
(B) Take aspirin
(C) Get a better computer
(D) Take a break once an hour

READING FAST

Read the passage as fast as you can. How long did it take?

_______ minutes _______ seconds

People are buying more cell phones. The country's largest cell phone company, Phonecom, reported its sales numbers yesterday. This year it has sold 38% more cell phones than it did last year. It has sold 25% of its phones to government offices, 40% to private companies, and 35% to individuals for personal use.

33. What does this report tell us? (A) (B) (C) (D)

(A) Government offices bought fewer cell phones last year.
(B) Cell phones are more expensive this year than last year.
(C) A phone company has sold 38,000 phones this year.
(D) This year people bought more cell phones than last year.

34. What is Phonecom? (A) (B) (C) (D)

(A) A large cell phone company
(B) A government office
(C) A marketing company
(D) A telephone store

35. Which group has bought the most cell phones? (A) (B) (C) (D)

(A) Government offices
(B) Private companies
(C) Individuals
(D) Phone companies

36. The word "reported" in line 2 is closest in meaning to (A) (B) (C) (D)

(A) stood by
(B) increased
(C) denied
(D) announced

READING FAST

Read the passage as fast as you can. How long did it take?

_______ minutes _______ seconds

ATTENTION ALL EMPLOYEES

We have 20 free tickets for the National Championship tennis match next Friday evening. If you are interested in these tickets, please contact Mr. Green in the accounting office before 5:00 PM on Wednesday. We can allow up to 4 tickets per employee.

37. When can the tickets be used? Ⓐ Ⓑ Ⓒ Ⓓ
(A) Before Wednesday
(B) Wednesday at 5:00 PM
(C) Friday at 5:00 PM
(D) Next Friday evening

38. How many tickets can one employee get? Ⓐ Ⓑ Ⓒ Ⓓ
(A) 1
(B) 4
(C) 5
(D) 20

READING FAST

Read the passage as fast as you can.
How long did it take?

_______ minutes _______ seconds

Come and say good-bye!

Please join Murray Jones
in a celebration of his retirement
after 40 years with the GY Camera Company

Place: Castle Restaurant
Date: March 10
Time: 6:00 PM

Kindly RSVP
(Lynn Mickleson, Office Manager, 555-7643)
by March 1.

We hope to see you there!

39. Who is Murray Jones? Ⓐ Ⓑ Ⓒ Ⓓ
(A) The office manager
(B) A company employee
(C) A restaurant owner
(D) A photographer

40. What is the party for? Ⓐ Ⓑ Ⓒ Ⓓ
(A) A birthday
(B) A retirement
(C) An anniversary
(D) A new employee

41. When is the event? Ⓐ Ⓑ Ⓒ Ⓓ
(A) Tomorrow
(B) On March 1
(C) On March 10
(D) In 40 years

READING FAST

Read the passage as fast as you can. How long did it take?

_______ minutes _______ seconds

Do you drink too much coffee?

How much coffee is too much? Most doctors say one cup a day is more than enough. However, most people who work in offices drink two or more cups a day. Many drink coffee during breaks, at lunch, and on their way to and from work. On the other hand, most people don't drink enough water. This is especially a problem for coffee drinkers. When people drink coffee, they don't drink water. Most doctors agree that everyone should drink at least eight glasses of water a day.

42. What type of reading is this? Ⓐ Ⓑ Ⓒ Ⓓ
(A) A letter
(B) A table
(C) An article
(D) A memo

43. How much coffee should people drink a day? Ⓐ Ⓑ Ⓒ Ⓓ
(A) One cup or less
(B) More than one cup
(C) Two or more cups
(D) At least three cups

44. The word "especially" in line 2, second column, is closest in meaning to Ⓐ Ⓑ Ⓒ Ⓓ
(A) only
(B) never
(C) hardly
(D) particularly

45. How much water should people drink every day? Ⓐ Ⓑ Ⓒ Ⓓ
(A) Less than four glasses
(B) Eight or more glasses
(C) One glass for every cup of coffee
(D) No more than two glasses

READING FAST

Read the passage as fast as you can. How long did it take?

_______ minutes _______ seconds

Questions 46–50 refer to the following two letters.

December 7, 20__

Edward James
Clampett, Inc.
362 Industrial Boulevard
Sedgwick, NH

Dear Mr. James,

I am writing in response to your notice in yesterday's Sedgwick Times . I understand you are looking for a market researcher. I have a bachelor's degree from Sedgwick College, where I majored in marketing. Since I graduated four years ago, I have been working in the research department of the Grover Advertising Agency. I have enjoyed my time at Grover. However, it is a very small company. At this point in my career, I would like to find a position in a larger company where there is room to grow and move up. I am eager to talk with you about the possibility of working for Clampett.

I am enclosing my résumé to give you a further idea of my background. You will see that prior to completing my marketing degree, I worked for three years as an office manager at a local law firm. I would be happy to provide you with the names of several references and any other information you may require. I look forward to hearing from you.

Sincerely,
Louise Troy
Louise Troy

December 14, 20__

Louise Troy
21345 Eastern Avenue
Apt. 56
Sedgwick, NH

Dear Ms. Troy,

I very much enjoyed meeting you the other day and discussing the possibility of your joining our team here at Clampett, Inc. I have checked your references and discussed the matter with my colleagues, and we feel certain that you are the most qualified candidate for the job. You are the only applicant, for example, who has the years of marketing experience we requested, and your degree from Sedgwick College means you have the best training available. You will be happy to know that we would like to offer you the position here at Clampett.

Peter Hockney, whom you will be replacing, plans to leave at the end of the year. Therefore, we would like you to begin during the first week of January. In the meantime, there are a number of papers you need to fill out. We would appreciate it if you could come to down to our Human Resources department and complete all the paperwork as soon as possible, but certainly before we close for the holidays on December 23.

Congratulations, and I look forward to seeing you here at Clampett.

Sincerely,
Edward James
Edward James
Hiring Manager

46. Why did Ms. Troy write the letter? (A) (B) (C) (D)

(A) To inquire about job openings
(B) To accept a job offer
(C) To apply for an advertised job
(D) To ask Mr. James for a reference

47. What did Ms. Troy send with her letter? (A) (B) (C) (D)
(A) Letters of reference
(B) Her résumé
(C) Her college transcripts
(D) A legal document

48. How many years experience are required for the job Ms. Troy is interested in? (A) (B) (C) (D)
(A) One
(B) Three
(C) Four
(D) Seven

49. What was Peter Hockney's job? (A) (B) (C) (D)
(A) Market researcher
(B) Hiring manager
(C) Lawyer
(D) College professor

50. When will Ms. Troy's new job start? (A) (B) (C) (D)
(A) On December 14
(B) Before December 23
(C) At the end of the year
(D) The first week of January

Double Passage: Form and Business Correspondence

Questions 51–55 refer to the following schedule and e-mail.

Great Northern Railway Schedule Mortonsville – Barrington Spring, 20__

Leave Mortonsville	Arrive Barrington	Leave Barrington	Arrive Mortonsville
6:30 AM	9:00 AM	7:30 AM	10:00 AM
7:15 AM	9:45 AM	9:00 AM	11:30 AM
8:30 AM	11:00 AM	11:45 AM	2:15 PM
11:15 AM	1:45 PM	1:30 PM	4:00 PM
2:30 PM	5:00 PM	3:15 PM	5:45 PM
3:45 PM	6:15 PM	4:10 PM	6:40 PM

Fares

Weekday: $45 one way, $80 round trip
Weekend: $40 one way, $70 round trip

Ten percent discount available on one-week advance purchase.

To:	Bill Wiggins	Date:	March 20
From:	Cynthia Jones	Subject:	Mortonsville Trip

Thank you for arranging the flight and hotel for my trip to Mortonsville next month for the annual meeting. I just found out that a factory tour has been arranged for me during that week at the Barrington facility, so I'll need you to make arrangements for that, as well. There's a train that runs between Mortonsville and Barrington, so please arrange train tickets for me. The tour is first thing the morning of April 5, that's a Wednesday. I think I should arrive Tuesday night, but I don't want to leave Mortonsville too early as I'll have a full agenda there. Please get me on the latest possible train Tuesday afternoon, and find a nice hotel in Barrington. After the tour, I won't be able to leave until 2:00 or so, but I'll need to be back in Mortonsville before 6:00, as I have theater tickets for that evening. Check the train schedule and see if this can be managed. If it can, go ahead and make the reservations and pay for the tickets. Also, before I leave, I'll need some background information on the Barrington factory. Do the research and put together an information packet for me. Thank you. —Cynthia

51. What will Cynthia do in Barrington? Ⓐ Ⓑ Ⓒ Ⓓ
(A) Visit a factory
(B) Attend a meeting
(C) Go to the theater
(D) Deliver a packet

52. What time will Cynthia probably arrive in Barrington? Ⓐ Ⓑ Ⓒ Ⓓ
(A) 11:00 AM
(B) 1:45 PM
(C) 5:00 PM
(D) 6:15 PM

53. What time will Cynthia probably leave Barrington? Ⓐ Ⓑ Ⓒ Ⓓ
(A) 2:00 PM
(B) 3:15 PM
(C) 4:10 PM
(D) 6:00 PM

54. How much will Cynthia's round-trip train ticket cost? Ⓐ Ⓑ Ⓒ Ⓓ
(A) $45
(B) $63
(C) $72
(D) $80

55. What is Bill's job? Ⓐ Ⓑ Ⓒ Ⓓ
(A) Travel agent
(B) Tour guide
(C) Factory owner
(D) Office assistant

Double Passage: Advertisement and Business Correspondence

Questions 56–60 refer to the following advertisement and e-mail.

For Rent

Pleasant and sunny corner office in East Gardens neighborhood. Five hundred square feet on third floor of small office building. Open space, can easily be divided into 3 or 4 offices. Free parking in rear. Bicycle lock-up area in basement. $1150 a month rent includes heat and hot water. Tenant pays electricity. One block from East Gardens subway station. Available June 1. Phone 555-0921 to see or for more information.

To: Sally Hillman
From: Luis Mendez
Date: April 1
Subject: Office rental

Hi Sally,

I saw an ad today for an office that could be just what we have been looking for. It isn't downtown, but I'm beginning to think we couldn't afford that kind of location, anyway. However, it's not far from there, just about a mile or so from the Marble River Bridge.

I called the landlord and he said the office has a great view of East Gardens Park right across the street, so that sounds really nice. I know we wanted a location near bus lines, but this one isn't far from the subway station, so it will still be accessible to our clients. Plus, there's a parking area in back, and a place for bicycles, too. The best thing is the rent is $100 less than we budgeted, and it includes utilities. I think that's really important. The downside is that we'll have to wait a month longer than we hoped to move in. I don't think that's a big deal, though. We can stay where we are now for a bit longer, and this will just give us more time to buy the new office furniture. I told the landlord I'd check with you about a time to look at it. Will tomorrow morning work for you? Let me know.

Luis

56. Where is the office located? (A) (B) (C) (D)

(A) Downtown
(B) Near a park
(C) By a river
(D) In a garden

57. What is included with the rent? (A) (B) (C) (D)

(A) Phone
(B) Furniture
(C) Electricity
(D) Heat

58. What desired feature is the office missing? (A) (B) (C) (D)

(A) Proximity to a bus stop
(B) Pleasant view
(C) Parking for clients
(D) Bicycle storage

59. How much monthly rent had Sally and Luis planned to pay? (A) (B) (C) (D)

(A) $100
(B) $1050
(C) $1150
(D) $1250

60. When had Sally and Luis wanted to move to a new office? (A) (B) (C) (D)

(A) April 1
(B) May 1
(C) June 1
(D) July 1

GRAMMAR TIP

Can in the Present and Future

The modal verb *can* is used for both present and future ideas.

Present

The new assistant *can* type very fast.
He *can* speak seven languages.
This room *can* hold fifty people.

Future

George *can* meet you at the airport tomorrow.
We *can* be ready by 5:00.
We *can* discuss it at the conference next week.

VOCABULARY TIP

Adjectives with _-ful_ or _-less_

In reading passages, you may see adjectives that end in the suffixes *-ful* or *-less*. The suffix *-ful* generally means *full of* and *-less* means *without*.

Adjective	Meaning
careful careless	full of care without care
helpful helpless	full of help without help
useful useless	full of use without use

When you type the document, be *careful* not to make mistakes.
If you are *careless* about your work, you will have to do it again.

The new assistant has been very *helpful* around the office.
Many people feel *helpless* when a computer does not work.

A laptop is very *useful* because you can take it anywhere.
This copy machine is *useless*; it always breaks down.

STRATEGY PRACTICE

Questions 1–20 refer to single passages, and questions 21–30 refer to double passages.

Single Passages

DIRECTIONS: Read the following passages and answer the questions. Use the reading strategies you have learned. Once you are finished, go over the questions again and identify the question type. Write whether they are detail questions, main idea questions, or inference questions.

Questions 1–2 refer to the following advertisement.

Glenville

7400 sq. ft. residential lot for sale.

The city of Glenville is selling houses, buildings, and lots seized by the city for nonpayment of taxes. These properties will be sold by local real estate brokers. The first such property to be sold, a residential lot, will be offered by John Michaels of the Glenville Leasing and Land Sales Company. 478-555-1253, ext. 5

1. What is the advertisement offering? (A) (B) (C) (D)

(A) A house for sale

(B) An apartment building for rent

(C) An office for lease

(D) A piece of land for sale

2. Who is John Michaels? (A) (B)  

(A) The owner of the property

(B) A real estate agent

(C) A stockbroker

(D) The city comptroller

Questions 3–6 refer to the following announcement.

Notice of Fare Increase and Bus Schedule Changes

Due to city budget cuts, the following changes will be made to the city bus service, effective April 1.

Fares on all city buses will be increased from $1.25 to $1.50.

Bus schedule changes will be made as follows:

- ➠ The #36 bus route from downtown to the airport will run every thirty minutes instead of every 20 minutes.
- ➠ The #5 bus route from downtown to City Park will run every 35 minutes instead of every 25 minutes.
- ➠ The #16 bus route from the university to the Outer City Shopping Mall will run once every hour instead of every 40 minutes.

There will be no bus service after 10:00 P.M. on weeknights and after 11:30 P.M. on Friday and Saturday nights.

3. Why will the bus schedules change? Ⓐ Ⓑ Ⓒ Ⓓ
(A) The city does not have enough money.
(B) There are not enough people to ride the buses.
(C) People don't like to take the bus at night.
(D) The buses are too slow.

4. The word "budget" in paragraph 1, line 1, is closest in meaning to Ⓐ Ⓑ Ⓒ Ⓓ
(A) rental
(B) transportation
(C) financial plan
(D) route

5. After April 1, how often will the bus to City Park run? Ⓐ Ⓑ Ⓒ Ⓓ
(A) Every 5 minutes
(B) Every 25 minutes
(C) Every 35 minutes
(D) Every hour

6. What will happen to bus fares? Ⓐ Ⓑ Ⓒ Ⓓ
(A) They will be higher on all buses.
(B) They will be lower on all buses.
(C) They will stay the same on some buses.
(D) They will be higher on some buses.

Questions 7–9 refer to the following form.

Educational Opportunities
Scholarship Fund
1701 University Circle
Orford, NY 12184

Your gift will make it possible for needy young people to get a college degree. We rely on gifts from people like you. Please be as generous as possible.

☐ $25 ☐ $75 ☐ $100 ☐ $250

Thank you!

Name ____________________

Street ____________________

City/State/Zip ____________________

Check one:

__ Check enclosed

__ Money order enclosed

__ Charge my credit card: No. ____________ Expiration date ________

Signature (required for credit card charges) ____________________

7. What is this form for? Ⓐ Ⓑ Ⓒ Ⓓ

(A) Ordering holiday gifts
(B) Contributing to a scholarship fund
(C) Paying college tuition
(D) Requesting information on educational opportunities

8. What possible form of payment is not listed? Ⓐ Ⓑ Ⓒ Ⓓ

(A) Cash
(B) Check
(C) Money order
(D) Credit card

9. Who should sign this form? Ⓐ Ⓑ Ⓒ Ⓓ

(A) Anybody who sends in a payment
(B) Anybody who has a credit card
(C) Anybody who needs a scholarship
(D) Anybody who pays by credit card

Questions 10–12 refer to the following paragraph.

> Thank you for becoming a National Bank credit card customer. Your new credit card is enclosed. Before using your card, please read the enclosed material describing your rights and responsibilities as a National Bank credit card user. If you have any questions, call 800-555-0998. To activate your card, call 800-555-4557 to confirm that you have received your card. Your card will not be valid for use until you call this number.

10. Who is this notice for? Ⓐ Ⓑ Ⓒ Ⓓ

(A) A person who has an account at the National Bank
(B) A person who has a new credit card from the National Bank
(C) A person who wants to work at the National Bank
(D) A person who wants to find out about services at the National Bank

11. Why would a bank customer call 800-555-0998? Ⓐ Ⓑ Ⓒ Ⓓ

(A) To ask questions about credit cards
(B) To order a new credit card
(C) To make the new credit card valid
(D) To order materials about credit cards

12. What must the customer do to receive his new card? Ⓐ Ⓑ Ⓒ Ⓓ

(A) Call 800-555-4557
(B) Answer some questions
(C) It is enclosed with this notice.
(D) Go to the bank

Questions 13–15 refer to the following memorandum.

Memorandum

TO: All Staff Members
FROM: Eric Sato, Office Manager
RE: New Photocopy Machine
DATE: October 18

I know you will all be pleased to learn that the new photocopy machine has finally arrived. The new machine has more features and performs more functions than the old one. While this will make things more convenient for us in the long run, it can make it more complicated to learn how to run the machine initially. In addition, we all want to avoid the problem of constant breakdowns that we had with the old machine. Therefore, I ask that if you have any questions or problems with the machine, please ask my assistant, Ms. Ono, to help you. Similarly, please do not attempt to remove paper jams, add toner, or refill the paper bin until Ms. Ono has shown you how to do this. Ms. Ono has received training from the manufacturer of the machine and is fully knowledgeable about how to run it and how to troubleshoot it. Thank you for your cooperation, and enjoy the new machine.

13. What is the purpose of this memo? Ⓐ Ⓑ Ⓒ Ⓓ
(A) To explain to the staff how to run photocopy machines
(B) To inform the staff that the old machine is broken
(C) To tell the staff about the new photocopy machine
(D) To let the staff know that Ms. Ono will receive training

14. What should staff members do if they have a problem with the machine? Ⓐ Ⓑ Ⓒ Ⓓ
(A) Speak to Ms. Ono
(B) Ask the Office Manager for assistance
(C) Call the manufacturer
(D) Read the training manual

15. Why is the new machine complicated? Ⓐ Ⓑ Ⓒ Ⓓ
(A) It needs toner.
(B) It's new.
(C) It breaks down a lot.
(D) It has many features and functions.

Questions 16–18 refer to the following advertisement.

> **Attention Sales and Marketing Professionals**
>
> # CAREER FAIR
>
> Thursday, May 25
> 9:30–3:30
> Hoover Hotel
> 1007 Elm Street
>
> If you are looking for a position as a:
>
> - Store Manager
> - Sales Associate
> - Sales Representative
> - Marketing Executive
> - Executive Assistant
>
> or other position in the Sales and Marketing field, then don't miss this event!
>
> **Free registration!**
>
> Register online at *www.salesmkting.com.*
> Onsite registration begins at 8:30. Doors open at 9:30.
> Complimentary lunch buffet from 12:00–1:00 for all registered participants.
> All day parking in the hotel garage half-price for registered participants.
> Call 633-555–9730 for more information.
>
> ***Don't miss our special Career Fair seminars:***
>
> *How to Write a Winning Résumé* 10:30–11:30
> *Preparing for the Job Interview* 1:00–2:00
>
> **Seminars are $12 each or $20 for both, payable at the door.**

16. Who is this advertisement for? (A) (B) (C) (D)
- (A) Hotel managers
- (B) Job seekers
- (C) Hotel guests
- (D) Employers

17. How can you register for the career fair? (A) (B) (C) (D)
- (A) Call 633-555-9730
- (B) Send a registration form by mail
- (C) Pay at the door
- (D) Arrive at the hotel at 8:30

18. How much does the lunch cost? (A) (B) (C) (D)
- (A) $12
- (B) $20
- (C) It's free.
- (D) It's half the usual price.

Questions 19–20 refer to the following report.

> The Jolly Hamburger restaurant chain reported that, because of cost cutting, it was able to double its profits this year to $52 million. Jolly Hamburger is the second largest fast-food company in the country, after Big Burgers, which reported profits this year of $60 million, up from $48 million last year. Jolly Hamburger plans to broaden its customer base by introducing a special low-fat, low-sodium menu geared toward senior citizens.

19. How was Jolly Hamburger able to increase its profits? Ⓐ Ⓑ Ⓒ Ⓓ

(A) By lowering its prices
(B) By introducing a new menu
(C) By getting more customers
(D) By decreasing its expenses

20. What were Jolly Hamburger's profits last year? Ⓐ Ⓑ Ⓒ Ⓓ

(A) $26 million
(B) $48 million
(C) $52 million
(D) $104 million

Questions 21–25 refer to the following advertisement and letter.

World Wide School of Languages

Classes in French, English, Spanish, Japanese, Korean, and Arabic

Beginning, Intermediate, Advanced, and Professional level classes

Small group classes

Tutoring available for French, Spanish, and Japanese only

Morning (three hours/day) and evening (two hours/week)

Weekend schedule also available

All our teachers are native speakers and are professionally trained in the latest methodologies.

Traveling? We also have locations in several other cities. Call our office to find out where. 888-555-4761

October 2

Dear Yoko,

I have exciting news for you. Do you remember how I've always wanted to learn Korean? Well now I'm finally doing it. I've found a fantastic language school not far from my apartment, and I'm taking classes there. Of course, I'm really busy at work all day, so I'm studying in the evening. The classes are really interesting and the homework load is not so bad. I'm really learning a lot. The best part of all is that my company is paying 100% of the class tuition.

You know you've been saying that you want to improve your English. You're in luck! I checked and found out that the World Wide School of Languages has a branch in your city. I really recommend their classes. I think their highest-level English class would be just right for you. Your company would probably pay for the classes because you use English a lot at work. You can also arrange to get university credit. I think it's a great deal.

The other good news is that my company is sending me on a trip next month to your city. So I'll see you soon.

Love,

Maki

21. Which language is NOT taught at the World Wide School of Languages? (A) (B) (C) (D)
   (A) French
   (B) English
   (C) German
   (D) Japanese

22. Where do Maki's Korean classes take place? (A) (B) (C) (D)
   (A) Near her work
   (B) At the university
   (C) Near her home
   (D) In Yoko's city

23. How many hours a week is Maki studying Korean? (A) (B) (C) (D)
   (A) Two
   (B) Three
   (C) Ten
   (D) Fifteen

24. What level class does Maki recommend for Yoko? (A) (B) (C) (D)
   (A) Beginning
   (B) Intermediate
   (C) Advanced
   (D) Professional

25. What will Maki do next month? (A) (B) (C) (D)
   (A) Take a business trip
   (B) Study English
   (C) Work at the university
   (D) Go on vacation

Questions 26–30 refer to the following ad and memo.

SUPPLY STATION

YOUR OFFICE SUPPLY COMPANY

Sale! Sale! Sale!

Don't miss this unique opportunity.
Printers, ink, and paper are discounted 15% or more.

BMX all-in-one printer, scanner, copier, fax
prints up to 30 pages/minute
prints top-quality color photos
was $325 now only **$250**

Maxi Systems printer
prints up to 25 pages/minute
scans and copies too
was $299 now only **$215**

Printer Ink
Type C ink cartridges, compatible with all BMX and Maxi Systems printers
1-cartridge pack: $30 sale price: **$24**
2-cartridge pack: $54 sale price: **$43**

Buy now. Sale lasts Monday–Friday only

To: Lucy Johnson, Assistant Office Manager
From: Mary Choi, Office Manager
Re: Office supply sale

Lucy,

Have you seen this ad? I think we should take advantage of it. Look at how fast that BMX printer prints. It's twice as fast as our old printer. I think that would make a big difference. And there's a big savings on printer ink, too. Let's get ten of the two-cartridge packs. While you're at the store, see what the sale prices are on paper. Have them charge it to our office account and check to see if we have a credit. I think we do from the cell phone I returned last month. The sale ends tomorrow, so you'd better get down there as soon as possible. Thanks.

Mary

26. What is on sale this week? Ⓐ Ⓑ Ⓒ Ⓓ
(A) Only printing supplies
(B) All office supplies
(C) Cameras
(D) Ink pens

27. How fast does the old printer print? Ⓐ Ⓑ Ⓒ Ⓓ
(A) 15 pages/minute
(B) 20 pages/minute
(C) 25 pages/minute
(D) 30 pages/minute

28. How much will Lucy spend on ink cartridges? Ⓐ Ⓑ Ⓒ Ⓓ
(A) $240
(B) $300
(C) $430
(D) $540

29. How will Lucy pay for her purchases? Ⓐ Ⓑ Ⓒ Ⓓ
(A) By cash
(B) With a credit card
(C) With a business check
(D) By charging it to an account

30. What day was the memo written? Ⓐ Ⓑ Ⓒ Ⓓ
(A) Monday
(B) Tuesday
(C) Thursday
(D) Friday

READING REVIEW

Do this Reading Review as if you were taking Parts 5, 6, and 7 of the TOEIC® test. You should take no more than 75 minutes to do this review. Use the Reading Review Answer Sheet on page 344.

READING TEST

In the Reading test, you will read a variety of texts and answer several different types of reading comprehension questions. The entire Reading test will last 75 minutes. There are three parts, and directions are given for each part. You are encouraged to answer as many questions as possible within the time allowed.

You must mark your answers on the separate answer sheet. Do not write your answers in the test book.

PART 5

Directions: A word or phrase is missing in each of the sentences below. Four answer choices are given below each sentence. Select the best answer to complete the sentence. Then mark the letter (A), (B), (C), or (D) on your answer sheet.

101. The files were _______ alphabetically.
(A) organization
(B) organizer
(C) organize
(D) organized

102. The business consultant suggested a _______ sales plan.
(A) modify
(B) modifies
(C) modified
(D) modifying

103. _______ there were so many customer complaints, we withdrew the item from the market.
(A) Therefore
(B) Because
(C) Although
(D) However

104. The contractor is _______ for his quality workmanship.
(A) respected
(B) respects
(C) respect
(D) respecting

105. Employees' work hours are _______ before the holidays.
(A) insisted
(B) installed
(C) increased
(D) intruded

106. The _______ report will be published next Monday.
(A) selling
(B) sales
(C) sell
(D) sells

107. The architect must consider every detail of a floor _______.
(A) planning
(B) plan
(C) plans
(D) planned

108. Mr. Lafferty wants to meet _______ six o'clock sharp.
(A) on
(B) upon
(C) at
(D) during

109. The sales personnel were given specific _______ about how to market the new product.
(A) instructions
(B) delays
(C) reservations
(D) adjustments

110. This construction project is as important as any other project _______ this year.
(A) undertaking
(B) undertook
(C) undertaken
(D) undertake

111. The supervisor talked about _______ changing patterns in consumer habits.
(A) slowly
(B) slowing
(C) slows
(D) slowed

112. This year tourism is growing _______ last year's predictions.
(A) outside
(B) inside
(C) beyond
(D) before

113. The grievance committee made _______ demands on management.
(A) reasonable
(B) reasonably
(C) reason
(D) reasoning

114. The _______ of the office party must take responsibility for the cleanup.
(A) plans
(B) planning
(C) planned
(D) planners

115. Mr. Shultz has _______ own plan for reorganizing the accounting department.
(A) him
(B) his
(C) he
(D) himself

116. There are early _______ that the market is beginning to recover.
(A) indications
(B) solutions
(C) proposals
(D) revisions

117. Before you leave, please _______ the data in the database.
(A) submerge
(B) propose
(C) admit
(D) enter

118. _______ the new product didn't sell well, it's still on the market.
(A) However
(B) So that
(C) Although
(D) Nevertheless

119. _______ have the employees complained so much about working conditions in the factory.
(A) Never
(B) Ever
(C) Soon
(D) Forever

120. Staff _______ an environmental group will be here to check for evidence of pollution.
(A) of
(B) by
(C) about
(D) from

121. The crew worked _______ to avoid problems in the future.
(A) careful
(B) carefully
(C) care
(D) more careful

GO ON TO THE NEXT PAGE

122. _______ job performance is awarded with a salary bonus.
(A) Except
(B) Exception
(C) Exceptional
(D) Exceptionally

123. The _______ on the merger lasted until midnight.
(A) negotiated
(B) negotiations
(C) negotiator
(D) negotiates

124. When it came to solving a mechanical problem, he did not have a _______.
(A) clue
(B) sense
(C) hint
(D) thought

125. _______ a good credit history, don't expect to get a loan easily.
(A) From
(B) Unless
(C) Without
(D) Since

126. The company managers _______ the union about any changes in employee vacation allowances.
(A) advice
(B) advising
(C) advised
(D) advisor

127. The president answers all his calls _______.
(A) himself
(B) he
(C) him
(D) his

128. To _______ disruption during the day, construction is done at night.
(A) criticize
(B) localize
(C) sanitize
(D) minimize

129. Mr. Nigel becomes _______ when he has to wait too long.
(A) evident
(B) extraordinary
(C) impatient
(D) inconclusive

130. The negotiations failed because _______ broke down.
(A) communicative
(B) communicated
(C) communications
(D) communicate

131. _______ amazes Ms. Fifel is the speed of her new computer.
(A) That
(B) Which
(C) Who
(D) What

132. Any changes to the employee handbook must be _______ in writing.
(A) proposed
(B) propelled
(C) preferred
(D) preordained

133. _______ to the directory will be published every month.
(A) Additional
(B) Additions
(C) Added
(D) Adding

134. The audience was asked to _______ from talking during announcements.
(A) refrain
(B) respect
(C) reserve
(D) restore

135. The news was so _______ that the company invested even more money in the project.

(A) encourage
(B) encouraged
(C) encouraging
(D) encourages

136. The job couldn't be finished because of an _______ supply of essential materials.

(A) improper
(B) unlikely
(C) unlucky
(D) inadequate

137. A positive _______ helps everyone be productive.

(A) alteration
(B) attitude
(C) anxiety
(D) ambivalence

138. Mr. Logan's instructions were _______ clear that no one had any questions.

(A) such
(B) ever
(C) so
(D) too

139. The _______ to the training has been very positive.

(A) respondent
(B) respond
(C) responsible
(D) response

140. Demand for the new line of cars is up; _______, production will increase.

(A) however
(B) despite
(C) therefore
(D) regardless

GO ON TO THE NEXT PAGE

PART 6

Directions: Read the texts that follow. A word or phrase is missing in some of the sentences. Four answer choices are given below each of the sentences. Select the best answer to complete the text. Then mark the letter (A), (B), (C), or (D) on your answer sheet.

Questions 141–143 refer to the following e-mail.

To: Naser Abdul
From: Nicholas Reed
Subject: Request for office equipment

Dear Naser,
My first week working for the Citron Company has been very good. I
_____________ my new job. Now I need some things for my office. Can you help me?

141. (A) enjoyed
(B) will enjoy
(C) am enjoying
(D) was enjoying

_____________, there is a problem with the computer. It works very

142. (A) First
(B) Also
(C) Then
(D) Finally

_____________, and it is difficult to get on the Internet. I think the computer

143. (A) slow
(B) slowly
(C) slower
(D) slowness

doesn't have enough memory.

There is also a problem with the heating system in my office. The office is very cold early in the day, but in the afternoon it is too hot. One last thing, my desk is very small. I need a bigger desk. Can you get me one?

Everything else is okay. Thank you for your help, Naser.

Sincerely,
Nicholas Reed, Office Specialist

Questions 144–146 refer to the following announcement.

ATTENTION
ALL EMPLOYEES

Our office is collecting money for the ____________ of last week's

144. (A) observers
(B) victims
(C) planners
(D) reporters

terrible floods. Many people in our city lost their homes and all their ____________ in the floods. We

145. (A) possesses
(B) possessed
(C) possessing
(D) possessions

would like to send money to help them. If you wish to make a ____________, please bring a

146. (A) cake
(B) friend
(C) salary
(D) donation

check or cash to Mr. Kim in Human Resources before 5:00 on Friday. We will send a check in the name of everyone in the office to the Flood Fund.

GO ON TO THE NEXT PAGE

Questions 147–149 refer to the following advertisement.

Are you looking for an economical car to rent?

Look no more. Come to

Mr. Miser's Car Rental Agency

Why pay more than you have to?

At Mr. Miser's, we have ____________ prices in town.

147. (A) low
(B) lower
(C) lowers
(D) the lowest

Why travel farther than you have to?

Mr. Miser's has three convenient ____________.

148. (A) cars
(B) prices
(C) locations
(D) schedules

We have offices at the airport, at the train station, and downtown on Main Street.

At Mr. Miser's we are always ready to serve you with a friendly smile.

Next time, ____________ your car from Mr. Miser's.

149. (A) rent
(B) rents
(C) renting
(D) will rent

Questions 150–152 refer to the following notice.

Crestfield Office Towers
Notice to Tenants

Due to the repair work currently taking place throughout the building, all electric power in the building will be turned ____________ tomorrow afternoon from 4:00 until 6:00. This

150. (A) off
(B) on
(C) in
(D) up

means the elevators will not be running, lights will not work, and you will not be able to use any electric office equipment during this time. We are very sorry for any ____________

151. (A) incompetence
(B) inconvenience
(C) incompleteness
(D) inconsistence

this may cause. Please direct any questions about this situation to the building superintendent. We hope to have all repair work finished soon. We thank you for your ____________.

152. (A) patience
(B) patients
(C) patiently
(D) patient

PART 7

Directions: In this part you will read a selection of texts, such as magazine and newspaper articles, letters, and advertisements. Each text is followed by several questions. Select the best answer for each question and mark the letter (A), (B), (C), or (D) on your answer sheet.

Questions 153–155 refer to the following announcement.

According to a new report, people now work more hours than before. Ten years ago, most professional people worked 40 hours a week or less. Now, 75% of professionals work 50 hours a week or more, and 15% of professionals work 55 hours a week or more. Researchers in the Labor Department released these numbers last week.

153. Who is the report about?
(A) Laborers
(B) Professionals
(C) All workers
(D) Researchers

154. Ten years ago, how many hours a week did most professional people work?
(A) 40 or less
(B) 50 or more
(C) 55 or more
(D) 75 or less

155. When did researchers report these figures?
(A) Yesterday
(B) 7 days ago
(C) 15 days ago
(D) 10 years ago

GO ON TO THE NEXT PAGE

Questions 156–159 refer to the following advertisement.

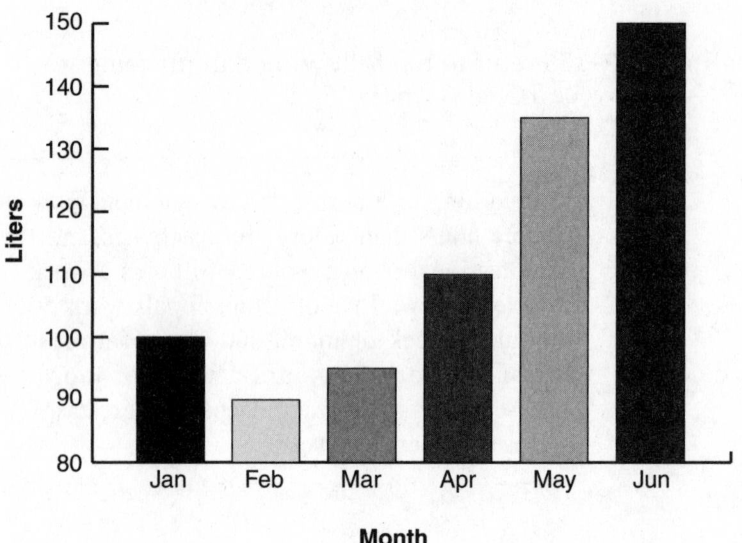

156. How many liters of ice cream did Ike sell in January?
(A) 90
(B) 95
(C) 100
(D) 110

157. When did Ike sell 135 liters of ice cream?
(A) March
(B) April
(C) May
(D) June

158. When did Ike sell the least amount of ice cream?
(A) January
(B) February
(C) March
(D) April

159. How much time does this graph cover?
(A) One month
(B) Six weeks
(C) Half a year
(D) One year

Questions 160–161 refer to the following form.

March 21, 20__

Amelia Greene
Director
Worldwide Travel Agency
78 North Street
Mayfield, TX 23450

Dear Ms. Greene:

I am interested in working at the Worldwide Travel Agency. I have five years' experience as a travel agent. I also have a lot of experience working with computers, and I can use different kinds of software.

I am enclosing my résumé. I hope to hear from you soon.

Sincerely,

Charles Chung

Charles Chung

160. Why did Charles Chung write this letter?
(A) He wants a job.
(B) He wants to buy a computer.
(C) He wants to take a trip.
(D) He wants help writing his résumé.

161. What did Charles Chung do for five years?
(A) He studied computers.
(B) He worked for Ms. Greene.
(C) He traveled around the world.
(D) He worked as a travel agent.

GO ON TO THE NEXT PAGE

Questions 162–164 refer to the following announcement.

> The Law Office of Murphy & Mann is moving.
>
> *Our new address, starting April 12, is:*
> 45 Oakland Avenue
> Suite 10
>
> (near the corner of Oakland Avenue and Broadwood Road, across the street from the National State Bank)
>
> Our new office hours are M–F 8:30–6:00
> Sat. 9–12:30
>
> Our phone number will stay the same:
> 301-555-7140

162. When will the new office open?
(A) April 1
(B) April 2
(C) April 12
(D) April 21

163. Where is the new office?
(A) On Oakland Avenue
(B) In Suite 45
(C) On Broadwood Road
(D) Next to a bank

164. What will NOT change?
(A) The suite number
(B) The office hours
(C) The telephone number
(D) The location

Questions 165–168 refer to the following announcement.

The new express train will begin service between Riverdale and Mayfield on October 24. The trip takes five hours on the older, slower train. On the express train it will take only three hours. The express train will have larger, more comfortable seats, and there will be free food for the passengers. There will be two express trains a day between Riverdale and Mayfield. There will also be four regular trains. Many people will prefer the regular trains because the tickets are cheaper.

165. How long is the trip on the express train?
(A) Two hours
(B) Three hours
(C) Four hours
(D) Five hours

166. How many regular trains will there be a day?
(A) Two
(B) Three
(C) Four
(D) Five

167. Why would people prefer the regular trains?
(A) The seats are larger.
(B) The tickets are less expensive.
(C) The food tastes better.
(D) They are more comfortable.

168. The word "service" in line 1 is closest in meaning to
(A) commuting
(B) setting up
(C) operation
(D) making do

GO ON TO THE NEXT PAGE

Questions 169–172 refer to the following advertisement.

ABC Market

Sale—this weekend only

Fresh Oranges—$1.50/kilo

Fresh Apples—$1.75/kilo

Beef—$1.25/2 kilos

Chicken—$1.25/kilo

Cookies—$2.50/bag OR *buy 2 bags, get the third bag free!*

Store hours:

M–F 8:30–6:30 Sat. & Sun. 12–5

169. What kind of business is advertised?
- (A) A grocery store
- (B) A school supply store
- (C) A restaurant
- (D) A bakery

170. When is the sale?
- (A) Today
- (B) Monday through Friday
- (C) Saturday and Sunday
- (D) All week

171. The word "Fresh" in line 3 is closest in meaning to
- (A) Inexpensive
- (B) Colorful
- (C) Newly picked
- (D) Special

172. How much do cookies cost?
- (A) $2 a bag
- (B) $2.50 a bag
- (C) $3 a bag
- (D) They're free.

Questions 173–174 refer to the following chart.

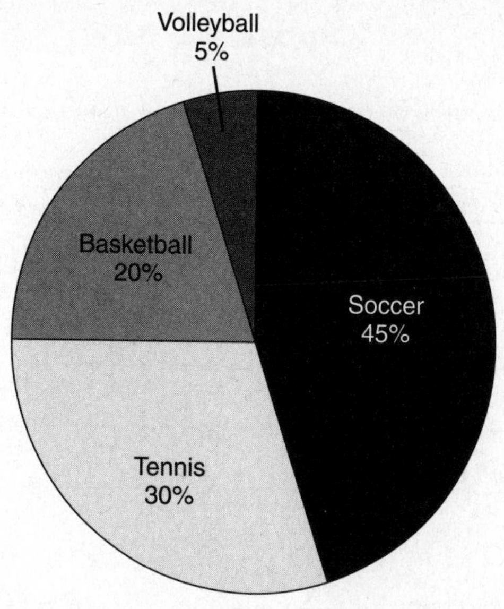

Favorite Sports

173. Which is the most popular sport?
(A) Volleyball
(B) Basketball
(C) Tennis
(D) Soccer

174. What percent of people prefer basketball?
(A) 5%
(B) 20%
(C) 30%
(D) 45%

GO ON TO THE NEXT PAGE

Questions 175–177 refer to the following form.

Subscribe now!

Receive *Business Times* in your home every month!

Six months — pay only $26
One year — pay only $45
Two years — pay only $75

Name: *Helena Bishop*

Address: *1776 Washington Street*

Eugene, OR 42308

check one: — 6 months X one year — two years

Payment method: — check — money order X credit card

175. What is *Business Times*?
(A) A TV show
(B) A book
(C) A magazine
(D) A radio program

176. How much will Helena Bishop pay?
(A) $26
(B) $45
(C) $75
(D) $90

177. How will she pay?
(A) Check
(B) Money order
(C) Credit card
(D) Cash

Questions 178–180 refer to the following letter.

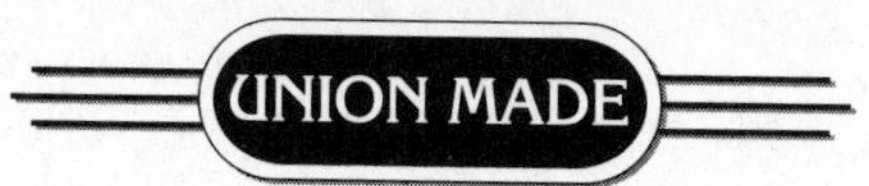

Mill Workers' Union, Local 806
3660 South River Trail
Two Rivers, ME 05601
March 19, 20____

Ms. Samantha Fagan, President & CEO
Lumber Yard Industries
9871 Kennewick Drive
Grove Isle, ME 05603

Dear Ms. Fagan:

As a union arbitrator, I have been asked by a number of your employees to write to you. It is in regard to your decision to make the mill off-limits to smokers. That means from now on, all employees who wish to smoke must go outdoors, but not near the main entrance.

Many of your employees who smoke consider this a very harsh decision. They appreciate that nonsmokers do not wish to be exposed to cigarette smoke, but they cannot understand why they are being treated as second-class citizens. They feel it is unfair to force them to have to go outdoors in order to smoke. You know that we get a lot of rain and cold temperatures in this area for a good part of the year. Should they go outside in the rain? Should they be out in freezing weather?

Your employees who smoke would like a meeting with you. They would like to offer suggestions that would be acceptable to both sides. For example, perhaps a separate employee lounge for smokers could be created within the mill. In that way, both parties would feel satisfied. A meeting between you and your employees who smoke would be most advantageous.

I hope you will consider this request and agree to meet with those employees. Thank you in advance for your time and consideration.

Sincerely yours,

Faith Dunnaway
Faith Dunnaway

GO ON TO THE NEXT PAGE

178. What outdoor area is currently off-limits to employees who smoke?

(A) The picnic area
(B) The parking lot
(C) The recycling area
(D) The main entrance

179. What is the primary issue?

(A) Some employees can smoke, while others can't.
(B) Employees who smoke don't think they're being treated fairly.
(C) The employee lounge needs to be enlarged.
(D) Weather conditions are making it hard for employees to work.

180. What is the request that Faith Dunnaway is making in the letter?

(A) Ms. Fagan should allow smoking in the mill.
(B) Ms. Fagan should meet with employees who smoke.
(C) Two employee lounges should be built.
(D) Ms. Fagan should come to the union offices.

Questions 181–185 refer to the following agenda and e-mail.

Multiple Marketing, Inc.
Department Heads Meeting
Monday, April 15 4:00 p.m.
Place: Company Cafeteria

AGENDA

1. Budget report
   Marguerite Rodin
2. Fall conference plans
   Cindy Lee
3. New hiring policy
   Yasser Ahmed
4. Office supplies issues
   Jan Petersen

To: Sam Blair
From: Rose Daniels
Subject: Yesterday's Meeting

Mr. Blair,
The meeting yesterday went as planned, for the most part. It started on time and everyone was there, except you, of course. We rearranged the order of the agenda a bit. We talked about the third item first because it's such a pressing issue for all of us. We were able to get to all the items on the agenda because we agreed to stay until everything was finished. The meeting lasted two and a half hours. Also, we changed the location. The cafeteria was being cleaned, so we moved the meeting to the lounge. It worked out fine. We set the date for next month's meeting. It will be on the 18th.
Rose

GO ON TO THE NEXT PAGE

181. Where was the meeting held?
(A) In the cafeteria
(B) In the director's office
(C) In the conference room
(D) In the lounge

182. What item was discussed first?
(A) The budget report
(B) The fall conference plans
(C) The new hiring policy
(D) The office supplies issues

183. Who did NOT attend the meeting?
(A) Sam Blair
(B) Rose Daniels
(C) Jan Petersen
(D) Marguerite Rodin

184. How long did the meeting last?
(A) Two hours
(B) Two and a half hours
(C) Four hours
(D) Four and a half hours

185. When will the next meeting be held?
(A) April 15
(B) April 18
(C) May 15
(D) May 18

Questions 186–190 refer to the following schedule and memo.

COMPUTER INSTITUTE OF TECHNOLOGY

FALL SCHEDULE

Keyboarding		
Beginning	Mon. and Wed.	5:30–6:30
Intermediate	Mon. and Wed.	6:30–7:30
Advanced	Tue. and Thur.	5:30–6:30
Word Processing		
Level I	Mon. and Wed.	6:00–7:30
Level II	Mon. and Wed.	7:30–9:00
Level III	Tue. and Thur.	6:00–7:30
Level IV	Tue. and Thur.	7:30–9:00
Web Page Design		
Basic	Mon., Tue., and Thur.	6:00–7:00
Advanced	Tue. and Wed.	7:00–8:00
All levels	Sat.	9:00–1:00

*Classes begin on the first Monday of every month.
Each class lasts one month. Tuition is $275 per class.
To register for classes, download a registration form from our website. Mail the completed form with your check or credit card information to:*

COMPUTER INSTITUTE OF TECHNOLOGY
811 Horseshoe Boulevard • Hilltown, MI 02046

To: G. Y. Kim
From: Elizabeth Jones
Re: Computer training

Mr. Kim,
I am interested in taking some computer classes that I think would give me some useful skills for my work. I hope the company can pay the tuition for these classes.
I am most interested in learning web page design. Then I could develop and maintain our company's web page, and we wouldn't have to pay an outside consultant to do it.
The Computer Institute of Technology offers a Beginning web page design class.
It starts at 6:00, which would give me half an hour to get there after I leave work. It's not far from the office, so that's plenty of time. That class ends at 7:00, so I could also take a word processing class that begins at 7:30 on Tuesdays and Thursdays.
I like this school because the schedule and the location are both very convenient.
I know this training would really improve the work I do for you, so I hope you can help me with the tuition. I have attached the class schedule for you to see.
Thank you.
Elizabeth Jones

GO ON TO THE NEXT PAGE

186. How many days a week are classes offered at the Computer Institute of Technology?

(A) Two
(B) Three
(C) Four
(D) Five

187. How can a student register for classes?

(A) Call the school
(B) Mail a form
(C) Visit the school
(D) Send an e-mail

188. What time does Elizabeth leave work?

(A) 5:30
(B) 6:00
(C) 7:00
(D) 7:30

189. Which word processing class does Elizabeth want to take?

(A) Level I
(B) Level II
(C) Level III
(D) Level IV

190. How much money will Elizabeth need to pay for her classes?

(A) $275
(B) $475
(C) $500
(D) $550

Questions 191–195 refer to the following memo and e-mail.

To: All personnel
From: Luis Mora, Office Manager
Re: Conference room painting

We all know that the painting of both conference rooms is long overdue. We've been waiting months for this to happen, and now it will. Painting of Conference Room 1 will begin next Tuesday and should take no more than two days. Meetings that you have scheduled for next week can be held in the cafeteria. The painting of Conference Room 2 will be scheduled for a later date. If you have any questions, don't hesitate to contact me. Thank you for your cooperation.

To: Luis Mora
From: George Werner
Subject: Conference room

Luis,
I know we've all been waiting for the conference rooms to be painted, but it couldn't be more inconvenient for me. I have an important meeting planned for the day the painting begins. I can't have it in my office because only four or five people can sit there comfortably, and I need room for ten people. Conference Room 2 is already booked through Friday. The meeting place you suggest is too informal for an important meeting. Would it be possible to schedule the painting so that it begins on Wednesday or Thursday? Please let me know.
George

GO ON TO THE NEXT PAGE

191. What will be painted next week?
(A) One conference room
(B) Two conference rooms
(C) The cafeteria
(D) Some offices

192. How long will the painting probably take?
(A) Two days
(B) A week
(C) A month
(D) Several months

193. Why did George write the e-mail?
(A) To invite Luis to a meeting
(B) To ask for his office to be painted
(C) To find a different room for his meeting
(D) To ask for the painting schedule to be changed

194. What day will George's meeting be?
(A) Tuesday
(B) Wednesday
(C) Thursday
(D) Friday

195. According to George, which place is too informal for his meeting?
(A) His office
(B) Luis's office
(C) The cafeteria
(D) Conference Room 2

Questions 196–200 refer to the following advertisement and letter.

RESEARCH ASSOCIATE

Top advertising firm seeks research associate to join our team of market researchers. Seeking creative, energetic team worker to work with a group of four other researchers. Must have a Master's in Business Administration and three to five years' experience in market research. Send résumé and cover letter to: Priscilla Kovacs, Director of Human Resources, Avid Advertising Associates, 1456 State Street, Suite 101, Springfield, OH 48804.

Jung Choi
25 Water Street, Apt. 10
Springfield, OH 48804

Dear Ms. Choi:

Thank you for your interest in our company. Unfortunately, the research associate position that we advertised has already been filled. However, you have a strong background, and we might be interested in considering you for a position in the future. Your résumé shows that you have the educational level we require, and your Bachelor's degree in Psychology strengthens your qualifications as a market researcher. You also have more years of experience in the field than we asked for. I would like to keep your résumé on file and contact you when we have another position available. If you don't hear from me in six months' time, please give me a call.

Sincerely,

Priscilla Kovacs

Priscilla Kovacs

GO ON TO THE NEXT PAGE

196. What is Priscilla Kovacs job?
- (A) Research associate
- (B) Director of Human Resources
- (C) Head researcher
- (D) Psychologist

197. Why wasn't Choi hired for the position?
- (A) Her résumé was lost.
- (B) She decided she didn't want it.
- (C) She didn't have the qualifications.
- (D) The position had already been filled.

198. What degree does Choi have?
- (A) Master of Psychology
- (B) Associate of Business
- (C) Master of Business Administration
- (D) Bachelor of Business Administration

199. How many years' experience does Choi have as a market researcher?
- (A) Less than 3 years
- (B) Three years
- (C) Five years
- (D) More than five years

200. What suggestion does Ms. Kovacs make to Ms. Choi?
- (A) Write a new résumé
- (B) Call her in six months
- (C) Get a job as a psychologist
- (D) Get more experience in the field

PRACTICE TEST ONE

Practice Test One is similar to an actual TOEIC® test. You can take this test before you study this book. Then, after you finish studying this book, take Practice Test Two and compare your score on Practice Test One with Practice Test Two in order to measure your improvement.

Read all directions carefully. This will help you become familiar with the TOEIC test directions and item types.

Use the Practice Test One Answer Sheet on page 345.

LISTENING TEST

In the Listening test, you will be asked to demonstrate how well you understand spoken English. The entire Listening test will last approximately 45 minutes. There are four parts, and directions are given for each part. You must mark your answers on the separate answer sheet. Do not write your answers in the test book.

PART 1

Directions: For each question in this part, you will hear four statements about a picture in your test book. When you hear the statements, you must select the one statement that best describes what you see in the picture. Then find the number of the question on your answer sheet and mark your answer. The statements will not be printed in your test book and will be spoken only one time.

Example

Sample Answer

 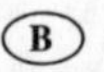  

Statement (C), "They're standing near the table," is the best description of the picture, so you should select answer (C) and mark it on your answer sheet.

1.

2.

GO ON TO THE NEXT PAGE

3.

4.

5.

6.

7.

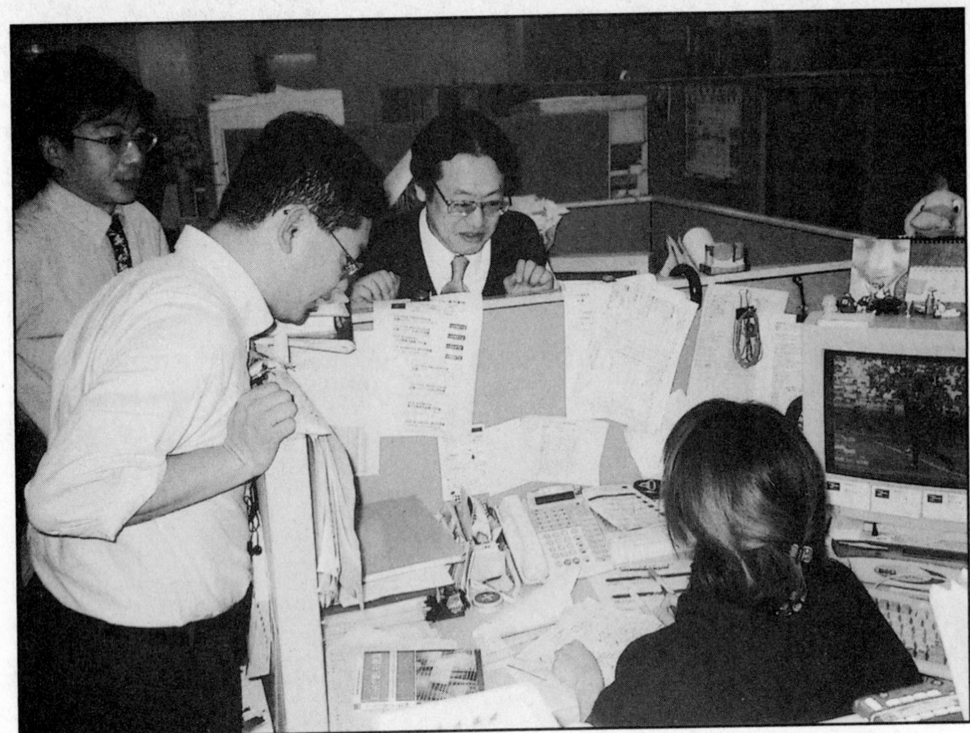

8.

9.

10.

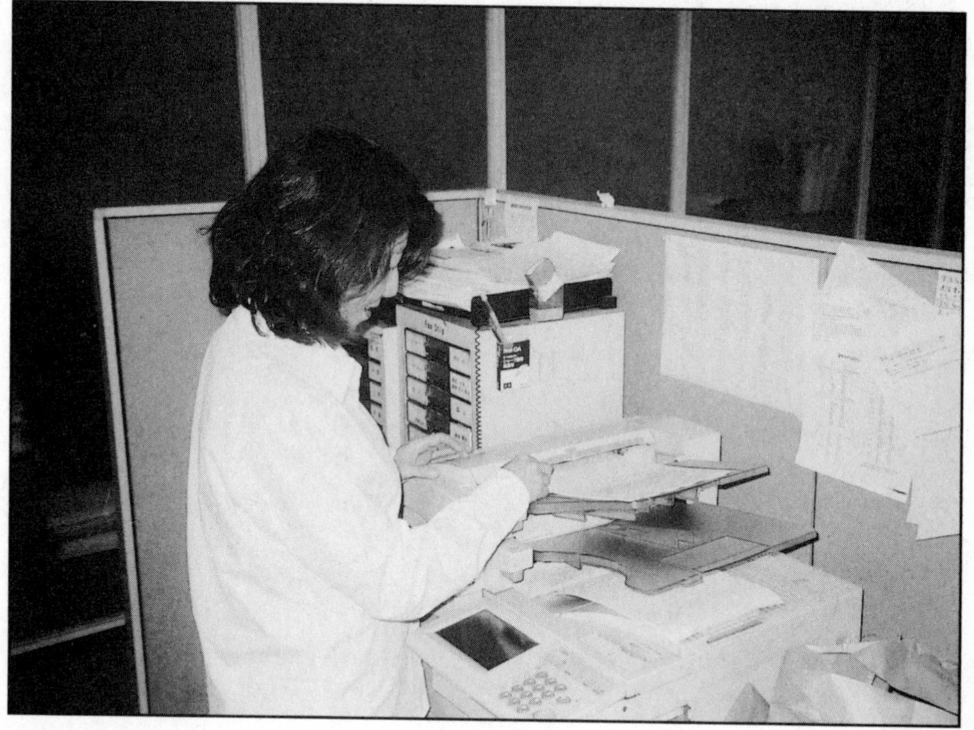

GO ON TO THE NEXT PAGE

PART 2

Directions: You will hear a question or statement and three responses spoken in English. They will not be printed in your test book and will be spoken only one time. Select the best response to the question or statement and mark the letter (A), (B), or (C) on your answer sheet.

Sample Answer

Example

You will hear: Where is the meeting room?

You will also hear: (A) To meet the new director.
(B) It's the first room on the right.
(C) Yes, at two o'clock.

Your best response to the question "Where is the meeting room?" is choice (B), "It's the first room on the right," so (B) is the correct answer. You should mark answer (B) on your answer sheet.

11. Mark your answer on your answer sheet.

12. Mark your answer on your answer sheet.

13. Mark your answer on your answer sheet.

14. Mark your answer on your answer sheet.

15. Mark your answer on your answer sheet.

16. Mark your answer on your answer sheet.

17. Mark your answer on your answer sheet.

18. Mark your answer on your answer sheet.

19. Mark your answer on your answer sheet.

20. Mark your answer on your answer sheet.

21. Mark your answer on your answer sheet.

22. Mark your answer on your answer sheet.

23. Mark your answer on your answer sheet.

24. Mark your answer on your answer sheet.

25. Mark your answer on your answer sheet.

26. Mark your answer on your answer sheet.

27. Mark your answer on your answer sheet.

28. Mark your answer on your answer sheet.

29. Mark your answer on your answer sheet.

30. Mark your answer on your answer sheet.

31. Mark your answer on your answer sheet.

32. Mark your answer on your answer sheet.

33. Mark your answer on your answer sheet.

34. Mark your answer on your answer sheet.

35. Mark your answer on your answer sheet.

36. Mark your answer on your answer sheet.

37. Mark your answer on your answer sheet.

38. Mark your answer on your answer sheet.

39. Mark your answer on your answer sheet.

40. Mark your answer on your answer sheet.

PART 3

Directions: You will hear some conversations between two people. You will be asked to answer three questions about what the speakers say in each conversation. Select the best response to each question and mark the letter (A), (B), (C), or (D) on your answer sheet. The conversations will not be printed in your test book and will be spoken only one time.

41. Where does the conversation take place?
(A) At a post office.
(B) At a park.
(C) At a business office.
(D) At an airport.

42. When were the contracts mailed?
(A) Earlier in the week.
(B) Yesterday morning.
(C) Last night.
(D) This morning.

43. What time is it now?
(A) 7:00.
(B) 7:45.
(C) 11:00.
(D) 11:45.

---

44. What level class does the man want to take?
(A) Basic.
(B) Beginning.
(C) Intermediate.
(D) Advanced.

45. How much will the class cost?
(A) $90.
(B) $400.
(C) $500.
(D) $600.

46. What time of day does the man want to study?
(A) Morning.
(B) Noon.
(C) Afternoon.
(D) Night.

---

47. When will Mr. Katz arrive?
(A) Today.
(B) Tonight.
(C) Tomorrow morning.
(D) Tomorrow night.

48. How is the weather in New York?
(A) It's raining.
(B) It's snowing.
(C) It's icy.
(D) It's nice.

49. How did the woman hear about the weather?
(A) Mr. Katz told her.
(B) On the radio.
(C) In the newspaper.
(D) On TV.

---

50. Where will they have the retirement party?
(A) In the conference room.
(B) In Mr. Lee's office.
(C) In the party room.
(D) In a restaurant.

51. How many guests will there be?
(A) 15.
(B) 16.
(C) 50.
(D) 60.

52. When will the party be?
(A) Tuesday.
(B) Wednesday.
(C) Thursday.
(D) Friday.

GO ON TO THE NEXT PAGE

53. Where does the conversation take place?
(A) In a restaurant.
(B) In a stadium.
(C) In a theater.
(D) In a train station.

54. How long will the woman have to wait?
(A) Four or five minutes.
(B) Ten minutes.
(C) Forty minutes.
(D) Forty-five minutes.

55. What does the man suggest doing?
(A) Making reservations.
(B) Waiting.
(C) Trying another place.
(D) Returning later.

---

56. Why can't the woman speak with Mr. Curtis right now?
(A) He's too busy.
(B) He's on a business trip.
(C) He went downtown.
(D) He's talking on the phone.

57. What will the woman do?
(A) Leave a message.
(B) Return later.
(C) Make an appointment.
(D) Call back.

58. Why does the woman want to see Mr. Curtis?
(A) To show him some contracts.
(B) To give him a book.
(C) To open a bank account.
(D) To sell him a boat.

---

59. Why did Mr. Cho stop work?
(A) He's been feeling tired.
(B) He's on vacation.
(C) He was fired.
(D) He retired.

60. When did Mr. Cho stop work?
(A) Two days ago.
(B) On Tuesday.
(C) Last week.
(D) Last month.

61. Why did the speakers like Mr. Cho?
(A) He told jokes.
(B) He worked hard.
(C) He cleaned the office.
(D) He brought them cookies.

---

62. How long have the speakers been waiting for Janet?
(A) Thirty minutes.
(B) One hour.
(C) Since 8:00.
(D) Since 9:00.

63. Why is Janet late this time?
(A) She had a dentist appointment.
(B) She had to work late.
(C) She had to stop at the store.
(D) She had to exercise.

64. How does the man feel?
(A) Happy.
(B) Annoyed.
(C) Sad.
(D) Relaxed.

---

65. What is the man's problem?
(A) The hotel lost his reservation.
(B) The room is too expensive.
(C) He doesn't like the room.
(D) He lost his key.

66. How long will the man stay at the hotel?
(A) One day.
(B) Two days.
(C) Three days.
(D) Four days.

67. How much does the room cost?
(A) $65.
(B) $155.
(C) $160.
(D) $165.

68. What happened to Carl?
(A) He got a promotion.
(B) He bought a new house.
(C) He got married.
(D) He painted his office.

69. How does the man feel about Carl's situation?
(A) He's unhappy.
(B) He's glad.
(C) He's fearful.
(D) He's mad.

70. What does the man want to do?
(A) Meet Carl's wife.
(B) Leave the office.
(C) Visit Carl's house.
(D) Give a party.

GO ON TO THE NEXT PAGE

PART 4

Directions: You will hear some talks given by a single speaker. You will be asked to answer three questions about what the speaker says in each talk. Select the best response to each question and mark the letter (A), (B), (C), or (D) on your answer sheet. The talks will not be printed in your test book and will be spoken only one time.

71. Who was responsible for the problem?
(A) A park ranger.
(B) A boy scout.
(C) A spokesperson.
(D) A smoker.

72. What was destroyed?
(A) Campgrounds.
(B) Houses.
(C) A car.
(D) A town.

73. When do authorities expect the fire to be put out?
(A) On Monday.
(B) On Wednesday.
(C) By today.
(D) In two days.

---

74. What type of place is the announcement about?
(A) A school.
(B) A church.
(C) A village.
(D) A hospital.

75. Who receives services at this place?
(A) Poor people.
(B) Middle-income people.
(C) Rich people.
(D) Retired people.

76. Why are they changing the name of the place?
(A) The old name was too long.
(B) Dr. Schweitzer was a popular physician.
(C) They would like to have a separate identity.
(D) Villa Hospitalis has moved to another city.

---

77. What is the specialty of Fuji House?
(A) Seafood.
(B) Chicken.
(C) Tempura.
(D) Pork.

78. What describes the food at Fuji House?
(A) It's very expensive.
(B) It's vegetarian only.
(C) It smells and tastes delicious.
(D) It comes from all over the world.

79. When is Fuji House open?
(A) Every day.
(B) Monday and Friday only.
(C) Saturday and Sunday only.
(D) Monday through Friday only.

---

80. Why are these people meeting?
(A) To discuss employee concerns.
(B) To elect the Manager of the Year.
(C) To choose the Employee of the Year.
(D) To vote for a new contract.

81. How will the employees vote?
(A) By using a ballot.
(B) By raising their hands.
(C) By calling out people's names.
(D) By registering a name electronically.

82. How many prizes will the winner get?
(A) One.
(B) Two.
(C) Three.
(D) Four.

---

83. When does this tour take place?
(A) In the morning.
(B) In the afternoon.
(C) In the evening.
(D) At night.

84. Where will the tour end?
(A) At the main gate.
(B) At Machu Picchu.
(C) At the main plaza.
(D) At the Temple of the Sun.

85. What does the tour guide request of the tourists?
(A) To use the litter cans.
(B) Not to wander away.
(C) Not to touch the monuments.
(D) Not to ask questions until he has finished.

---

86. Why is the woman calling?
(A) To return a phone call.
(B) To ask for Max's address.
(C) To verify her phone number.
(D) To make an appointment with Max.

87. What is she confused about?
(A) The reason for Max's phone call.
(B) The time she should call back.
(C) The name of her street.
(D) Max's last name.

88. When can Max call her back?
(A) Before noon.
(B) At noon.
(C) This afternoon.
(D) After three days.

---

89. Why did the county residents lose electric power?
(A) There was a big storm.
(B) There are too many residents in the county.
(C) Work crews are installing a new system.
(D) Power Company employees are on strike.

90. How many residents don't have power?
(A) 15,000.
(B) 50,000.
(C) 100,000.
(D) 150,000.

91. Who will have power this evening?
(A) Power Company employees.
(B) The western part of the county.
(C) Just a few lucky residents.
(D) The entire county.

---

92. What is being announced?
(A) A golf tournament.
(B) The opening of a sports facility.
(C) The start of a renovation project.
(D) Reduced-price orientation sessions.

93. When will the event take place?
(A) November 1.
(B) November 21.
(C) December 1.
(D) December 21.

94. What special offer is being announced?
(A) Free golf clubs.
(B) Private swim lessons.
(C) Two-for-one memberships.
(D) Overnight rooms for guests.

GO ON TO THE NEXT PAGE

95. When will the train for Springdale leave?
(A) In five minutes.
(B) In fifteen minutes.
(C) At 7:30.
(D) At 10:30.

96. Who will be allowed to get on the train first?
(A) Passengers with reservations.
(B) Passengers with children.
(C) Passengers with no bags.
(D) Passengers with pets.

97. What are passengers allowed to take on the train?
(A) Nothing.
(B) Small bags.
(C) Large suitcases.
(D) Musical instruments.

98. How many lectures are there in the series?
(A) Seven.
(B) Ten.
(C) Eleven.
(D) Seventeen.

99. What is the topic of tonight's lecture?
(A) Butterflies.
(B) Deserts.
(C) Oceans.
(D) Plants.

100. What will happen after the talk?
(A) A trip to Central America will be organized.
(B) There will be a display of butterflies.
(C) The speaker will show a video.
(D) There will be a sale of photos.

This is the end of the Listening test. Turn to Part 5 in your test book.

READING TEST

In the Reading test, you will read a variety of texts and answer several different types of reading comprehension questions. The entire Reading test will last 75 minutes. There are three parts, and directions are given for each part. You are encouraged to answer as many questions as possible within the time allowed.

You must mark your answers on the separate answer sheet. Do not write your answers in the test book.

PART 5

Directions: A word or phrase is missing in each of the sentences below. Four answer choices are given below each sentence. Select the best answer to complete the sentence. Then mark the letter (A), (B), (C), or (D) on your answer sheet.

101. Can you explain all the _______ I see on my pay statement?
(A) deduct
(B) deductions
(C) deductibles
(D) deducting

102. I'm sorry, but this area is _______ to bank personnel only.
(A) restricted
(B) restriction
(C) restrict
(D) restricts

103. The human resources manager hasn't arrived _______, so please have a seat.
(A) already
(B) still
(C) soon
(D) yet

104. Management has _______ to make a reasonable offer at the next contract bargaining session.
(A) promises
(B) promise
(C) promised
(D) promising

105. Employees are _______ to put in for vacation time at least two months in advance.
(A) requested
(B) referred
(C) rejected
(D) reported

106. The sales manager didn't care for our _______ about last quarter's sales slump.
(A) remarking
(B) remarkable
(C) remarked
(D) remarks

107. My cousin's _______ advice about selling our stock saved us thousands.
(A) amazingly
(B) amazed
(C) amazing
(D) amazement

108. I'm surprised _______ how fast customers get served in this restaurant.
(A) on
(B) at
(C) in
(D) for

109. In order to get a _______, you must bring in the defective product with a valid receipt.
(A) reimbursement
(B) premium
(C) duplication
(D) refund

110. Ms. Kim is learning Russian _______ she can communicate with her new father-in-law.
(A) so that
(B) because
(C) although
(D) then

GO ON TO THE NEXT PAGE

111. The CFO believes that a _______ large volume of sales is the reason we are out of the red.
(A) surprised
(B) surprising
(C) surprisingly
(D) surprise

112. Making decisions about layoffs isn't _______ our supervisor's job description.
(A) within
(B) into
(C) about
(D) inside

113. When starting a new business, it isn't _______ to expect profits during the first year.
(A) real
(B) realistic
(C) realistically
(D) really

114. It is only through a _______ effort on the part of all employees that a company will prosper.
(A) collaboration
(B) collaborative
(C) collaborator
(D) collaboratively

115. That decision of _______ to repaint the house now was a very smart one.
(A) your
(B) you
(C) yourself
(D) yours

116. Before investing in a new drug, we carry out extensive _______ to see if there is a need for one.
(A) investigation
(B) investing
(C) planning
(D) research

117. All branch managers must _______ a semi-annual report for the main office by the end of May.
(A) compensate
(B) deliver
(C) apply
(D) prepare

118. Doing business in 2010 will be extremely _______ what it was like in 1910.
(A) different from
(B) different to
(C) different
(D) different then

119. _______ has there been more of a demand for e-business courses at universities than there is now.
(A) Always
(B) Never
(C) Rare
(D) Often

120. The company's new database system will be installed and running _______ the end of the year.
(A) in
(B) from
(C) by
(D) on

121. The head of the space program will not be satisfied unless all work is done with the utmost _______.
(A) accurate
(B) accurately
(C) accuracy
(D) more accuracy

122. Clients will receive _______ questionnaires to see if they are satisfied with our gym equipment.
(A) periodical
(B) periodic
(C) periodically
(D) period

123. With the approach of the holiday season, employees are _______ awaiting their bonuses.
(A) anxiety
(B) anxious
(C) anxiousness
(D) anxiously

124. We have just received a troubling ______ on the expected rise in health care costs.
(A) accounting
(B) documentation
(C) report
(D) observance

125. Could you please elaborate ______ your claim that housekeeping didn't keep your room clean?
(A) on
(B) over
(C) for
(D) into

126. It is recommended that potential investors ______ the help of financial advisors before investing.
(A) are seeking out
(B) seek out
(C) to seek out
(D) sought out

127. With globalization now a part of our lives, it is impossible for a country to do business by ______.
(A) itself
(B) it
(C) its own
(D) it's self

128. The government's decision to lower tariffs will allow the volume of imports to ______ tremendously.
(A) extrapolate
(B) exhibit
(C) expand
(D) exhale

129. Our ______ cost-cutting measures will ensure greater profits for the company in the next fiscal year.
(A) outrageous
(B) lucrative
(C) aggressive
(D) astounding

130. Our hotel has every ______ of making your annual convention the most memorable one ever.
(A) intent
(B) intently
(C) intend
(D) intention

131. Shopping on the Internet is for those consumers for ______ going to malls has become a nightmare.
(A) who
(B) whom
(C) which
(D) that

132. Because of security concerns, all job applicants are ______ carefully before interviews are granted.
(A) screamed
(B) screened
(C) scrawled
(D) scraped

133. Mr. Hansen's ______ from his position as chief comptroller has been a shock to all of us.
(A) resigning
(B) resigned
(C) resigns
(D) resign

134. Investors are relieved that all ______ say the stock market will bounce back in the next six months.
(A) predicaments
(B) predilections
(C) predictions
(D) predicates

135. This new trade agreement has created all kinds of ______ possibilities for both our countries.
(A) excited
(B) exciting
(C) excitement
(D) excitable

136. The use of e-mail has caused an ______ leap in business communications throughout the world.
(A) unacceptable
(B) implacable
(C) inadvertent
(D) unimaginable

137. Because of renovations to our offices, future social ______ will be held in the company cafeteria.
(A) events
(B) reunions
(C) councils
(D) invocations

GO ON TO THE NEXT PAGE

138. The last company blood drive was _______ a success that we plan on having one every two months.

(A) such
(B) so
(C) too
(D) much

139. The staff breathed a _______ sigh of relief when it was announced that there would be no layoffs.

(A) collected
(B) collective
(C) collecting
(D) collectible

140. Consumers are spending less these days _______ reports that the economy is steadily improving.

(A) in spite
(B) because of
(C) although
(D) despite

PART 6

Directions: Read the texts that follow. A word or phrase is missing in some of the sentences. Four answer choices are given below each of the sentences. Select the best answer to complete the text. Then mark the letter (A), (B), (C), or (D) on your answer sheet.

Questions 141–143 refer to the following announcement.

Bournesville Bank

is pleased to announce the opening of a new branch at 1109 South Boulevard in the Green Lake section of town.

This ____________ a full-service branch where you can be sure of

141. (A) has been
(B) will be
(C) being
(D) was

receiving the professional, prompt, and friendly service that you are accustomed to at all Bournesville Bank branches.

Please join us for the grand opening of our new branch on Monday, May 22 during our regular business hours 9:00 A.M. to 3:00 P.M.

There will be refreshments, live ____________, and prizes.

142. (A) entertain
(B) entertainer
(C) entertaining
(D) entertainment

Bank staff will be on hand to explain all the services available to our customers. Everyone who opens a new ____________ during the

143. (A) vault
(B) ledger
(C) account
(D) entrance

Grand Opening will receive a special bonus gift. This gift is our way of saying "Thank you" for doing business with us.

Bournesville Bank, your partner in all your business and personal financial needs.

GO ON TO THE NEXT PAGE

Questions 144–146 refer to the following article.

Profits Up In ________ Sector

144. (A) Transportation
(B) Agriculture
(C) Technology
(D) Finance

Galaxy Systems reported a fourth quarter profit of $250,000, compared to a loss of nearly $2 million during the same period last year. This was the first quarter with a profit for the computer company, which began operations five years ago.

According to the year-end report from Goldsboro, Inc., the company's profits rose 20%, or $2.5 million since the end of last year. This is good news for the financial software company, which had been suffering losses during the past several years. The rise in profits is attributed to the introduction of a new software system for personal finance accounting. The company hopes to further increase its ________ next year by

145. (A) debts
(B) products
(C) factories
(D) earnings

expanding its markets overseas.

Profits for Providence Communications Company were up only 5% at the end of the fourth quarter. This is a much smaller increase than the company has reported for several years running. Providence has been losing a significant portion of its market share to competitors, but the company is optimistic about the future. "We're confident that our plans for bringing more efficient and less ________ wireless service to our

146. (A) cost
(B) costly
(C) coasted
(D) costing

customers will result in increased market share and greater profits than the company has ever enjoyed in the past," said Thomas P. Witherspoon, CEO.

Questions 147–149 refer to the following letter.

Rita Harwood
Manager
Tinkum Square Hotel
Portsmouth, NJ 14689

Dear Ms. Harwood:

I am writing to let you know of the exemplary care and service I received from _____________ staff during my stay at the Tinkum Square Hotel last July. From the

147. (A) my
(B) our
(C) your
(D) their

moment of my arrival until the day I departed, I received nothing but courteous and efficient service from all members of the hotel staff.

I especially want to bring to your attention two staff members who provided me with assistance above and beyond the call of duty. On my way to the airport after a pleasant week at Tinkum Square, I discovered that I had left my computer behind. I immediately called the manager on duty, Robert Dunstan, who supervised an emergency search for my computer. After it was discovered in the hotel restaurant, Mr. Dunstan's assistant, Martha Jones, got into a taxi and personally delivered the computer to me at the airport. It was all done so _____________ that I had my computer in hand well before I had to board the plane.

148. (A) speedy
(B) speeded
(C) speeding
(D) speedily

I know that you would want to hear about this example of the loyalty and professionalism of Mr. Dunstan and Ms. Jones. I look forward to _____________ at Tinkum Square during

149. (A) staying
(B) working
(C) looking
(D) existing

my next business trip to Portsmouth.

Sincerely,
James L. Keenan
James L. Keenan

GO ON TO THE NEXT PAGE

Questions 150–152 refer to the following notice.

Migdalia Cleaning Services

Service Contract Notification

Office Cleaning Services for:
Bower Company
Suite 253
210 Benson Boulevard
Farmington, CT 06726

This is to notify you that your service cleaning contract will expire on May 10. If you would like to __________ your contract, fill out the form below.

150. (A) sign
(B) renew
(C) cancel
(D) review

Complete information about our services is available on our website: www.migdaliaclean.com. __________ the form to our offices before May 1.

151. (A) Submit
(B) To submit
(C) Submitting
(D) Submission

Payment is required at the same time.

Please enclose a check with the form or provide your credit card information. Your contract will not go into effect __________ we receive your payment.

152. (A) until
(B) after
(C) when
(D) while

Send it in today to avoid any disruptions to your cleaning service. Thank you for your business.

PART 7

Directions: In this part you will read a selection of texts, such as magazine and newspaper articles, letters, and advertisements. Each text is followed by several questions. Select the best answer for each question and mark the letter (A), (B), (C), or (D) on your answer sheet.

Questions 153–154 refer to the following announcement.

FEELING STRESSED?

Need a *real* break during working hours?
Having trouble relaxing after work?

Human Resources is bringing you
"The Stress Buster"

- 15 minutes of total relaxation free of charge
- Choose the table for full bodywork.
- Choose the chair for neck, shoulders, and back.

Where: Employee Lounge
When: Mondays, Wednesdays, Fridays
Times: During breaks, lunchtime, after work

153. What is this announcement about?
(A) Length of breaks
(B) Massages
(C) Furniture sales
(D) Language classes

154. How much will this service cost the employees?
(A) Fifteen dollars for fifteen minutes
(B) They pay nothing.
(C) It depends on the service.
(D) Human Resources has the rate.

Questions 155–157 refer to the following memorandum.

MEMORANDUM

TO: All Atlantis Corporation Employees
FROM: Myrtle Sternbridge, Chief Financial Officer *MS*
RE: Two-day unpaid leave
DATE: June 3

It is my unhappy duty to inform you that the Board of Directors has voted to impose a two-day layoff for all employees in order to avoid an operating budget shortfall. The company is facing a serious crisis due to poor profits over the past two quarters. The budget is short by about $13 million and, according to our bylaws, the budget must be balanced by June 30, the end of this fiscal year.

It is necessary for all employees to give up two days' pay in order to put an end to the budget crisis. Employees are to speak to their supervisors regarding scheduling the two days that they are not to report to work.

According to the agreement reached between Atlantis Corp. and the union, employees will be reimbursed for the days they lose during the first six months of the next fiscal year if profits improve.

I sincerely regret the need to take such drastic measures to end the current budget crisis, but with your cooperation, we can see this through.

155. Why must employees give up two days' pay at this time?
(A) To pay back money they were overpaid
(B) To contribute to a company charity
(C) To end a budget crisis in this fiscal year
(D) The bylaws state they have to.

156. What is causing this budget crisis?
(A) There is a surplus of $13 million.
(B) There is a shortage of $13 million.
(C) The CFO did not plan out the operating budget properly.
(D) Nobody can pinpoint the reasons for this budget crisis.

157. How will the days be taken off?
(A) Employees will arrange days off with their supervisors.
(B) All employees are to stay home starting June 30.
(C) A specific plan has not been worked out yet.
(D) Employees can arrange to take two days off this or next fiscal year.

Questions 158–160 refer to the following notice.

> ***Miami-Dade County Transit Authority***
>
> **LANE CLOSURES**
>
> Due to continued construction on Interstate 95, the two left lanes on the north side will be closed from NE 79th St. to NE 135th St. between the hours of midnight and 6:00 A.M., Monday to Friday, and 10:00 P.M. to 7 A.M. weekends.
>
> Lane closures are scheduled to begin on October 16 and continue until November 6.
>
> We regret any inconvenience to motorists.

158. Which part of the highway will have lane closures?
(A) All north side lanes
(B) One lane on each side
(C) The two left lanes on each side
(D) The two left lanes on the north side

159. Who is authorizing the lane closures?
(A) The city
(B) The county
(C) The state
(D) The district

160. Which of the following exits will NOT be in the affected area?
(A) NE 125th Street
(B) NE 95th Street
(C) NE 151st Street
(D) NE 82nd Street

GO ON TO THE NEXT PAGE

Questions 161–163 refer to the following article.

Those old *Movie Goer* magazines in the basement may be worth more than you would imagine. A 1952 copy featuring Clark Gable can be worth over $750, and an old Lucille Ball is valued at $900. But it's not just the oldies that are worth so much money. A collection of twenty-five *Lost in Space* covers from June, 2001, sells for more than $450 online. "The Internet has been great for collecting and has made it a lot easier to find things," says George Boulis, 58, a Boston-based collector who has all the *Movie Goer Magazine* covers. They're worth about $28,000. And what do you think is the most valuable issue? The first one, of course: A mint-condition copy goes for more than $1,850.

161. What is this article about?
(A) The literary value of *Movie Goer Magazine*
(B) How George Boulis became a very rich man
(C) The monetary value of old issues of *Movie Goer Magazine*
(D) The monetary value of old covers of *Movie Goer Magazine*

162. Where does the writer assume the readers may have old issues of this magazine?
(A) In the attic
(B) In the basement
(C) Under their beds
(D) In their garages

163. Which is the most valuable issue of this magazine?
(A) The premier issue
(B) The ultimate issue
(C) The one with Lucille Ball
(D) The one with Clark Gable

Questions 164–168 refer to the following television schedule.

BCAST	8:00	8:30	9:00	9:30	10:00	10:30
2	Washington Week	Wall Street Week Ⓑ	McLaughlin Report		Hurricane Watch	
4	48 Hours		Diagnosis Murder: Town Without Pity (2006) Ⓜ			
5	Dateline NBC				Law and Order: Special Victims Unit	
6	Dateline NBC				Law and Order: Special Victims Unit	
7	Sports Extra		X-Files		News	
10	Financial Success with Sonya Ozman Ⓑ		Lilo & Stitch: Aloha from Hollywood		20/20	
CABLE						
A&E	Biography		Tea with Mussolini (1999) Ⓜ			
AMC	Working Girl (1988) Ⓜ				Working Girl (1988) Ⓜ	
BPL	Business Week in Review Ⓑ		Business Week in Review Ⓑ		It's Your Money Ⓑ	
CNN	Live from . . .		Larry King Live		NewsNight with Aaron Brown	
DSC	U.S. Mint Ⓑ		Inside the World's Mightiest Bank Ⓑ		Three Gorges	
MTV	To Be Announced					

Ⓑ = Business Ⓜ = Movies

164. How long is *Financial Success with Sonya Ozman* on the air?
(A) Thirty minutes
(B) One hour
(C) Two hours
(D) Three hours

165. How many different shows about business are being televised in this schedule?
(A) Two
(B) Four
(C) Six
(D) Eight

166. Which financial show is repeated on the same station?
(A) *Business Week in Review*
(B) *Law and Order: Special Victims Unit*
(C) *Working Girl*
(D) *Dateline NBC*

167. Which station shows only business programs?
(A) DSC
(B) BPL
(C) 2
(D) AMC

168. The word "Unit" in line 3 of the first box is closest in meaning to
(A) Apartment
(B) Individual
(C) Department
(D) Investigation

GO ON TO THE NEXT PAGE

Questions 169–172 refer to the following news article.

LONDON—In May, Great Britain's Home Office, deciding on compensation for a man who served four years in prison for industrial espionage that he did not commit, ruled that he was entitled to about $1.1 million. They said, however, that he would have to reimburse the prison about $23,000 for four years' room and board. The outraged Michael O'Brien, age 34, was freed by a Court of Appeal. He said, "They don't charge guilty people for bed and board. They only charge innocent people!"

169. Who decided that Michael O'Brien should be released from prison?
(A) The Queen
(B) A group of judges
(C) A government agency
(D) Popular opinion

170. What had Mr. O'Brien been convicted of?
(A) Robbing a bank
(B) Forging documents
(C) Spying on other companies
(D) Embezzling thousands from his company

171. The word "commit" in line 5 is closest in meaning to
(A) believe in
(B) profit from
(C) condone
(D) carry out

172. What is upsetting Mr. O'Brien?
(A) He has to pay back money to the prison.
(B) He has to pay money to the Home Office.
(C) He will have more money than he ever dreamed of.
(D) The authorities never caught the real spy.

Questions 173–175 refer to the following advertisement.

easy ways to
shop

shop over 350 stores
call 1.800.GOTRENDY

shop by mail
call 1.800.555.8183

shop online
trendymale.com

3181 River Road
Rockville, NM 13579
909–555–5208

buy one sale or
clearance item, **get one**
50% off*

*2nd item must be of equal or lesser value. Applies to sale and clearance merchandise only. May not be combined with any other coupon offer, promotion, or previous purchases. Excludes fragrance, gift certificate, catalogue, or online purchases. Not valid on designer merchandise. Not valid on Trendy Male Outlets. Sale Monday, June 17 through Sunday, July 7.

Trendy Male

save
up to 60%
or more off
original
prices

173. How many ways can you buy merchandise at "Trendy Male"?
(A) One
(B) Two
(C) Three
(D) Four

174. If you buy a shirt on sale for $46.00, how much will you pay for another, similar shirt?
(A) $15.00
(B) $23.00
(C) $27.60
(D) $46.00

175. How long will this offer last?
(A) Eleven days
(B) Sixteen days
(C) Twenty-one days
(D) Twenty-six days

Questions 176–178 refer to the following instructions.

> Connect the lead from the charger to the bottom of your cellular phone or to a charging stand. Then plug the charger into a standard wall outlet. When the battery is charging, the battery strength indicator on the right side of the display scrolls.
> *Note:* When you charge the battery for the first time, the battery strength indicator will not scroll the entire time; this is normal.
>
> If your phone displays **Not charging,** charging is suspended. Check that the battery is connected to an approved charging device. If the battery is very hot or cold, wait for a while; charging will automatically resume after the battery is restored to its normal operating state. If charging still fails, contact your dealer.

176. What device are these instructions for?
- (A) A portable phone
- (B) A palm pilot
- (C) A cell phone
- (D) A laptop computer

177. What should you do if the battery is not charging?
- (A) Check that the battery is connected to the charger
- (B) Call the factory
- (C) Call your dealer immediately
- (D) Check the normal operating time

178. What should you do if the device fails to charge properly?
- (A) Return it to the company
- (B) Get in touch with the place you bought it from
- (C) Send it back to the factory
- (D) Throw it away and buy another one

GO ON TO THE NEXT PAGE

Questions 179–180 refer to the following advertisement.

Prepare for a New Career
Or get your H.S. Diploma at home.

You've always wanted to start a new career, but could never find the time to get the training you need. Until now. The Learning Center can help you study at home in your spare time to get the skills you need to succeed!

Get your career diploma as a private investigator or medical transcriptionist in as little as six months! Earn your high school diploma in as little as nine months. In as little as two years, you could even have your degree in accounting!

Join the 8 million men and women who enrolled with The Learning Center to change their lives for the better. Call, write, or visit our website today for FREE information!

For fastest service, call toll free:
1-800-555-9878 ext. 834
Visit our website **www.thelearningcenter.com**

Choose ONE of the programs below:

06 High School	57 Private Investigator
86 Accounting	21 Medical Transcriptionist

Dept. LV168R
456 Elm Road
Boynton Cove, FL 31245

179. When does the ad say you would be able to study for a career?
(A) In the mornings
(B) In the evenings
(C) On the weekends
(D) Whenever you had free time

180. How long would it take you to get a degree in accounting?
(A) Six months
(B) Nine months
(C) Eighteen months
(D) Two years

Questions 181–185 refer to the following two e-mails.

To: Ronald Richards, Peter Kim, Hiro Sachimoto, Giovanna Bertini
From: Isabelle Santelli
Subject: Meeting reminder

This is a reminder that this month's department meeting will take place this Thursday at 12:00 in Conference Room 2. Please note location change. The meeting will NOT take place in my office. We will review progress on the Lockerman project and look at the budget for the rest of the year. This is a lunchtime meeting and sandwiches and coffee will be served. Please let me know by Wednesday if you won't be able to make the meeting. Thank you.

Isabelle Santelli

To: I. Santelli
From: R. Richards
Subject: Re: Meeting reminder

Isabelle,

I'm sorry I won't be able to make the meeting. I'm leaving for Sydney that morning and can't get a later flight. Before I go, I'll put on your desk the figures you'll need for the second item on the meeting agenda. I've prepared a thorough report, so you'll be able to have that part of the discussion without me. Also, Peter worked with me on this and can probably answer any questions.

I'll be meeting with Mr. Lockerman first thing Friday and will send you the particulars later that day, or by Saturday morning at the latest.

Ronald

181. Who should attend the meeting on Thursday?
- (A) Conference committee members
- (B) All company personnel
- (C) Department members
- (D) Mr. Lockerman

182. Where will the meeting take place?
- (A) In a conference room
- (B) In a sandwich shop
- (C) In a cafeteria
- (D) In an office

183. When will Mr. Richards go to Sydney?
- (A) Wednesday
- (B) Thursday
- (C) Friday
- (D) Saturday

184. Who worked on a report with Mr. Richards?
- (A) Mr. Sachimoto
- (B) Ms. Santelli
- (C) Ms. Bertini
- (D) Mr. Kim

185. What will Mr. Richards leave for Ms. Santelli?
- (A) Information for the meeting
- (B) Mr. Lockerman's address
- (C) An agenda
- (D) His Sydney itinerary

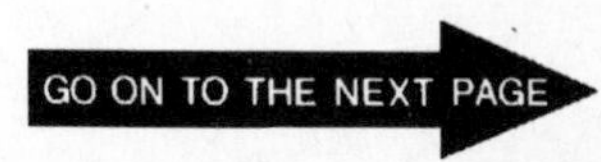

Questions 186–190 refer to the following invoice and letter.

Peninsula Office Supplies and Equipment
105978 Rutherford Drive • Suite 110
Greensboro, RI 45790

Invoice No. 1078
Date: November 10
Ship Date: November 15

Item		**Price**
1 computer stand—model B		$150
2 desk chairs model ZY		$225
1 large watercooler		$ 85
3 paper cutters		$180
	subtotal	$640
	shipping & handling	$ 75
	amount due	$715

The above amount has been charged to your credit card.
Thank you for doing business with us.

November 21

Customer Service Department
Peninsula Office Supplies and Equipment
105978 Rutherford Drive, Suite 110
Greensboro, RI 45790

Dear Customer Service:

On November 18, we received a shipment of office furniture and equipment from your company. Unfortunately, the items we received were not the same as the items we ordered. I am enclosing a copy of the bill so that you can see exactly what was delivered to us. We did order a computer stand, but requested model D, which is half the price of model B. We also asked for only one desk chair, and we didn't order any paper cutters at all. At least the watercooler was correct.

I have tried calling your Customer Service number repeatedly, but the line is always busy. Several attempts at e-mailing have also resulted in no response. Please let me know how we can return the office furniture which was erroneously delivered and receive instead the furniture that we actually ordered. I would like to resolve this matter as quickly as possible.

Sincerely yours,

H. J. Simpson

H. J. Simpson
Office Manager

186. How long was the shipment in transit?
(A) 3 days
(B) 5 days
(C) 8 days
(D) 11 days

187. Why did Mr. Simpson write the letter?
(A) Because he received the wrong order
(B) Because the furniture arrived damaged
(C) Because he didn't like what he ordered
(D) Because the furniture was too expensive

188. How much does a model D computer stand cost?
(A) $50
(B) $75
(C) $150
(D) $300

189. How many watercoolers did Mr. Simpson order?
(A) None
(B) One
(C) Two
(D) Three

190. What happened when Mr. Simpson called the Customer Service number?
(A) He was asked to send an e-mail.
(B) His order was reshipped.
(C) He received a refund.
(D) He got a busy signal.

GO ON TO THE NEXT PAGE

Questions 191–195 refer to the following schedule and e-mail.

High-Speed Train Service
Mitteldorf-Kohlberg Line

LV MITTELDORF	ARR KOHLBERG
5:45*	10:30
7:30**	11:50
8:15	**12:35**
11:00**	**3:20**
12:20*	**5:05**
4:35	**8:55**

Times listed in bold are P.M.
* Makes intermediate stops at Badstein and Grauling
** Monday, Wednesday, and Friday only

Reservations are required on all trains.

One-way ticket prices as of April 1:
Business Class: $175
Tourist Class: $135

Round-trip fares are double the one-way fare.

To: Park Travel Agency
From: Hilda Heinz
Subject: Train ticket

Dear Mr. Park,

Thank you for forwarding the train schedule to me. I'm not an early riser, but I need to be in Kohlberg by the early afternoon, so I'll take the second train in the morning next Tuesday the 22nd. I'll return the following Friday. I haven't seen the return schedule, but time is not so important for my return. Would you please make me a reservation that would have me back in Mitteldorf by about 5 or 6 in the afternoon? I prefer to travel business class, of course. Please bill my account and have the ticket sent to my office.

Thank you, as always, for your kind and efficient service.

Hilda Heinz

191. What time does the earliest train arrive in Kohlberg?
(A) 3:20
(B) 5:05
(C) 8:55
(D) 10:30

192. How long is a nonstop trip between Mitteldorf and Kohlberg?
(A) Three and a half hours
(B) Four hours and twenty minutes
(C) Four hours and forty-five minutes
(D) Five and a half hours

193. Which train does Ms. Heinz plan to take on Tuesday?
(A) 5:45
(B) 7:30
(C) 8:15
(D) 11:00

194. How much will Ms. Heinz pay for her round-trip ticket?
(A) $135
(B) $175
(C) $270
(D) $350

195. When does Ms. Heinz want to arrive in Mitteldorf on her return?
(A) As early as possible
(B) Before noon
(C) In the early afternoon
(D) In the late afternoon

Questions 196–200 refer to the following advertisement and e-mail.

Have your next company banquet at the

Hotel Grandiflor

We offer:

- Table seating for up to 250 guests
- A choice of catered meals prepared by our European-trained chefs
- Two world-class dance floors

We also provide on request professional assistance in selecting decorations, music, and seating arrangements.

Rooms are available for both midday and evening banquets.

Meal options include buffet, 3-course, and 5-course meals.

Impress your clients and reward your employees by inviting them to lunch or dinner at the Hotel Grandiflor.

Contact Cathy Chang, Events Manager, or Lois Street, Head Manager

To: Cathy Chang
From: Georgette Blanc
Subject: Banquet plans

Dear Ms. Chang:

I saw your hotel's ad in the May 23 issue of the *Business Gazette*. I am planning the annual employee appreciation banquet for my company, Agrix International, and am interested in the possibility of hosting it at the Hotel Grandiflor.

Our banquet is scheduled for the evening of July 15. We only plan to have half the number of guests mentioned in your ad, so I am sure you can accommodate our numbers. I think a five-course dinner would be too much, but I am interested in discussing with you the other two meal options. Mostly I am concerned about having both vegetarian and meat choices available for our guests.

I am also interested in your professional assistance in planning other aspects of the evening. We would need seating arrangements that are conducive to conversation but that will also accommodate the awards ceremony that is the main focus of the evening. We also would like to have dancing after the meal and would appreciate your assistance in selecting a suitable and affordable band.

Please call me or my assistant, Robert de Luc, at 656-555-0987 to discuss arrangements and costs.

Georgette Blanc

196. What is the name of the hotel's events manager?
(A) Cathy Chang
(B) Lois Street
(C) Georgette Blanc
(D) Robert de Luc

197. What is the main purpose of the banquet mentioned in the e-mail?
(A) To celebrate an anniversary
(B) To honor employees
(C) To discuss business
(D) To impress clients

198. When will the banquet take place?
(A) May 3
(B) May 23
(C) July 5
(D) July 15

199. How many guests will be invited to the banquet?
(A) 15
(B) 125
(C) 250
(D) 500

200. Which type of meal would be of interest to the banquet planner?
(A) Meat-only three-course meal
(B) Five-course meal
(C) Light lunch
(D) Vegetarian and meat buffet

Stop! This is the end of the test. If you finish before time is called, you may go back to Parts 5, 6, and 7 and check your work.

PRACTICE TEST TWO

Practice Test Two is similar to an actual TOEIC® test. You can take this test anytime while studying this book in order to measure your improvement.

Read all directions carefully. This will help you become familiar with the actual TOEIC test directions and item types.

Use the Practice Test Two Answer Sheet on page 346.

LISTENING TEST

In the Listening test, you will be asked to demonstrate how well you understand spoken English. The entire Listening test will last approximately 45 minutes. There are four parts, and directions are given for each part. You must mark your answers on the separate answer sheet. Do not write your answers in the test book.

PART 1

Directions: For each question in this part, you will hear four statements about a picture in your test book. When you hear the statements, you must select the one statement that best describes what you see in the picture. Then find the number of the question on your answer sheet and mark your answer.The statements will not be printed in your test book and will be spoken only one time.

Example

Sample Answer

Statement (C), "They're standing near the table," is the best description of the picture, so you should select answer (C) and mark it on your answer sheet.

1. 

2. 

GO ON TO THE NEXT PAGE

3. 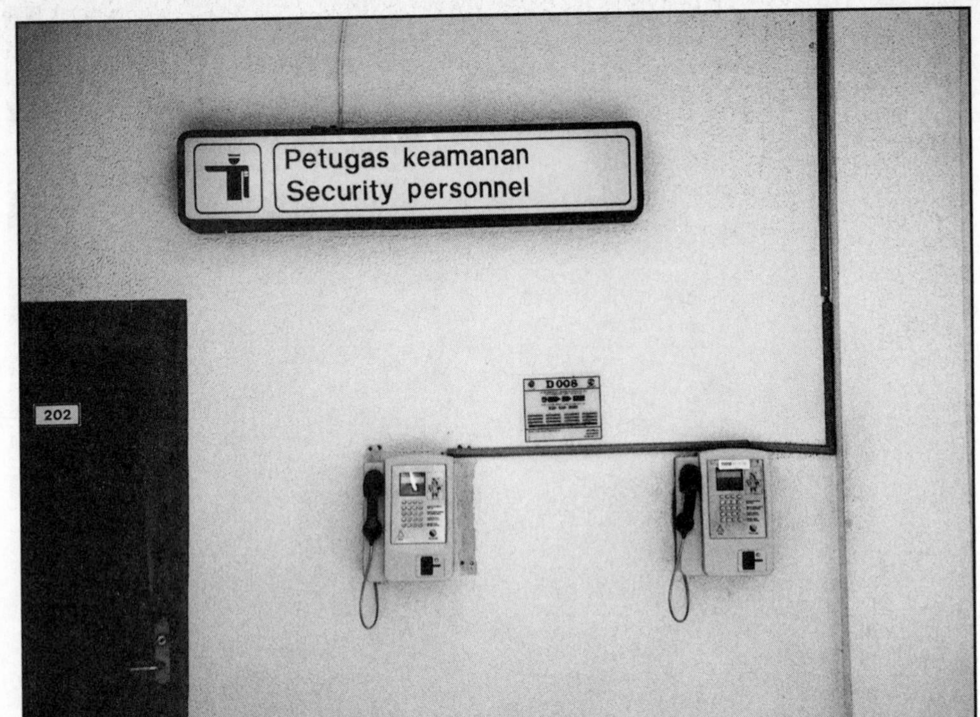

4. 

5.

6.

GO ON TO THE NEXT PAGE

7.

8.

9.

10.

PART 2

Directions: You will hear a question or statement and three responses spoken in English. They will not be printed in your test book and will be spoken only one time. Select the best response to the question or statement and mark the letter (A), (B), or (C) on your answer sheet.

Sample Answer

(A) 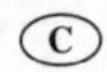 (C)

Example

You will hear: Where is the meeting room?

You will also hear: (A) To meet the new director.
(B) It's the first room on the right.
(C) Yes, at two o'clock.

Your best response to the question "Where is the meeting room?" is choice (B), "It's the first room on the right," so (B) is the correct answer. You should mark answer (B) on your answer sheet.

11. Mark your answer on your answer sheet.

12. Mark your answer on your answer sheet.

13. Mark your answer on your answer sheet.

14. Mark your answer on your answer sheet.

15. Mark your answer on your answer sheet.

16. Mark your answer on your answer sheet.

17. Mark your answer on your answer sheet.

18. Mark your answer on your answer sheet.

19. Mark your answer on your answer sheet.

20. Mark your answer on your answer sheet.

21. Mark your answer on your answer sheet.

22. Mark your answer on your answer sheet.

23. Mark your answer on your answer sheet.

24. Mark your answer on your answer sheet.

25. Mark your answer on your answer sheet.

26. Mark your answer on your answer sheet.

27. Mark your answer on your answer sheet.

28. Mark your answer on your answer sheet.

29. Mark your answer on your answer sheet.

30. Mark your answer on your answer sheet.

31. Mark your answer on your answer sheet.

32. Mark your answer on your answer sheet.

33. Mark your answer on your answer sheet.

34. Mark your answer on your answer sheet.

35. Mark your answer on your answer sheet.

36. Mark your answer on your answer sheet.

37. Mark your answer on your answer sheet.

38. Mark your answer on your answer sheet.

39. Mark your answer on your answer sheet.

40. Mark your answer on your answer sheet.

PART 3

Directions: You will hear some conversations between two people. You will be asked to answer three questions about what the speakers say in each conversation. Select the best response to each question and mark the letter (A), (B), (C), or (D) on your answer sheet. The conversations will not be printed in your test book and will be spoken only one time.

41. Who sent the package?
(A) Mr. Ozawa.
(B) Ms. Jones.
(C) Mr. Ozawa's boss.
(D) Mr. Ozawa's secretary.

42. When is the meeting with Ms. Jones?
(A) Right now.
(B) This morning.
(C) Tonight.
(D) Tomorrow.

43. Where is Mr. Ozawa now?
(A) At lunch.
(B) At his desk.
(C) In a meeting.
(D) In the mailroom.

---

44. Where are the speakers?
(A) At home.
(B) At a bank.
(C) At the office.
(D) At a restaurant.

45. What will the woman do?
(A) Buy a card.
(B) Pay the bill.
(C) Play a game.
(D) Cook a meal.

46. What will the man give the woman?
(A) Some money.
(B) Some letters.
(C) A wallet.
(D) A meal.

---

47. How many people will eat dinner?
(A) Two.
(B) Three.
(C) Eight.
(D) Nine.

48. What time will they eat dinner?
(A) 8:30.
(B) 8:45.
(C) 9:00.
(D) 10:00.

49. What will they do before dinner?
(A) Visit the kitchen.
(B) Look for a table.
(C) Sit in the bar.
(D) Fix the car.

---

50. What are the speakers discussing?
(A) Washing the windows.
(B) Buying new chairs.
(C) Painting the room.
(D) Cleaning the rug.

51. What color is the rug?
(A) Green.
(B) White.
(C) Yellow.
(D) Blue.

52. When will they start work on the project?
(A) Tonight.
(B) Tomorrow.
(C) On Friday.
(D) Next week.

GO ON TO THE NEXT PAGE

53. Why did Jim miss the meeting?
(A) He was feeling sick.
(B) He had to type a memo.
(C) He left his watch at home.
(D) The copy machine didn't work.

54. What time was the meeting?
(A) 3:00.
(B) 4:00.
(C) 6:00.
(D) 8:00.

55. Why does the man have to hurry?
(A) The meeting starts soon.
(B) He has to mail a letter.
(C) It's starting to rain.
(D) He has to catch a train.

---

56. Where will the speakers go to work?
(A) The conference room.
(B) The business office.
(C) The elevator.
(D) Their desks.

57. What will they take with them?
(A) Pens.
(B) Notepads.
(C) A computer.
(D) Computer paper.

58. What kind of work are they doing?
(A) Ordering office supplies.
(B) Planning a conference.
(C) Fixing a computer.
(D) Writing a report.

---

59. Who will be in the office tomorrow?
(A) Sam.
(B) Sam's boss.
(C) Sam's friend.
(D) Sam's assistant.

60. What does the woman want help with?
(A) Cooking lunch.
(B) Finding a book.
(C) Going over accounts.
(D) Planning a conference.

61. When will the woman go to the office?
(A) After work.
(B) After lunch.
(C) Before lunch.
(D) At dinnertime.

---

62. What does the man want to buy?
(A) A fax machine.
(B) A newspaper.
(C) A telephone.
(D) A briefcase.

63. How much is the sale?
(A) 10 percent off.
(B) 15 percent off.
(C) 20 percent off.
(D) 50 percent off.

64. When does the sale end?
(A) Today.
(B) Tomorrow.
(C) On Saturday.
(D) Next week.

---

65. What is broken?
(A) The air conditioner.
(B) The photocopier.
(C) The telephone.
(D) The light.

66. When will the repair person arrive?
(A) At noon.
(B) Next week.
(C) Right away.
(D) This afternoon.

67. What will the man do while he is waiting?
(A) Eat a meal.
(B) Read e-mail.
(C) Write a report.
(D) Make a phone call.

---

68. Why can't the man meet with the woman this week?
(A) He has to meet with another person.
(B) He needs to rest this week.
(C) He'll be away on a trip.
(D) His office won't be open.

69. What does the woman want to discuss?
(A) Conference plans.
(B) A letter.
(C) Money.
(D) A class.

70. What time will the woman be at the man's office?
(A) 9:00.
(B) 10:00.
(C) 11:00.
(D) 1:00.

GO ON TO THE NEXT PAGE

PART 4

Directions: You will hear some talks given by a single speaker. You will be asked to answer three questions about what the speaker says in each talk. Select the best response to each question and mark the letter (A), (B), (C), or (D) on your answer sheet. The talks will not be printed in your test book and will be spoken only one time.

71. What time will the train leave?
(A) 10:10.
(B) 10:15.
(C) 10:30.
(D) 10:40.

72. Who should arrive at the gate early?
(A) Passengers who can offer help.
(B) Passengers with luggage.
(C) Passengers who have questions.
(D) Passengers who have children.

73. What form of payment is accepted for tickets on the train?
(A) Cash.
(B) Check.
(C) Credit card.
(D) Money order.

---

74. Who is talking?
(A) A news reporter.
(B) A weather forecaster.
(C) A pilot.
(D) A travel agent.

75. When is the speaker talking?
(A) In the early morning.
(B) At noon.
(C) In the evening.
(D) Late at night.

76. How will the weather be tomorrow?
(A) Rainy.
(B) Cloudy.
(C) Sunny.
(D) Cold.

---

77. Where would you hear this announcement?
(A) At a grocery store.
(B) At a department store.
(C) At a restaurant.
(D) At a library.

78. What is on sale?
(A) Beef.
(B) Vegetables.
(C) Fruit.
(D) Suits.

79. Who can use the express check-out lanes?
(A) People buying ground beef.
(B) People buying sale items.
(C) People buying vegetables.
(D) People buying only 15 items.

---

80. Who is talking?
(A) A student.
(B) A professor.
(C) An author.
(D) A medical doctor.

81. What is the subject of the class?
(A) Math.
(B) Computers.
(C) Finance.
(D) Health.

82. How many tests will there be?
(A) One.
(B) Two.
(C) Seven.
(D) Ten.

---

83. Who was Bob Wilson?
(A) A mayor.
(B) A bus driver.
(C) A war hero.
(D) An artist.

84. How long will they stay at the Wilson House?
(A) Half an hour.
(B) One hour.
(C) One hour and ten minutes.
(D) Two hours.

85. Where will they go after visiting the Wilson House?
(A) To a restaurant.
(B) To a bus station.
(C) To a monument.
(D) To a museum.

---

86. What are the tickets for?
(A) A city bus tour.
(B) A theater.
(C) A sports event.
(D) An awards ceremony.

87. Where can you get tickets?
(A) At the stadium.
(B) At the front desk.
(C) At the bus station.
(D) At the ticket counter.

88. What time will the bus leave?
(A) 3:00 in the morning.
(B) 6:00 in the morning.
(C) 3:00 in the afternoon.
(D) 6:00 in the evening.

---

89. What is Ms. Park's book about?
(A) Public speaking.
(B) Sports.
(C) Making money.
(D) Retail business.

90. What will Ms. Park do?
(A) Introduce someone.
(B) Receive an award.
(C) Read from her book.
(D) Make copies of the book.

91. What can you do at the back of the auditorium?
(A) Buy a book.
(B) Read some signs.
(C) Play a game.
(D) Answer questions.

---

92. Who is Pamela Jones?
(A) A telephone operator.
(B) A scientist.
(C) An assistant.
(D) A newspaper reporter.

93. Why can't she answer the telephone right now?
(A) She's at a conference.
(B) She's talking to someone else.
(C) She's reading the newspaper.
(D) She's working on a story.

94. What should you do if you want to leave a message?
(A) Talk to Ms. Jones's assistant.
(B) Call the main switchboard.
(C) Stay on the line.
(D) Send a message by e-mail.

95. Which flight will arrive on time?
(A) The flight from Hong Kong.
(B) The flight from Sydney.
(C) The flight from London.
(D) The flight from Paris.

96. Why was a flight canceled?
(A) Because of rain in London.
(B) Because of a blizzard in Paris.
(C) Because no tickets were sold.
(D) Because the schedule changed.

97. When does the special sale end?
(A) This evening.
(B) On the weekend.
(C) Next week.
(D) Next month.

98. How many shows will the theater have today?
(A) One.
(B) Two.
(C) Three.
(D) Five.

99. What is half price?
(A) The midnight show.
(B) Tickets for people younger than 18.
(C) Shows before five o'clock.
(D) Snacks sold in the lobby.

100. What is not allowed inside the theater?
(A) Popcorn.
(B) Drinks.
(C) Any snack.
(D) Outside food.

This is the end of the Listening test. Turn to Part 5 in your test book.

READING TEST

In the Reading test, you will read a variety of texts and answer several different types of reading comprehension questions. The entire Reading test will last 75 minutes. There are three parts, and directions are given for each part. You are encouraged to answer as many questions as possible within the time allowed.

You must mark your answers on the separate answer sheet. Do not write your answers in the test book.

PART 5

Directions: A word or phrase is missing in each of the sentences below. Four answer choices are given below each sentence. Select the best answer to complete the sentence. Then mark the letter (A), (B), (C), or (D) on your answer sheet.

101. Customer ______ is one of the top priorities of this company.
(A) satisfied
(B) satisfying
(C) satisfy
(D) satisfaction

102. Remember that feeling confident and ______ is an important part of giving a presentation.
(A) relaxing
(B) relaxes
(C) relaxed
(D) relax

103. Final arrangements for the board of directors' meeting haven't ______ been made.
(A) already
(B) still
(C) while
(D) yet

104. We have ______ all project managers to turn in their reports by the end of the week.
(A) asking
(B) asked
(C) ask
(D) asks

105. Nobody will be ______ to the room after the meeting has started.
(A) admitted
(B) omitted
(C) permitted
(D) submitted

106. Customer ______ representatives are available to answer your questions twenty-four hours a day.
(A) servants
(B) serving
(C) serve
(D) service

107. While some people enjoy receiving calls from telemarketers, other people find such calls ______.
(A) annoys
(B) annoying
(C) annoyingly
(D) annoyed

108. If you are interested ______ receiving free samples of our product, simply fill out the enclosed card.
(A) to
(B) in
(C) of
(D) about

109. Because of the mild climate and rich soil, a wide variety of crops can be ______ in this region.
(A) grown up
(B) increased
(C) raised
(D) enlarged

GO ON TO THE NEXT PAGE

110. ______ she has worked very hard during the past year, Ms. Gomez has still failed to get a promotion.
(A) Although
(B) Because
(C) So
(D) In spite of

111. The new advertising campaign resulted in a ______ large increase in sales.
(A) surprised
(B) surprisingly
(C) surprise
(D) surprises

112. A fine will be charged for all materials that are returned to the library ______ the due date.
(A) past
(B) over
(C) later
(D) above

113. We felt that the recent reports were not particularly ______.
(A) informs
(B) information
(C) informative
(D) inform

114. The slow ______ on this project has been a cause for concern.
(A) progress
(B) progressed
(C) progressive
(D) progresses

115. After you have had a chance to look over the enclosed documents, please return ______ to the front office.
(A) they
(B) them
(C) their
(D) theirs

116. Due to the ______ weather conditions, all flights have been postponed until further notice.
(A) current
(B) abundant
(C) actual
(D) eventual

117. We need all the help we can get and would like everyone in the office to ______ us in getting this job completed on time.
(A) resist
(B) desist
(C) insist
(D) assist

118. The new computer does not seem to work ______ the old one did.
(A) as well
(B) as well than
(C) as good as
(D) as well as

119. ______ have market conditions been as favorable as they are now.
(A) Reliably
(B) Fortunately
(C) Never
(D) Usually

120. Most ______ the people who responded to the survey were pleased with the new product.
(A) of
(B) for
(C) to
(D) from

121. Fill out this form ______ before turning it in to your supervisor.
(A) completed
(B) complete
(C) completion
(D) completely

122. All new staff members should become ______ with the standard office procedures.
(A) family
(B) familiar
(C) familiarly
(D) familiarize

123. The recent changes in the economy have led to greater ______ in our company's products.
(A) interest
(B) interesting
(C) interested
(D) interestingly

124. Weather conditions _______ the region have had a negative impact on agricultural production.
(A) whole
(B) during
(C) throughout
(D) entire

125. While we understand the desire to save money, we usually advise _______ choosing an insurance plan merely because it has the lowest price.
(A) for
(B) from
(C) against
(D) over

126. Please call the travel agent this afternoon to _______ your travel plans.
(A) confirmation
(B) confirm
(C) confirmed
(D) confirming

127. The manager has asked that all vacation requests be handed in to _______ office by 9:00 on Monday morning.
(A) she's
(B) her
(C) she
(D) hers

128. _______ for improvements in current economic conditions have been met with nothing but disappointment.
(A) Expectations
(B) Experiences
(C) Experiments
(D) Expressions

129. Any personal items left in the lockers will be _______ at the end of the month.
(A) reminded
(B) remarked
(C) remodeled
(D) removed

130. The director would like to express his appreciation for the _______ efforts made by all members of the staff during this time of crisis.
(A) admirable
(B) admired
(C) admirably
(D) admiral

131. The person to _______ you submitted your request is no longer in charge of this section.
(A) whom
(B) which
(C) who
(D) where

132. We would be very interested in hearing your _______ of the current political crisis.
(A) reaction
(B) mind
(C) reason
(D) opinion

133. While negative criticism is rarely appreciated, _______ advice is always welcome.
(A) constructive
(B) construction
(C) construct
(D) constructing

134. We hope that you will _______ all of the evidence before making your final decision in this matter.
(A) confuse
(B) convince
(C) consider
(D) concur

135. Mr. Chang will serve as _______ director until a permanent director can be found.
(A) act
(B) acting
(C) actor
(D) acted

GO ON TO THE NEXT PAGE

136. It is important to respond to customer complaints with as pleasant an _______ as possible.

(A) assertion
(B) attitude
(C) assignment
(D) attendant

137. While it is _______ to know the final results this soon, we have received some preliminary information.

(A) impossible
(B) impatient
(C) improper
(D) impolite

138. Our team worked _______ hard on that project that we finished it two days before the deadline.

(A) too
(B) so
(C) such
(D) a lot

139. _______ can be the cause of many work delays.

(A) Careless
(B) Cared
(C) Carelessness
(D) Carelessly

140. _______ the growing demand for our product, we are making plans to increase production.

(A) Although
(B) In spite of
(C) Because of
(D) Consequently

PART 6

Directions: Read the texts that follow. A word or phrase is missing in some of the sentences. Four answer choices are given below each of the sentences. Select the best answer to complete the text. Then mark the letter (A), (B), (C), or (D) on your answer sheet.

Questions 141–143 refer to the following announcement.

The National Museum of Art

is proud to announce the upcoming ____________ *of European Expressionist*

141. (A) exhibit
(B) lecture
(C) auction
(D) purchase

paintings and prints, from January 15 through March 15.

We are very fortunate to be able to bring this opportunity to area residents and visitors. This show includes works on loan from museums and collectors all around the world. It is the first time this area has seen such a wide representation of Expressionist works together in one place.

____________ *for the show are available by calling the museum's Special Events*

142. (A) Guides
(B) Tickets
(C) Brochures
(D) Schedules

office at 342-555-0980, or by visiting our website: www.artmuseum.org. Prices are $25 general admission and $20 for senior citizens and students with a valid ID. Children under 12 will be charged half price. Entrance prices also include admission to the museum's permanent collection. A recorded tour and headphones will be available at the exhibit for $6.

During the show, the Museum Gift Store ____________ *on sale catalogues,*

143. (A) has had
(B) had
(C) has
(D) will have

art reproductions, calendars, coffee mugs, and other souvenirs of the show.

GO ON TO THE NEXT PAGE

Questions 144–146 refer to the following letter.

April 17

To whom it may concern:

This letter is _______________ for Mr. Young Kim, who has worked for this company as an administrative

144. (A) a background
(B) an instruction
(C) a reference
(D) an acceptance

assistant for the past three years.

During most of his time here, Mr. Kim has worked directly under _______________ supervision. He has

145. (A) your
(B) his
(C) her
(D) my

served as an assistant to a busy accounting office with a staff of five. He has always shown himself to be reliable and hardworking. He has never shirked his duties, even when the office workload has required him to work late into the evening or on a weekend. I always feel sure that whatever task I may give him, it will be done promptly and with a smile. Mr. Kim's friendliness and upbeat attitude have been a real contribution to the office environment.

We will miss Mr. Kim, but we understand that he is ready to move on to a _______________ that will make

146. (A) position
(B) degree
(C) residence
(D) professor

better use of his skills and provide him with more opportunities for his future. I can recommend him without reservation and know he will make a great contribution to any work environment.

Sincerely,

Ivan Sokolow
Ivan Sokolow

Questions 147–149 refer to the following memo.

To: All personnel
From: Marina Petrowski, Director
Re: Travel expenses

We are all aware that the procedures for charging and reporting expenses for business trips taken on behalf of the company have long been out of hand. As a result of recommendations from the Budget Office, the following procedures will be adopted.

Company personnel will no longer be given company credit cards to cover expenses while on out of town trips. Instead, all travel expenses, with the _____________ of

147. (A) excepts
(B) excepted
(C) exception
(D) excepting

airline tickets which will continue to be charged directly to the company, will be paid for out of pocket. In order to receive _____________, an expense report must be

148. (A) bonuses
(B) assistance
(C) supervisors
(D) reimbursement

submitted to your department head within ten days of returning from a trip. All charges must be itemized on the report and accompanied by receipts. Approval of each item will be made at the discretion of each department head, following, of course, the company expense guidelines (see attached). Generally, charges for hotels, meals, and transportation will be _____________. Non-work related items such as

149. (A) reported
(B) expensive
(C) authorized
(D) unallowable

entertainment, excessive taxi rides, and bar bills will not. I am sure you will all understand the necessity of this strict attitude toward expense reporting. I am counting on everyone's cooperation.

GO ON TO THE NEXT PAGE

Questions 150–152 refer to the following e-mail.

To: Charmaine Hochul
From: customerservice@execgifts.com
Subject: Re: recent order
Date: June 1

Dear Ms. Hochul,

Thank you for your e-mail about your lost order. Although we say that orders generally arrive within 15 days of ______________, sometimes unexpected delays occur. A package

150. (A) payment
(B) shipment
(C) replacement
(D) announcement

may ______________ longer to arrive. We do not consider an order lost until 30 days have

151. (A) will take
(B) taking
(C) to take
(D) take

passed from the date it was sent. If your order has not arrived by June 15, please contact us then and we will resend your order. Or, we can reimburse your money, if you prefer that ______________. Please let us know if we can be of any further assistance. Thank you for

152. (A) option
(B) opt
(C) opting
(D) optimal

your business.

Sincerely,

Sanford Jones

Customer Service
Executive Gifts

PART 7

Directions: In this part you will read a selection of texts, such as magazine and newspaper articles, letters, and advertisements. Each text is followed by several questions. Select the best answer for each question and mark the letter (A), (B), (C), or (D) on your answer sheet.

Questions 153–154 refer to the following advertisement.

JOB FAIR

A job fair will be held at the Downtown Convention Center on Saturday, April 15, from 9:00 A.M. to 5:00 P.M.

If you are interested in a career in:

- Computer Programming
- Hotel Management
- Marketing
- Business Administration
- Journalism

. . . then this is your opportunity to meet people who are currently working in these and other fields and who have job openings for you. The job fair will be held in Conference Room 1 and doors open at 9:00 A.M. Bring ten copies of your résumé and a list of references.

The Downtown Convention Center is located at 125 South State Street, across from the Seward Hotel. It can be reached by the Main Street and Cross City bus lines. The job fair is sponsored by the City Chamber of Commerce.

153. What can you do at the job fair?
(A) Learn how to write a résumé
(B) Meet potential employers
(C) Attend a conference
(D) Buy things on sale

154. Where will the job fair be held?
(A) In the convention center
(B) On Main Street
(C) On South State Street
(D) At the Chamber of Commerce

GO ON TO THE NEXT PAGE

Questions 155–157 refer to the following instructions.

Capital Motel

Telephone Instructions

This telephone has been provided for your convenience.

- To reach the front desk, dial 1.
- To reach room service, dial 2.
- To reach maid service, dial 3.
- To make a local call, dial 9 and then the number.
- To make a long distance call, dial 1 to ask for assistance.

Local Numbers of Interest

Movie Hotline 567-555-2113
Tourist Information...... 567-555-3456
Airport Shuttle 567-555-5525
City Public Transportation 567-555-1014

155. What should you do to call someone in another city?
(A) Call Tourist Information
(B) Call room service
(C) Call City Public Transportation
(D) Call the front desk

156. If you dial 9-567-555-1014, what information can you find out?
(A) Which bus to take downtown
(B) Which movies are showing tonight
(C) Where to eat dinner
(D) How to make a local call

157. How can you ask someone to clean your room?
(A) Make a long distance call
(B) Dial 3
(C) Call room service
(D) Ask for Tourist Information

Questions 158–160 refer to the following letter.

New World Computers, Inc.

Sept. 12, 20__

Mary Matta
27 High Road
Ipswich, MA 01801

Dear Ms. Matta:

According to our records, you recently contacted the New World Computers Technical Support Service and spoke with our representative, Joan Kim. We hope your experience was pleasant and effective. We would appreciate your giving us feedback on your experience with Technical Support by taking a few minutes to fill out the enclosed Customer Survey form. By letting us know about the quality of the support you received, you will help us ensure that we continue to provide you and all our customers with the excellent service that you deserve.

Please return the form in the enclosed envelope, or you can complete it online by going to our website at www.nwc.com/customersurvey. If you have any questions, please contact the Customer Support Office at 800-555-8978. Thank you for being a New World Computers' customer.

Sincerely,

Samuel Lee

Samuel Lee, Support Service Manager

158. What is the purpose of this letter?
- (A) To ask for the customer's opinion
- (B) To offer technical support
- (C) To sell a new computer
- (D) To advertise a website

159. How can the customer complete the form?
- (A) By calling the Customer Support Office
- (B) By going online
- (C) By contacting Ms. Kim
- (D) By writing to Mr. Lee

160. Who did the customer speak with?
- (A) The Support Service Manager
- (B) A Technical Support representative
- (C) Someone in the Customer Support Office
- (D) A New World Computers customer

Questions 161–162 refer to the following notice.

Office Center Towers

This is to inform all tenants that tomorrow morning, October 10, service work will be performed on the building fire alarm system between the hours of 8:30 and 10:00. As part of this procedure, it will be necessary to test the alarm and you may hear it go off three or four times in the course of the morning. Do not be concerned when you hear the alarm go off. It is part of the normal service routine. If you have any questions, please contact the building superintendent's office. Thank you for your patience.

161. What is the purpose of this notice?
- (A) To let tenants know that the fire alarm system will be repaired
- (B) To tell tenants about a fire that occurred in the building
- (C) To warn tenants about the danger of fires
- (D) To inform tenants about what to do in case of fire

162. What should tenants do if they hear the fire alarm during 8:30 and 10:00?
- (A) Leave the building immediately
- (B) Contact the building superintendent
- (C) Continue with their usual activities
- (D) Wait patiently for the fire department to arrive

Questions 163–165 refer to the following notice.

Are you getting ready to put your house on the market? Are you thinking of selling it yourself? Don't do it on your own!

Research has shown that on the average real estate agents get a 30% higher sales price on single-family homes than owners who try to do the selling themselves.

Come learn the ins and outs of the real estate market and how to get the best possible price for your house. On Friday, January 20, at 7:30 P.M., Ms. Miranda Ortiz, a real estate agent with over twenty years' experience in the field, will talk about the current competitive real estate market and strategies for pricing and selling your single-family home or apartment. A question and answer session will follow the talk and refreshments will be served. Admission to this event is free, but because of the high level of interest, reservations are required.

Please call Mr. Jones at 676-555-0944 to reserve your space.

163. Who is this notice aimed at?
- (A) Real estate agents
- (B) Home owners
- (C) Researchers
- (D) Marketing experts

164. What kind of event does it advertise?
- (A) An estate sale
- (B) A party
- (C) A lecture
- (D) A competition

165. What should you do if you want to attend the event?
- (A) Put your house on the market
- (B) Send in some money
- (C) Call Ms. Ortiz
- (D) Make a reservation

Questions 166–169 refer to the following instructions.

Thank you for buying a product from the Office Ware mail-order catalog. We hope you are satisfied with your purchase of our quality merchandise. Please examine the contents of this package immediately to make sure that your order has arrived complete and in undamaged condition. In the event that you are not totally satisfied with your purchase for any reason, you can return it to us within thirty days for a full refund, no questions asked. Just repack it in the same box you received it in, and apply the enclosed return shipping label to the outside of the box. Return postage will be paid by the customer. If you wish to return a product after thirty days from the purchase date, please call the customer service office at 800-555-1002 and ask to speak with a purchase order representative.

166. Where would you find these instructions?
(A) In a catalog
(B) Enclosed in a package
(C) Hanging up in a post office
(D) At a store

167. The word "condition" in line 6 is closest in meaning to
(A) fitness
(B) appearance
(C) state
(D) shipment

168. What should you do to return a product the day after receiving it?
(A) Repack it and mail it back
(B) Wait for thirty days
(C) Call the customer service office
(D) Order a new catalog

169. What will happen if you return a product before thirty days have passed?
(A) The company will ask you some questions.
(B) A customer service representative will call you.
(C) You will get all your money back.
(D) You will have to send in a new purchase order.

Questions 170–173 refer to the following letter.

> **World Travel Tours**
> 32 Palm Tree Boulevard
> Playa del Coco, Florida, 39539
>
> Mr. and Mrs. Ivan Thomas
> 78 Putnam Street
> River City, New York, 10131
>
> Dear Mr. and Mrs. Thomas,
>
> Thank you for joining the World Travel tour to Emerald Island. We look forward to seeing you at the Ocean Breezes Hotel on April 2nd. At your request we have reserved for you an ocean view room with twin beds. Please notify hotel staff in advance of your arrival if you wish to make any changes in this room arrangement.
>
> When you check in at the hotel, mention that you are a participant in the World Travel tour, and the staff will inform the tour leader of your arrival. Tour participants will gather in the Ocean Breezes restaurant at 6:30 for dinner and a chance to meet each other. A complete itinerary for the tour will be distributed at that time. The tour leader will explain the tour activities and you will have the opportunity to ask questions.
>
> Your hotel room and three meals a day at the hotel restaurant are included in the price of the tour. The cost of transportation between the airport and the hotel will be paid by the individual participants. I have enclosed some informational brochures that may be of interest to you. Please don't hesitate to contact me if you have any questions.
>
> Sincerely,
>
> *George Harris*
> George Harris
> Assistant Director of Tours
>
> encl. Emerald Island Airport Shuttle Schedule
> *Your Guide to Emerald Island*

170. When should Mr. and Mrs. Thomas tell the hotel if they want to change their room reservation?
- (A) As soon as they arrive at the hotel
- (B) When the tour leader arrives at the hotel
- (C) Before they arrive at the hotel
- (D) After all the tour participants have arrived at the hotel

171. When will Mr. and Mrs. Thomas find out the complete tour schedule?
- (A) It is enclosed with the letter.
- (B) During dinner at the hotel restaurant.
- (C) When they check in at the hotel.
- (D) They already know it.

172. The word "distributed" in paragraph 2, line 4, is closest in meaning to
- (A) disturbed
- (B) revised
- (C) itemized
- (D) sent around

173. Who wrote the letter?
- (A) A tour participant
- (B) A travel agency employee
- (C) A hotel employee
- (D) The tour leader

Questions 174–175 refer to the following memo.

To: All personnel
From: Joseph Oh
Re: Training seminar
Date: July 15

This is a reminder that a training seminar in the use of the new software package we have adopted will take place next Monday, Tuesday, and Wednesday from 9:30 to 3:00. All seminar participants should be seated in Conference Room B by 9:30. Participation in this training seminar is mandatory for all staff of the Finance Office. Any other staff members who wish to participate should contact Mr. Oh in the Human Resources Office before Friday.

We are pleased to have Patricia Rossi of Intelligent Software Design, Inc., as our trainer. Ms. Rossi brings to this seminar years of experience as a computer consultant, and her previous seminars at our company have been well-received.

174. Who must attend the seminar?
(A) All personnel
(B) Everybody in the Finance Office
(C) Anybody who wants to
(D) People contacted by Mr. Oh

175. Where will the seminar take place?
(A) At the Intelligent Software Design Company
(B) In the Human Resources Office
(C) In Conference Room B
(D) In the Finance Office

GO ON TO THE NEXT PAGE

Questions 176–177 refer to the following notice.

NOTICE!!!

We regret that due to problems with the heating system in the auditorium, tonight's talk by Edward James entitled "My Thirty Years as a Career Diplomat" has been canceled. We are sorry for any inconvenience this may cause.

The auditorium should reopen by Friday and our weekly lecture series will resume next Monday at 8:00 P.M. with what promises to be an exciting talk by Sharon Rockford about her canoe trip down the Amazon River.

Don't miss it!

176. Why won't Mr. James speak tonight?
- (A) He's busy working.
- (B) It's inconvenient for him.
- (C) The auditorium is closed for repairs.
- (D) The weather is too hot.

177. What will happen next Monday?
- (A) The auditorium will close at 8:00 P.M.
- (B) There will be a new talk.
- (C) Mr. James will return to the auditorium.
- (D) There will be a class about writing résumés.

Questions 178–180 refer to the following guide.

Travelers' Guide to Greenville International Airport

Airport Services

- Business Centers can be found in Terminals 1, 4, and 7. Postage and mailboxes, photocopy machines, Internet access, conference rooms, pay phones, and a hotel hotline are available in all centers.
- A variety of food stands can be found in every terminal but Terminal 5. In addition, you can enjoy fine dining at the Runway View Restaurant in Terminal 3. The Worldwide Cafe in Terminal 6 serves sandwiches, desserts, and coffee, and provides Internet connection for your laptop computer.
- The Travelers Help Center, located in Terminal 2, can provide you with city maps and public transportation information. Taxi stands and bus stops are located in the front of each terminal.

178. Where can you go to send e-mail?
(A) Terminal 2
(B) Terminal 3
(C) Terminal 5
(D) Terminal 6

179. What is one thing you cannot do at a Business Center?
(A) Buy stamps
(B) Send a fax
(C) Make hotel reservations
(D) Have a meeting

180. What is available in all the terminals?
(A) Business Centers
(B) Food
(C) Transportation
(D) Maps

Questions 181–185 refer to the following advertisement and letter.

Office Assistant
Busy architectural firm seeks independent hard worker to be our office assistant. Responsible for answering phones, making appointments and schedules, maintaining database, typing letters and documents, and other tasks as needed. High school diploma required, some college desirable. Must have knowledge of word processing and database software. Send résumé to Mr. J. Woo, Architect, Modern Designs, Inc., 51 River Street, Middletown, California 94945

Mr. J. Woo
Modern Designs, Inc.
51 River Street
Middletown, California 94945

Dear Mr. Woo:
I saw your ad in last Sunday's *City Times* looking for an office assistant. I am well-qualified for the position you offer. I am very organized and hardworking. I have the computer skills and educational level you require. I am particularly interested in this position since in the future I would like to enter your profession. In fact, I am taking a night class at the university now, and hope to enter as a full-time student after I gain a few years of work experience. I am enclosing my résumé, and you may call my high school if you would like to see a copy of my high school record. I hope to hear from you soon.

Sincerely,
Lu Wang
Lu Wang

181. According to the ad, what will the new office assistant have to do?
(A) Photocopy documents
(B) Make phone calls
(C) Maintain computers
(D) Make appointments

182. What kind of computer program does Lu Wang know how to use?
(A) E-mail
(B) Web browser
(C) Word processing
(D) Architectural software

183. What kind of job does Lu Wang want in the future?
(A) Architect
(B) High school teacher
(C) University professor
(D) Computer programmer

184. What is Lu Wang doing now?
(A) Studying in high school
(B) Taking a university class
(C) Seeking a job as an architect
(D) Working as an office assistant

185. What has Lu Wang enclosed with her letter?
(A) Her résumé
(B) Her schedule
(C) Her high school record
(D) Her university's catalog

GO ON TO THE NEXT PAGE

Questions 186–190 refer to the following invitation and e-mail.

You're invited!

What: Farewell party
Where: Conference Room 2
When: Thursday, 4:30 P.M.

As you all know, Martha Cunningham and her family are moving to another city. Let's show her how much we appreciate all the hard work she's done for us.

Please bring a refreshment to share. Call Ted Jones in the accounting office by Tuesday to let him know if you'll attend and what food you'll bring. Also, we're taking up a collection to buy a gift for Martha. If everyone contributes just $15, we'll have $300 to buy her something really special.

Thanks, Susan Billings

To: Susan Billings
From: Tom Williamson
Subject: Farewell Party

Hi Susan,
I'm sorry I couldn't attend the party yesterday, as I'd planned, but I had a family emergency. Everything is OK now. I heard that everyone had a great time at the party and that you were able to raise $75 more than you expected. Fantastic. I'm sure Martha loved her gift. I did get a chance to sign the card before I left the office. Did you get the cake I sent over? It was a chocolate one from the Paris Bakery, so I hope it arrived on time for everyone to enjoy.
See you at the meeting this afternoon.
Tom

186. Who was the party for?
(A) Tom
(B) Ted
(C) Susan
(D) Martha

187. When did Tom write the e-mail?
(A) Tuesday
(B) Wednesday
(C) Thursday
(D) Friday

188. Why couldn't Tom attend the party?
(A) He had an emergency.
(B) He had made other plans.
(C) He had to attend a meeting.
(D) He had to work on the accounts.

189. How much money was raised for the gift?
(A) $15
(B) $75
(C) $300
(D) $375

190. What did Tom send to the party?
(A) Money
(B) A card
(C) Food
(D) A gift

Questions 191–195 refer to the following notice and e-mail.

The Dental Office of
Dr. Lilia Molari, DDS
Notice to all patients

OUR POLICY

We are here to serve you. In order to do so, the following policies are in effect.

Cancellation Policy

When you make an appointment, we reserve that time for you. Cancellations must be made 24 hours in advance or a $40 cancellation fee will be charged.

Payment Policy

We expect payment in full upon receipt of services. Payment may be made by check, credit card, or money order only.

Office Hours: Mon.–Thurs. 9–5, Fri. 12–8
Emergency phone: 555-9754
when the office is closed.

During normal office hours,
call us at 555-4825.

To: Dental Office
From: Jim Wilson
Subject: my appointment

I'm sorry I can't make my appointment this morning. I have to attend an emergency meeting in the afternoon and will have to spend the morning preparing for it. I know this is less than 24 hours notice so I'll be charged the cancellation fee. I'll have my assistant write and send a check today.

I'd like to reschedule my appointment, but my days are really full for the next several weeks. You have evening hours don't you? Please give me the next available appointment you have after 5:30 in the evening. Let me know by e-mail or phone. My office phone: 555-8977, and cell phone: 555-6295.
Jim Wilson

191. What form of payment is NOT accepted by the dental office?
(A) Cash
(B) Check
(C) Credit Card
(D) Money Order

192. If a patient has an emergency on Saturday morning, what number should he call?
(A) 555-9754
(B) 555-4825
(C) 555-8977
(D) 555-6295

193. What will Jim Wilson do this afternoon?
(A) Go to the dentist
(B) Attend a meeting
(C) Call for an appointment
(D) Send a check to his assistant

194. How much will Jim Wilson pay for his appointment today?
(A) $24
(B) $40
(C) $240
(D) $400

195. What day of the week will Jim Wilson's next appointment be?
(A) Monday
(B) Tuesday
(C) Thursday
(D) Friday

GO ON TO THE NEXT PAGE

Questions 196–200 refer to the following two phone messages.

While you were out . . .

To: *Harry Pak*
Pamela Lopez of One World called.
Time: *11:15 A.M.*
About: *Your upcoming trip.*

She can't get you a flight on Tuesday morning. There is a flight late Tuesday afternoon and one on Wednesday morning. Which do you prefer? Also, she can get you a room at the Grand Hotel, as you requested, but she can get you a better deal at the Marionette Hotel or the Riverside Hotel. Which hotel do you prefer? What day do you want to return? Please let her know before 3:00 this afternoon.

While you were out . . .

To: *Pamela Lopez*
Harry Pak of Pak and Associates called.
Time: *12:30 P.M.*
About: *Flights and hotels.*

About the flight, he'll take the second option, but he'll stay with his first choice for his hotel. He plans to stay the weekend and would like a flight back on Monday evening, arriving no later than 8:30, if possible. Also, he has a vacation next month and would like to go to the beach. Can you look into travel arrangements for him?

196. What is Pamela Lopez's job?
(A) Secretary
(B) Hotel clerk
(C) Travel agent
(D) Airline ticket agent

197. What time did Pamela Lopez call Harry Pak?
(A) 3:00
(B) 8:30
(C) 11:15
(D) 12:30

198. When does Harry Pak want to start his trip?
(A) Monday evening
(B) Tuesday morning
(C) Tuesday afternoon
(D) Wednesday morning

199. Which hotel does Harry Pak want to stay at?
(A) The Grand Hotel
(B) The Marionette Hotel
(C) The Riverside Hotel
(D) The One World Hotel

200. When will Mr. Pak take a vacation at the beach?
(A) Next weekend
(B) Next week
(C) Next month
(D) Next year

Stop! This is the end of the test. If you finish before time is called, you may go back to Parts 5, 6, and 7 and check your work.

PRACTICE TEST THREE

Practice Test Three is similar to an actual TOEIC® test. You can take this test after you finish studying this book in order to measure your improvement.

Read all directions carefully. This will help you become familiar with the actual TOEIC test directions and item types.

Use the Practice Test Three Answer Sheet on page 347.

LISTENING TEST

In the Listening test, you will be asked to demonstrate how well you understand spoken English. The entire Listening test will last approximately 45 minutes. There are four parts, and directions are given for each part. You must mark your answers on the separate answer sheet. Do not write your answers in the test book.

PART 1

Directions: For each question in this part, you will hear four statements about a picture in your test book. When you hear the statements, you must select the one statement that best describes what you see in the picture. Then find the number of the question on your answer sheet and mark your answer.The statements will not be printed in your test book and will be spoken only one time.

Example *Sample Answer*

Statement (C), "They're standing near the table," is the best description of the picture, so you should select answer (C) and mark it on your answer sheet.

1. 

2. 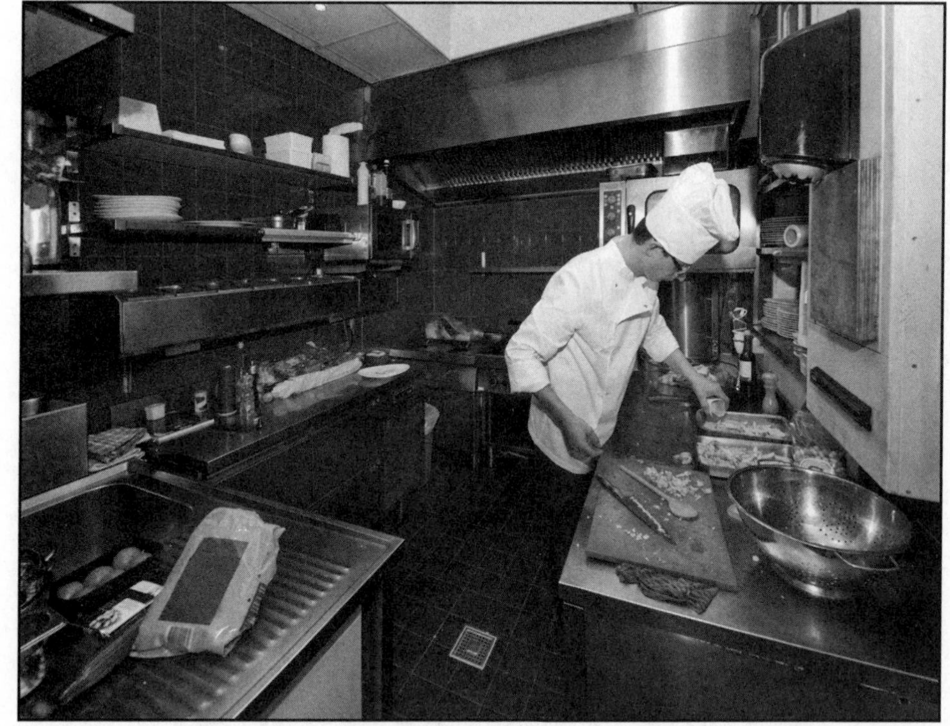

GO ON TO THE NEXT PAGE

3.

4.

5.

6.

GO ON TO THE NEXT PAGE

7. 

8. 

9. 

10. 

GO ON TO THE NEXT PAGE

PART 2

Directions: You will hear a question or statement and three responses spoken in English. They will not be printed in your test book and will be spoken only one time. Select the best response to the question or statement and mark the letter (A), (B), or (C) on your answer sheet.

Example

Sample Answer

You will hear: Where is the meeting room?

You will also hear: (A) To meet the new director.
(B) It's the first room on the right.
(C) Yes, at two o'clock.

Your best response to the question "Where is the meeting room?" is choice (B), "It's the first room on the right," so (B) is the correct answer. You should mark answer (B) on your answer sheet.

11. Mark your answer on your answer sheet.

12. Mark your answer on your answer sheet.

13. Mark your answer on your answer sheet.

14. Mark your answer on your answer sheet.

15. Mark your answer on your answer sheet.

16. Mark your answer on your answer sheet.

17. Mark your answer on your answer sheet.

18. Mark your answer on your answer sheet.

19. Mark your answer on your answer sheet.

20. Mark your answer on your answer sheet.

21. Mark your answer on your answer sheet.

22. Mark your answer on your answer sheet.

23. Mark your answer on your answer sheet.

24. Mark your answer on your answer sheet.

25. Mark your answer on your answer sheet.

26. Mark your answer on your answer sheet.

27. Mark your answer on your answer sheet.

28. Mark your answer on your answer sheet.

29. Mark your answer on your answer sheet.

30. Mark your answer on your answer sheet.

31. Mark your answer on your answer sheet.

32. Mark your answer on your answer sheet.

33. Mark your answer on your answer sheet.

34. Mark your answer on your answer sheet.

35. Mark your answer on your answer sheet.

36. Mark your answer on your answer sheet.

37. Mark your answer on your answer sheet.

38. Mark your answer on your answer sheet.

39. Mark your answer on your answer sheet.

40. Mark your answer on your answer sheet.

PART 3

 **Directions:** You will hear some conversations between two people. You will be asked to answer three questions about what the speakers say in each conversation. Select the best response to each question and mark the letter (A), (B), (C), or (D) on your answer sheet. The conversations will not be printed in your test book and will be spoken only one time.

41. What time will the speakers leave for the meeting?
(A) 8:00.
(B) 6:45.
(C) 7:30.
(D) 11:30.

42. How will they get to the meeting?
(A) Bus.
(B) Taxi.
(C) Subway.
(D) Private car.

43. Where will the meeting be held?
(A) Downtown.
(B) At the hotel.
(C) At the office.
(D) At the conference center.

---

44. Where does this conversation take place?
(A) A bank.
(B) An accountant's office.
(C) A driving school.
(D) An office supply store.

45. What does the woman ask the man to give her?
(A) An identification card.
(B) A check.
(C) A pen.
(D) Cash.

46. What does the woman ask the man to do?
(A) Check his license.
(B) Write his name.
(C) Read a sign.
(D) Pay cash.

47. Where will the man be next week?
(A) Downtown.
(B) At a ranch.
(C) At the branch office.
(D) At the accountant's office.

48. When will the speakers meet?
(A) Next week.
(B) The following Monday.
(C) The following Friday.
(D) Next month.

49. What will the man do now?
(A) Look at his calendar.
(B) Call his assistant.
(C) Write a check.
(D) Go to New York.

---

50. When will the budget report be ready?
(A) At 10:00.
(B) This afternoon.
(C) Tomorrow morning.
(D) On Friday.

51. Where does the man want the woman to leave the report?
(A) In his office.
(B) In his mailbox.
(C) In the post office.
(D) In the conference room.

52. What does the woman offer to do?
(A) Pass out the report at the meeting.
(B) Make copies of the report.
(C) Clean the man's desk.
(D) Work until 8:00.

GO ON TO THE NEXT PAGE

53. How many nights does the man want to stay at the hotel?
(A) 1.
(B) 2.
(C) 3.
(D) 4.

54. When will the man arrive at the hotel?
(A) Friday.
(B) Saturday.
(C) Sunday.
(D) Monday.

55. What does the woman ask the man for?
(A) His room number.
(B) His flight number.
(C) His reservation number.
(D) His credit card number.

---

56. How did the man plan to travel to Toronto?
(A) By bus.
(B) By car.
(C) By plane.
(D) By train.

57. What's the weather like?
(A) Rain.
(B) Snow.
(C) Hot.
(D) Clear.

58. When will the weather change?
(A) This morning.
(B) This afternoon.
(C) Tonight.
(D) Tomorrow.

---

59. What does the man want to do?
(A) Visit the park.
(B) Park his car.
(C) Buy groceries.
(D) Repair his car.

60. How far does he have to go?
(A) 1 block.
(B) 3 blocks.
(C) 1 mile.
(D) 3 miles.

61. How much will he have to pay?
(A) $0.
(B) $4.
(C) $8.
(D) $20.

---

62. How does the woman feel?
(A) Sad.
(B) Bored.
(C) Happy.
(D) Angry.

63. When will they celebrate the man's promotion?
(A) Now.
(B) Tonight.
(C) At 10:00.
(D) Next Monday.

64. What does the woman offer to do?
(A) Help the man with his work.
(B) Prepare dinner for the man.
(C) Pay for the man's lunch.
(D) Give the man her seat.

---

65. Why is the woman hosting the dinner?
(A) She's having a meeting.
(B) She's entertaining clients.
(C) She's having a birthday party.
(D) She's celebrating her retirement.

66. How many people will be at the dinner?
(A) 15.
(B) 16.
(C) 50.
(D) 60.

67. What food does the woman order?
(A) Rice.
(B) Fish.
(C) Steak.
(D) Chicken.

---

68. What does the woman want new shoes for?
(A) A trip.
(B) A party.
(C) A present.
(D) An interview.

69. What color shoes does the woman want?
(A) White.
(B) Gray.
(C) Blue.
(D) Black.

70. When does she need to wear them?
(A) Now.
(B) Sunday.
(C) Monday.
(D) Next month.

GO ON TO THE NEXT PAGE

PART 4

Directions: You will hear some talks given by a single speaker. You will be asked to answer three questions about what the speaker says in each talk. Select the best response to each question and mark the letter (A), (B), (C), or (D) on your answer sheet. The talks will not be printed in your test book and will be spoken only one time.

71. Where would this announcement be heard?
(A) On a bus.
(B) On a plane.
(C) On a train.
(D) On a ship.

72. When will they arrive at their destination?
(A) In 13 minutes.
(B) In 30 minutes.
(C) In one hour.
(D) In two hours.

73. What are passengers asked to do?
(A) Read a schedule.
(B) Order drinks.
(C) Eat a meal.
(D) Sit down.

---

74. What days is the dental office open?
(A) Tuesday and Friday only.
(B) Tuesday through Friday only.
(C) Tuesday through Saturday only
(D) Tuesday, Friday, and Saturday only.

75. What should a caller do in case of emergency?
(A) Call another number.
(B) Call during office hours.
(C) Press 1.
(D) Press 2.

76. How can a caller make an appointment?
(A) Speak with the dentist.
(B) Call back later.
(C) Leave a message.
(D) Ask for an assistant.

---

77. Who is this talk for?
(A) Office workers.
(B) Police officers.
(C) Health experts.
(D) Gym teachers.

78. How much exercise should adults get every day?
(A) 4 to 5 minutes.
(B) 45 minutes.
(C) One hour.
(D) Three hours.

79. What does the speaker recommend about exercise for adults?
(A) They should exercise at the gym.
(B) They should exercise once a day.
(C) They should exercise in the afternoon.
(D) They should exercise several times a day.

---

80. What kind of business is Branwell's?
(A) Café.
(B) Sports store.
(C) Clothing store.
(D) Travel agency.

81. What size discount is offered?
(A) 5%.
(B) 10%.
(C) 20%.
(D) 25%.

82. When does the sale begin?
(A) Saturday.
(B) Sunday.
(C) Monday.
(D) Tuesday.

---

83. What kind of service is advertised?
(A) Employment agency.
(B) Computer training.
(C) Office rental.
(D) Hotel.

84. What fee is charged for the service?
(A) $0.
(B) $13.
(C) $30.
(D) $35.

85. What are listeners asked to do?
(A) Write a letter.
(B) Call the office.
(C) Visit the office.
(D) Make an appointment.

---

86. What is the weather today?
(A) Cold.
(B) Wind.
(C) Rain.
(D) Snow.

87. What problem has the weather caused?
(A) School closings.
(B) Trains delayed.
(C) Loss of electricity.
(D) Damage to bridge.

88. When will the weather change?
(A) This afternoon.
(B) This evening.
(C) Tomorrow morning.
(D) Next week.

---

89. What time will the workshops begin?
(A) 2:00.
(B) 10:00.
(C) 10:15.
(D) 12:15.

90. Where will lunch be served?
(A) In the lobby.
(B) In the auditorium.
(C) On the ground floor.
(D) On the second floor.

91. What will happen after lunch?
(A) Coffee will be served.
(B) There will be a discussion.
(C) Workshops will be held.
(D) Registration will end.

---

92. Why is there no train service to New York?
(A) The tracks are flooded.
(B) The train is damaged.
(C) There aren't enough seats.
(D) There isn't any heating.

93. What are passengers asked to do?
(A) Speak with a ticket agent.
(B) Travel on another date.
(C) Buy another ticket.
(D) Take a bus.

94. When will the trains run again?
(A) It is not certain.
(B) Later in the evening.
(C) At 4:00.
(D) At 6:30.

GO ON TO THE NEXT PAGE

95. What will be constructed?
(A) A park.
(B) A bridge.
(C) Some monuments.
(D) A new City Hall.

96. When will construction begin?
(A) In the fall.
(B) In the winter.
(C) In September.
(D) In November.

97. What will the mayor do tomorrow?
(A) Meet with the budget committee.
(B) Give a press conference.
(C) Visit a museum.
(D) Give a speech.

98. When will Dr. Jones talk?
(A) After the meeting.
(B) During lunch.
(C) Next week.
(D) Next month.

99. What will Dr. Jones talk about?
(A) Office management.
(B) Public speaking.
(C) International relations.
(D) Making videos.

100. What are the listeners asked to do?
(A) Attend a lunch.
(B) Pay with a check.
(C) Mark their calendars.
(D) Got to a press conference.

This is the end of the Listening test. Turn to Part 5 in your test book.

READING TEST

In the Reading test, you will read a variety of texts and answer several different types of reading comprehension questions. The entire Reading test will last 75 minutes. There are three parts, and directions are given for each part. You are encouraged to answer as many questions as possible within the time allowed.

You must mark your answers on the separate answer sheet. Do not write your answers in the test book.

PART 5

Directions: A word or phrase is missing in each of the sentences below. Four answer choices are given below each sentence. Select the best answer to complete the sentence. Then mark the letter (A), (B), (C), or (D) on your answer sheet.

101. Each of these documents has to be _______ by both parties.

(A) sign
(B) signing
(C) signed
(D) signature

102. The person who spoke to you _______ the company's managing director.

(A) is
(B) are
(C) have
(D) were

103. Since _______ is mandatory, everyone will have to go to the meeting.

(A) attend
(B) attendance
(C) attention
(D) attentive

104. Some people are _______ to change and always want things to remain the same.

(A) persistent
(B) resistant
(C) consistent
(D) assistant

105. If I don't get a reply by tomorrow, I _______ to reach him directly by phone.

(A) will try
(B) have tried
(C) try
(D) am trying

106. All the computer supplies are _______ the lower shelf of the supply closet.

(A) to
(B) at
(C) in
(D) on

107. Nobody wants to take _______ for the difficulty we find ourselves in.

(A) respond
(B) responsible
(C) responsibly
(D) responsibility

108. If we hadn't submitted the budget on time, we _______ adequate funding for the project.

(A) didn't get
(B) won't get
(C) wouldn't get
(D) wouldn't have gotten

109. _______ it is late, we can't go home until the work is finished.

(A) Meanwhile
(B) Since
(C) Although
(D) Because

110. I keep envelopes and stamps _______ the top drawer of my desk.

(A) on
(B) in
(C) between
(D) through

GO ON TO THE NEXT PAGE

111. Mrs. Brown's health problems are causing her difficulty at work, and she may have to ______ from her job.
(A) resign
(B) assign
(C) design
(D) consign

112. We couldn't ______ on the best place to hold next year's conference.
(A) agree
(B) agreed
(C) agreeing
(D) agreeable

113. I am happy to recommend Mr. Jung for a promotion as he has done a very ______ job at his current position.
(A) satisfy
(B) satisfactory
(C) satisfaction
(D) satisfactorily

114. You must ______ the document carefully for mistakes before you make copies.
(A) respect
(B) aspect
(C) inspect
(D) prospect

115. ______ those papers back in the file after you have finished looking at them.
(A) Put
(B) Puts
(C) Putting
(D) Will put

116. We don't ______ to quiet conversations in the office, but we would like to keep noise to a minimum.
(A) subject
(B) project
(C) reject
(D) object

117. After the speaker ______ her presentation, there will be time for a question and answer session.
(A) finished
(B) finishes
(C) finishing
(D) will finish

118. ______ tomorrow is a holiday, the office will be closed.
(A) Unless
(B) Though
(C) Since
(D) However

119. We plan to ______ the planned merger of the two companies as soon as possible.
(A) public
(B) publicize
(C) publicity
(D) publicly

120. ______ the documents were completed, they were mailed to the client's office.
(A) As soon as
(B) By the time
(C) While
(D) Afterwards

121. Sales ______ significantly since we started the new advertising campaign.
(A) increase
(B) increased
(C) are increasing
(D) have increased

122. If you ______ the meeting, you will miss some important information.
(A) won't attend
(B) didn't attend
(C) don't attend
(D) weren't attending

123. There is a new ______ regarding funding requests, which states that they must first be approved by the department head.
(A) direct
(B) director
(C) directive
(D) directed

124. There is a bank on the next block ______ the café and the bookstore.
(A) between
(B) next
(C) under
(D) through

125. We had to put _______ the meeting because so many people were unable to attend.
(A) on
(B) off
(C) up
(D) down

126. The main business of this company is to _______ food products from foreign countries.
(A) deport
(B) import
(C) report
(D) purport

127. You are allowed an hour for lunch, and you may _______ it at any time you wish.
(A) will take
(B) taking
(C) take
(D) took

128. We suggest _______ a lawyer about this matter.
(A) consult
(B) will consult
(C) consulting
(D) to consult

129. We cannot go ahead with the project until we have the _______ of our supervisor.
(A) resent
(B) consent
(C) absent
(D) present

130. _______ the problem over with another person might help you find a good solution.
(A) Talk
(B) Talks
(C) Talking
(D) Will talk

131. This new computer is very different _______ the one I am accustomed to working with.
(A) from
(B) for
(C) to
(D) of

132. The announcement will be made this afternoon _______ precisely 2:00.
(A) at
(B) to
(C) on
(D) in

133. The woman who wrote those books _______ a great deal of experience in the field.
(A) has
(B) have
(C) are
(D) did

134. After thinking it over carefully, George finally decided _______ the job offer.
(A) accepts
(B) accepted
(C) accepting
(D) to accept

135. I keep the important papers _______ a locked cabinet.
(A) inner
(B) enclosed
(C) inside
(D) under

136. Check to make sure there are enough chairs _______ you set up the room for the meeting.
(A) after
(B) before
(C) while
(D) by

137. Harry _______ to punch his time card when he left the building last night.
(A) forget
(B) forgets
(C) forgot
(D) to forget

138. All the walls _______ when we renovated the office last year.
(A) paint
(B) painted
(C) were painting
(D) were painted

139. Do not speak _______ when asking for a salary increase, as that could lead to an unfavorable response.

(A) hesitate
(B) hesitant
(C) hesitation
(D) hesitantly

140. Write out the instructions clearly and simply because you don't want to _______ your reader.

(A) confuse
(B) diffuse
(C) profuse
(D) refuse

PART 6

Directions: Read the texts that follow. A word or phrase is missing in some of the sentences. Four answer choices are given below each of the sentences. Select the best answer to complete the text. Then mark the letter (A), (B), (C), or (D) on your answer sheet.

Questions 141–143 refer to the following newspaper article.

Wonderford, one of the nation's largest retail chains, ____________ that

141. (A) annulled
(B) annexed
(C) annotated
(D) announced

it will be opening a branch store near the city of Midville next year. "Our research has shown that there is potentially an excellent customer base in that region," said Wonderford spokesperson, George Jones, at a press conference at corporate headquarters yesterday afternoon. Rather than locating the new store in Midville's shopping district, the company has decided to build it in the ____________ of the city. A store situated close to the city's edge is

142. (A) middle
(B) outskirts
(C) downtown
(D) neighborhoods

more accessible to the majority of shoppers, ____________ actually live in

143. (A) who
(B) whom
(C) whose
(D) which

the city's suburbs, Mr. Jones explained. Construction on the new store is scheduled to begin before the first of next year and is expected to take no longer than nine months.

GO ON TO THE NEXT PAGE

Questions 144–146 refer to the following notice.

The Clydesdale Corporation
Professional Development Opportunities

We are pleased to announce a special professional development opportunity. All company employees are invited to a workshop on "Creating a Cooperative Work Environment" with guest speaker Myrtle Wilson, author of The Coopertive Workplace. The workshop will take place next June 30 in the company Conference Center. ______________ there will be no charge for

144. (A) Although
(B) Because
(C) Since
(D) Despite

the workshop, advance registration is required due to space limitations. All those interested in attending are asked to register for the workshop before June 25 by giving their names to Ms. Smithers in the Human Resources Department. Depending on the amount of interest generated, the workshop may be repeated later in the year. Upcoming workshops for the rest of the summer ______________ "Sharpening Your Writing Skills" and "Advanced Word Processing."

145. (A) invoke
(B) include
(C) inspire
(D) incline

Times and dates will be announced later. Please see Ms. Smithers for further information or to sign ______________ for either of these opportunities.

146. (A) off
(B) in
(C) on
(D) up

Questions 147–149 refer to the following letter.

February 3, 20_

Franklin Rogers
Tropical Tours
12 Juneau Street
Anchorage, AK

Dear Mr. and Mrs. Thomas,

I am writing to let you know what a wonderful experience I had on the trip my husband and I recently took to Hawaii with ____________ company,

147. (A) our
(B) his
(C) your
(D) my

Tropical Tours. I can sincerely say it was the trip of a lifetime. Everything about the trip, down to the smallest detail, was well organized and professionally managed. The tour guide for our group, Amanda Price, was extremely ____________ about the area, provided us with a lot of

148. (A) knows
(B) known
(C) knowledge
(D) knowledgeable

interesting information, and good-naturedly answered our constant questions. She was very patient and always managed to remain ____________ even when faced with frequent delays and complaints. The

149. (A) punctual
(B) calm
(C) present
(D) informed

hotel where we stayed was extremely comfortable and the sights we visited were fascinating. I will happily recommend Tropical Tours to anyone who asks me for the name of a reliable tour company.

Sincerely,

Rose Ashton

GO ON TO THE NEXT PAGE

Questions 150–152 refer to the following article.

Tips for the Business Traveler

Travel across time zones is ______________ to sleep routines, increasing the

150. (A) disrupt
(B) disruptor
(C) disruptive
(D) disruption

stress of business travel. The more quickly you are able to adjust to the new time zone, the more alert and productive you will be as you conduct your business. Certain habits can help you adapt your sleep patterns more easily to a new time zone. Many business travelers have the practice of setting ______________ watches to the local time even before getting off the plane.

151. (A) their
(B) your
(C) you
(D) them

This helps them adjust themselves psychologically. It is also a good idea to go to bed at your usual time, according to the local hour. If you find you cannot fall asleep quickly, get up for a short while and engage in some quiet activity such as reading a novel or taking a stroll. In the morning, get up at the correct local time. Eat a good breakfast and avoid excessive amounts of caffeine. ______________ a moderate amount of exercise everyday will also

152. (A) Get
(B) Gets
(C) To get
(D) Getting

help make your adjustment easier.

PART 7

Directions: In this part you will read a selection of texts, such as magazine and newspaper articles, letters, and advertisements. Each text is followed by several questions. Select the best answer for each question and mark the letter (A), (B), (C), or (D) on your answer sheet.

Questions 153–156 refer to the following brochure.

OPTIONS Software Training and Consulting Company

All our classes are offered online.

We provide training in all the most commonly-used business software for the busy businessperson. Other companies require you to disrupt your schedule by spending a day or weekend at a hotel or conference center. With an OPTIONS training course, you don't have to devote an entire day to the course, and you never have to leave the comfort of your own office. You simply log on to our website from your own computer and participate in a live webinar. We offer both morning and afternoon courses, so you can pick the schedule that is most convenient for you.

OPTIONS Software Training and Consulting Company offers courses in word processing, accounting, database, and other types of business software at both beginning and advanced levels. All courses are scheduled for an hour a day, Monday-Friday and last just one week. Try out one of our courses for the low, low price of $250. Sign up for two together for $470. That's just $235 each. To register, call our offices at 900-111-5252, or visit our website at www.optionstraining.com.

153. Where can you take an OPTIONS course?
(A) At a hotel
(B) At a conference center
(C) At your office
(D) At the OPTIONS office

154. The word "devote" in line 5 is closest in meaning to
(A) give
(B) plan
(C) pay
(D) enjoy

155. How many hours does it take to complete an OPTIONS course?
(A) 1
(B) 2
(C) 4
(D) 5

156. How much would it cost to take a beginning level word processing course only?
(A) $235
(B) $250
(C) $470
(D) $500

Questions 157–159 refer to the following article.

A dinner was hosted at the Creighton Hotel last night by the Pottsville Bank in honor of Marcella Inman, who will be retiring after 35 of service to the bank. Ms. Inman started her career at the bank as a teller at the original branch in downtown Pottsville. She was soon promoted to branch manager at the bank's Riverview branch. She served in that position for close to twenty years and was responsible for the expansion of the bank's customer base in the Riverview region, which eventually led to the establishment of three more regional branches. Ms. Inman has served as the bank's president for the past ten years. "It has been my great honor to lead this fine institution all these years," she said at last night's dinner. "Experience is a great teacher, and I am grateful for the many things I have learned during my experience with the bank." Harry Plunkett will serve as the new president of the Pottsville Bank.

157. What was celebrated at the dinner?
(A) A promotion
(B) A retirement
(C) A 35th birthday
(D) A branch opening

158. What was Ms. Inman's job before she became a branch manager?
(A) teller
(B) hotel clerk
(C) teacher
(D) server

159. How many years was Ms. Inman president of the bank?
(A) 10
(B) 20
(C) 25
(D) 35

Questions 160–163 refer to the following letter.

Dear Editor,

I am writing to commend our mayor for his support of an improved public transportation system for our city. We need to bring businesses to our city, not drive them away, and Mayor Wilson understands how important a viable public transportation system is to creating an attractive business climate. Every business owner knows that there is no business without customers, and our city's crowded streets make it difficult for customers to access our city's business establishments. When customers drive downtown and then cannot find a place to park, they end up going elsewhere to spend their money.

At its annual meeting last month, the Downtown Business Association expressed its strong approval for the proposed expansion of bus and subway service in the downtown business district. As president of that entity, I strongly encourage City Council members to listen to the voice of the business community when voting next week on whether to approve the mayor's proposal to increase the public transportation budget next year. It is sensible measures like this that will keep our downtown alive.

Sincerely,

Alicia Johnson

160. Why did Ms. Johnson write this letter?
- (A) To promote her business
- (B) To encourage people to reelect the mayor
- (C) To discuss the work of the Business Association
- (D) To express her opinion about public transportation

161. The word *commend* in line 1 is closest in meaning to
- (A) approve
- (B) suggest
- (C) oppose
- (D) praise

162. What problem do downtown businesses have?
- (A) High rents
- (B) Crowded stores
- (C) Not enough parking
- (D) Unattractive streets

163. When will there be a vote?
- (A) Next week
- (B) Next month
- (C) In a year
- (D) In two years

GO ON TO THE NEXT PAGE

Questions 164–165 refer to the following advertisement.

Rosebud's
Does this scene sound familiar: You have an important business meeting coming up this afternoon, and you just spilled coffee on your suit.

Don't Despair!
Rosebud's to the rescue!

Rosebud's offers the fastest cleaning service in town. We pick up your clothes at your office and deliver them back to you within ONE HOUR. GUARANTEED.

Rosebud's.
We're located at
483 East State Street.
Call us at 349-0977.
To view our low, low rates, visit our website at
www.rosebuds.com

164. What kind of business is Rosebud's?
(A) Clothing store
(B) Dry cleaners
(C) Office cleaners
(D) Meeting organizers

165. How can you find out the prices they charge?
(A) Go to their office.
(B) Call them.
(C) Visit their website.
(D) Send an e-mail.

Questions 166–168 refer to the following advertisement.

Winston Realty
Offices for Rent

1
This fifth floor office space offers spectacular views of Riverside Park. Includes large open area suitable for a waiting room, plus two private offices. Sign a five-year lease and pay only $1200 a month.

2
Now available. The entire first floor of the Centerville Professional Building. Reception area, 2 conference rooms, and a small kitchen are included. Ample parking for staff and clients in rear of building. $5000 a month, with possibilities for subletting part of the space.

3
Large, sunny office available on top floor of Sullivan Street building. Prime downtown location. Approximately 650 square feet. No parking lot, but on-street parking is available. Low, low rent includes all utilities. $1350/month.

4
Modern office space available next to Simpson Park shopping mall. Space includes two private offices and small kitchen. Approximately 975 square feet. Manager in building. Must see to appreciate. $2000/monthly.

Visit our website to see more listings: www.winstonrealty.com. All listed spaces are currently available for showing. Please call our offices at 593-0922 to make an appointment.

166. How much is the lowest rent advertised?
(A) $650
(B) $975
(C) $1200
(D) $1350

167. How many offices include parking with the rent?
(A) 1
(B) 2
(C) 3
(D) 4

168. How can an appointment be made to see a rental space?
(A) Call the realty office.
(B) Visit the website.
(C) Wait in the reception area.
(D) Contact the building manager.

GO ON TO THE NEXT PAGE

Questions 169–172 refer to the following article.

> ***Making an Impression***
> by Jack Schultz
>
> Preparing for a job interview can be stressful, and it is important to get the best advice possible. Career counselors can be helpful, but for this month's column we decided to go right to the person who matters–the hiring manager. We asked Melissa Wayman of the Candle Store what she looks for in a potential employee. "When I advertise a job opening, typically I get maybe two, three hundred résumés," Ms. Wayman told us. "Out of those, I narrow it down to the fifteen strongest candidates. Those are the ones I interview. Of those, usually I'll end up with three or four who I'm interested in hiring." How does she decide among those top three or four? It's all about confidence, Ms. Wayman explains. People often focus on things such as how they dress for an interview or being punctual. "By the time I've narrowed it down to the last few candidates, we're way past that," says Ms. Wayman. "All else being equal, I'll hire the person who shakes my hand, looks me in the eye, and answers questions without hesitation. I know I can rely on a person with that sort of confidence." Ms. Wayman admits that she enjoys hiring for new positions. "My job is never boring," she says. "Interviewing people is difficult for many managers, but I like it."

169. Who is this article for?
- (A) Job seekers
- (B) Résumé editors
- (C) Hiring managers
- (D) Career counselors

170. How many people does Ms. Wayman interview for a job opening?
- (A) Two
- (B) Three or four
- (C) Fifteen
- (D) Three hundred

171. What advice is given?
- (A) Be punctual
- (B) Ask questions
- (C) Dress correctly
- (D) Act confident

172. How does Ms. Wayman feel about her job?
- (A) It's stressful.
- (B) It's enjoyable.
- (C) It's boring.
- (D) It's difficult.

Questions 173–174 refer to the following letter.

Northeast Electrical Services
120 Bayview Boulevard
Upton, ME 00121

May 30, 20__

Customer
Jones and Smith, PC
49 River Road
Upton, ME 00122

For:

Rewiring of offices at 49 River Road	$1500
Replacement of outlets	$125
Installation of water heater	$750

Amount due payable in full within fifteen days of the date of this invoice. Ten percent of total charged as late fee after that date.

Thank you for being a Northeast customer. We value your business.

173. How much is owed to Northeast Electrical Services?
(A) $125
(B) $750
(C) $1500
(D) $2375

174. When is it due?
(A) May 15
(B) May 30
(C) June 15
(D) June 30

GO ON TO THE NEXT PAGE

Questions 175–178 refer to the following notice.

> **Oglethorpe's Office Supply**
>
> **Return Policy**
>
> We want you to be satisfied with your purchase. If for any reason you are not completely satisfied, you may return most items for a refund within 90 days of purchase, or within 30 days for computers and computer peripherals. DVDs, CDs, and unopened software may be returned for exchange only within 14 days of purchase. Snack and other edible items may not be returned under any circumstances.
>
> All items must be returned undamaged in their original packaging and accompanied by a receipt. Items returned in open boxes will be inspected for damage. A return charge of 15% of the original purchase price will be made on all items, except for CDs, DVDs, and software being returned for exchange, that are returned after 24 hours of purchase.
>
> Executive brand office furniture, the only brand we carry, comes with a lifetime guarantee. If you are ever unsatisfied with a piece of Executive brand furniture, you may return it to any Oglethorpe's branch for a full refund, no questions asked. The 15% return charge does not apply to Executive brand furniture, and there are no time limits on the return.

175. What must be returned within two weeks?
(A) Computers
(B) Software
(C) Snacks
(D) Peripherals

176. The word "circumstances" in line 5 is closest in meaning to
(A) Time
(B) Reason
(C) Location
(D) Situation

177. When is there a 15 percent charge on a returned item?
(A) It is returned after 24 hours have passed.
(B) It is returned with minor damage.
(C) It is returned in an open box.
(D) It is returned without a receipt.

178. When can furniture be returned?
(A) Never
(B) Within 30 days
(C) Within 90 days
(D) Anytime

Questions 179–180 refer to the following article.

The Department of Transportation announced on Monday that an increase in city bus fares has been approved. Regular bus fares will rise 15%, which means a bus trip within city limits will go up by $.30 to $2.30 for a one-way adult fare. The 25% senior citizen's discount will still be in effect, however, there will no longer be a reduced weekend rate. This is the first bus fare increase in 5 years and has been determined in response to rising fuel costs. The increase is scheduled to go into effect next month.

179. How much will bus fares increase?
(A) 5%
(B) 15%
(C) 25%
(D) 30%

180. When will bus fares increase?
(A) On Monday
(B) On the weekend
(C) Next month
(D) Next year

GO ON TO THE NEXT PAGE

Questions 181–185 refer to the following advertisement and letter.

WANTED: Busy downtown engineering firm seeks manager for office of three engineers, an assistant, and interns. Manage appointment calendar, maintain website, oversee supplies, answer phones, greet clients. Light bookkeeping. Good people skills. Familiarity with word processing and database software necessary. Five years experience in a similar setting required. Send résumé and references before July 10 to: Anne Green, Bing and Rogers Engineering, Box 77, North Concord, N.H. No phone calls please.

June 30, 20__

Anne Green
Bing and Rogers Engineering
Box 77
North Concord, N.H. 03301

Dear Ms. Green,
I am writing in reference to Edward Sharpe, who is interested in applying for the position at your engineering firm, advertised in yesterday's newspaper. I run a small editorial service and Mr. Sharpe has worked as my office assistant for the past two years. It has been a great pleasure working with Mr. Sharpe. When I hired him, he had had no previous experience in an office, but I found him to be a fast learner. He also has many personal qualities that suit him for this type of work. He is punctual and reliable and runs my office in an extremely well-organized way. He is always courteous with my clients and generally has good "people skills." He is also quite proficient in the use of word processing and database software. I depend on him a great deal to keep my office running smoothly. I will be sorry to see him leave, but I support his efforts to seek a more challenging position. Please let me know if you need any further information about Mr. Sharpe, or if I can help you in any other way.

Sincerely,

Carolyn Peters
Peters Editorial

181. Who is Carolyn Peters?

(A) Anne Green's supervisor
(B) Edward Sharpe's supervisor
(C) Owner of an engineering firm
(D) A client of Bing and Rogers

182. What job is Edward Sharpe applying for?

(A) Office manager
(B) Engineer
(C) Editor
(D) Bookkeeper

183. When was the job advertised?

(A) June 10
(B) June 29
(C) June 30
(D) July 10

184. What should Edward Sharpe do to apply for the job?

(A) Look for instructions on the website
(B) Call the office for an appointment
(C) Mail in his résumé and references
(D) Visit the office in person

185. Why won't Edward Sharpe get the job?

(A) He doesn't have enough experience.
(B) He isn't familiar with the right software.
(C) He doesn't have a good reference.
(D) He isn't polite with clients.

GO ON TO THE NEXT PAGE

Questions 186–190 refer to the following agenda and e-mail.

The Stridus Corporation
Staff Meeting Agenda for
September 15, 20__

Budget Review ....Sam Chang
Market Report ....Liz Lopez
Hiring Procedures .... Polly Andrews
New Client Report ....Mark Pavlis

Lunch

Product Development ..... Patty Brown

This month's meeting will begin at the usual hour, 9:00, in Conference Room B. Because of the unusually full agenda, we will reconvene immediately following lunch, in the auditorium, to hear Patty's presentation. For those who wish it, lunch will be served from 12:00 – 1:15 in Conference Room A.

From: Liz Lopez
Date: Monday, Sept. 11
To: Sam Chang
Subject: Monthly Meeting

Hi Sam,
I just discovered that I have a meeting with a client next Friday morning which can't be changed, so I'm going to be two hours late for the monthly meeting. Don't worry, I've already discussed this with Mark and he has given me permission to arrive late. However, he doesn't want to rearrange the meeting format, so we agreed that you would give my presentation for me. I think you have all the necessary information, but why don't you drop by my office after lunch on Thursday and we can go over everything then. You won't have to talk very long, anyway, since Mark plans to have Polly begin by 10:00 so that she and he will have time to complete their presentations before lunch. Thanks so much for your help.
Liz

186. What day of the week will the staff meeting take place?
(A) Monday
(B) Tuesday
(C) Thursday
(D) Friday

187. Who will present the market report?
(A) Sam Chang
(B) Liz Lopez
(C) Polly Andrews
(D) Mark Pavlis

188. Which presentation will begin at 10:00?
(A) Budget Review
(B) Market Report
(C) Hiring Procedures
(D) New Client Report

189. Where will lunch be served?
(A) Conference Room A
(B) Conference Room B
(C) The auditorium
(D) Liz's office

190. What time will the presentation on product development begin?
(A) 9:00
(B) 9:15
(C) 12:00
(D) 1:15

GO ON TO THE NEXT PAGE

Questions 191–195 refer to the following memo and form.

To: All personnel
From: Janet Howland, Office Manager
Re: Office supplies
Date: Thursday, December 1

This is to inform you of a change in the way office supplies will be distributed, effective next Monday, December 5. Recently, too many supplies have been disappearing too fast from the supply room. Unfortunately, as a result, we will have to limit access to the supply room. My assistant, Mr. Wang, will be the only person authorized to enter the supply room and remove supplies from it. In order to get supplies, you will need to complete a supply request form and submit it to Mr. Wang. Supply requests will be filled within two days so, for example, if you submit the form on a Monday, you should have your supplies the following Wednesday. The one exception to this is business cards, which normally take a week since we have to specially request them from the printing company. For your convenience, the form is available on line. I have placed a link on the company website, so it will be quite easy to fill it out and e-mail it to Mr. Wang whenever you need supplies. Please see me in Room 5 if you have any questions. Thank you for your cooperation.

Supply Request Form

Date: *Wednesday, December 14*
Name: *Sara Soto*
Room: *10A*

Item	**Quantity**
Printer paper	1 package
Note pads (indicate size)	5 (legal)
Ink cartridges	1
Paper clips	3 boxes
Staples	
Pens (indicate ink color)	2 boxes (blue)
Rubber bands	4 bags
Index cards	
Business cards	
Other	

Supplies will be delivered to your office unless another location is indicated here: *Please deliver to Conference Room 2B.*

191. Who will Sara submit the form to?

(A) Ms. Howland
(B) Mr. Wang
(C) Mr. Wang's assistant
(D) Her own assistant

192. When do business cards have to be ordered?

(A) Two days ahead of time
(B) A week ahead of time
(C) On Thursdays
(D) In December

193. When will Sara get her supplies?

(A) Monday
(B) Wednesday
(C) Thursday
(D) Friday

194. How many paper clips does Sara want?

(A) 3 bags
(B) 4 bags
(C) 3 boxes
(D) 4 boxes

195. Which room will Sara's supplies be delivered to?

(A) Room 5
(B) Room 10
(C) Room 10 A
(D) Room 2B

GO ON TO THE NEXT PAGE

Questions 196–200 refer to the following two letters.

July 18, 20__

Wigford Hotel
125 North Main Street
Whitefish, Montana
USA

Dear Manager,

I am a frequent guest at the Wigford Hotel. I have been spending my vacation there every summer for the past seven years, and have always enjoyed comfortable accommodations and courteous service. In fact, it is such a pleasant place to stay that I feel it is well worth the $350 a night price. Unfortunately, during my visit to the Wigford last month, I found that some things were not up to the usual standard. I understand that renovations of several areas of the hotel were done last winter and spring and were only just completed before my arrival, so it would be natural to expect some confusion. Things did seem to be slightly disorganized, but that did not create any serious problems. I was very surprised, however, at the poor quality of the meals. The restaurant at the Wigford has such a good reputation but has not lived up to it this summer. I ended up eating several meals at other restaurants because the Wigford kitchen was serving such indifferent meals. It is a shame to see such a fine hotel fail in this respect. I hope the situation can be improved before my vacation there next year.

Sincerely,

Elizabeth Springer

July 18, 20__

Elizabeth Springer
20 Tulalip Road
Vancouver, British Columbia
Canada

Dear Ms. Springer,

I have received your letter about your recent stay at the Wigford. Thank you for bringing to my attention the issues with the meal service that occurred during your recent stay. You may not be aware that the renovation work was still under way during your visit. In fact, work on the kitchen began exactly during the week you were with us. Our kitchen staff made a great deal of effort to maintain the usual high quality of the menu despite the disruptions caused by the renovation work. I am sorry they were not entirely successful. Please accept my apologies on their behalf. I am sending with this letter a coupon for a free meal at our restaurant. In addition, I would like to offer you a 20% discount on your room charge during your next visit. Again, thank you for your letter, and we look forward to seeing you at the Wigford.

Sincerely,

James Grayson
Manager

196. Why did Ms. Springer write the letter?
(A) To complain about the food
(B) To praise the accommodations
(C) To reserve a room at the hotel
(D) To find out about the renovations

197. How many times has Ms. Springer stayed at the Wigford Hotel?
(A) 5
(B) 6
(C) 7
(D) 8

198. When was the hotel kitchen renovated?
(A) Last winter
(B) Last spring
(C) In June
(D) In July

199. What did Mr. Grayson enclose with the letter?
(A) A refund
(B) A letter from the staff
(C) A menu
(D) A coupon for a meal

200. How much will Ms. Springer pay per night the next time she visits the hotel?
(A) 20
(B) 330
(C) 280
(D) 350

Stop! This is the end of the test. If you finish before time is called, you may go back to Parts 5, 6, and 7 and check your work.

ANSWER SHEETS

ANSWER SHEET: Listening Comprehension and Reading Review

Name ____________________

Listening Comprehension

Part 1 | Part 2 | Part 3 | Part 4

	Answer		Answer		Answer		Answer		Answer		Answer		Answer		Answer		Answer		Answer
	A B C D		A B C		A B C		A B C		A B C D		A B C D		A B C D		A B C D		A B C D		A B C D
1	Ⓐ Ⓑ Ⓒ Ⓓ	11	Ⓐ Ⓑ Ⓒ	21	Ⓐ Ⓑ Ⓒ	31	Ⓐ Ⓑ Ⓒ	41	Ⓐ Ⓑ Ⓒ Ⓓ	51	Ⓐ Ⓑ Ⓒ Ⓓ	61	Ⓐ Ⓑ Ⓒ Ⓓ	71	Ⓐ Ⓑ Ⓒ Ⓓ	81	Ⓐ Ⓑ Ⓒ Ⓓ	91	Ⓐ Ⓑ Ⓒ Ⓓ
2	Ⓐ Ⓑ Ⓒ Ⓓ	12	Ⓐ Ⓑ Ⓒ	22	Ⓐ Ⓑ Ⓒ	32	Ⓐ Ⓑ Ⓒ	42	Ⓐ Ⓑ Ⓒ Ⓓ	52	Ⓐ Ⓑ Ⓒ Ⓓ	62	Ⓐ Ⓑ Ⓒ Ⓓ	72	Ⓐ Ⓑ Ⓒ Ⓓ	82	Ⓐ Ⓑ Ⓒ Ⓓ	92	Ⓐ Ⓑ Ⓒ Ⓓ
3	Ⓐ Ⓑ Ⓒ Ⓓ	13	Ⓐ Ⓑ Ⓒ	23	Ⓐ Ⓑ Ⓒ	33	Ⓐ Ⓑ Ⓒ	43	Ⓐ Ⓑ Ⓒ Ⓓ	53	Ⓐ Ⓑ Ⓒ Ⓓ	63	Ⓐ Ⓑ Ⓒ Ⓓ	73	Ⓐ Ⓑ Ⓒ Ⓓ	83	Ⓐ Ⓑ Ⓒ Ⓓ	93	Ⓐ Ⓑ Ⓒ Ⓓ
4	Ⓐ Ⓑ Ⓒ Ⓓ	14	Ⓐ Ⓑ Ⓒ	24	Ⓐ Ⓑ Ⓒ	34	Ⓐ Ⓑ Ⓒ	44	Ⓐ Ⓑ Ⓒ Ⓓ	54	Ⓐ Ⓑ Ⓒ Ⓓ	64	Ⓐ Ⓑ Ⓒ Ⓓ	74	Ⓐ Ⓑ Ⓒ Ⓓ	84	Ⓐ Ⓑ Ⓒ Ⓓ	94	Ⓐ Ⓑ Ⓒ Ⓓ
5	Ⓐ Ⓑ Ⓒ Ⓓ	15	Ⓐ Ⓑ Ⓒ	25	Ⓐ Ⓑ Ⓒ	35	Ⓐ Ⓑ Ⓒ	45	Ⓐ Ⓑ Ⓒ Ⓓ	55	Ⓐ Ⓑ Ⓒ Ⓓ	65	Ⓐ Ⓑ Ⓒ Ⓓ	75	Ⓐ Ⓑ Ⓒ Ⓓ	85	Ⓐ Ⓑ Ⓒ Ⓓ	95	Ⓐ Ⓑ Ⓒ Ⓓ
6	Ⓐ Ⓑ Ⓒ Ⓓ	16	Ⓐ Ⓑ Ⓒ	26	Ⓐ Ⓑ Ⓒ	36	Ⓐ Ⓑ Ⓒ	46	Ⓐ Ⓑ Ⓒ Ⓓ	56	Ⓐ Ⓑ Ⓒ Ⓓ	66	Ⓐ Ⓑ Ⓒ Ⓓ	76	Ⓐ Ⓑ Ⓒ Ⓓ	86	Ⓐ Ⓑ Ⓒ Ⓓ	96	Ⓐ Ⓑ Ⓒ Ⓓ
7	Ⓐ Ⓑ Ⓒ Ⓓ	17	Ⓐ Ⓑ Ⓒ	27	Ⓐ Ⓑ Ⓒ	37	Ⓐ Ⓑ Ⓒ	47	Ⓐ Ⓑ Ⓒ Ⓓ	57	Ⓐ Ⓑ Ⓒ Ⓓ	67	Ⓐ Ⓑ Ⓒ Ⓓ	77	Ⓐ Ⓑ Ⓒ Ⓓ	87	Ⓐ Ⓑ Ⓒ Ⓓ	97	Ⓐ Ⓑ Ⓒ Ⓓ
8	Ⓐ Ⓑ Ⓒ Ⓓ	18	Ⓐ Ⓑ Ⓒ	28	Ⓑ Ⓒ ○	38	Ⓐ Ⓑ Ⓒ	48	Ⓐ Ⓑ Ⓒ Ⓓ	58	Ⓐ Ⓑ Ⓒ Ⓓ	68	Ⓐ Ⓑ Ⓒ Ⓓ	78	Ⓐ Ⓑ Ⓒ Ⓓ	88	Ⓐ Ⓑ Ⓒ Ⓓ	98	Ⓐ Ⓑ Ⓒ Ⓓ
9	Ⓐ Ⓑ Ⓒ Ⓓ	19	Ⓐ Ⓑ Ⓒ	29	Ⓐ Ⓑ Ⓒ	39	Ⓐ Ⓑ Ⓒ	49	Ⓐ Ⓑ Ⓒ Ⓓ	59	Ⓐ Ⓑ Ⓒ Ⓓ	69	Ⓐ Ⓑ Ⓒ Ⓓ	79	Ⓐ Ⓑ Ⓒ Ⓓ	89	Ⓐ Ⓑ Ⓒ Ⓓ	99	Ⓐ Ⓑ Ⓒ Ⓓ
10	Ⓐ Ⓑ Ⓒ Ⓓ	20	Ⓐ Ⓑ Ⓒ	30	Ⓐ Ⓑ Ⓒ	40	Ⓐ Ⓑ Ⓒ	50	Ⓐ Ⓑ Ⓒ Ⓓ	60	Ⓐ Ⓑ Ⓒ Ⓓ	70	Ⓐ Ⓑ Ⓒ Ⓓ	80	Ⓐ Ⓑ Ⓒ Ⓓ	90	Ⓐ Ⓑ Ⓒ Ⓓ	100	Ⓐ Ⓑ Ⓒ Ⓓ

Reading

Part 5 | Part 6 | Part 7

	Answer		Answer		Answer		Answer		Answer		Answer		Answer		Answer		Answer		Answer
	A B C D		A B C D		A B C D		A B C D		A B C D		A B C D		A B C D		A B C D		A B C D		A B C D
101	Ⓐ Ⓑ Ⓒ Ⓓ	111	Ⓐ Ⓑ Ⓒ Ⓓ	121	Ⓐ Ⓑ Ⓒ Ⓓ	131	Ⓐ Ⓑ Ⓒ Ⓓ	141	Ⓐ Ⓑ Ⓒ Ⓓ	151	Ⓐ Ⓑ Ⓒ Ⓓ	161	Ⓐ Ⓑ Ⓒ Ⓓ	171	Ⓐ Ⓑ Ⓒ Ⓓ	181	Ⓐ Ⓑ Ⓒ Ⓓ	191	Ⓐ Ⓑ Ⓒ Ⓓ
102	Ⓐ Ⓑ Ⓒ Ⓓ	112	Ⓐ Ⓑ Ⓒ Ⓓ	122	Ⓐ Ⓑ Ⓒ Ⓓ	132	Ⓐ Ⓑ Ⓒ Ⓓ	142	Ⓐ Ⓑ Ⓒ Ⓓ	152	Ⓐ Ⓑ Ⓒ Ⓓ	162	Ⓐ Ⓑ Ⓒ Ⓓ	172	Ⓐ Ⓑ Ⓒ Ⓓ	182	Ⓐ Ⓑ Ⓒ Ⓓ	192	Ⓐ Ⓑ Ⓒ Ⓓ
103	Ⓐ Ⓑ Ⓒ Ⓓ	113	Ⓐ Ⓑ Ⓒ Ⓓ	123	Ⓐ Ⓑ Ⓒ Ⓓ	133	Ⓐ Ⓑ Ⓒ Ⓓ	143	Ⓐ Ⓑ Ⓒ Ⓓ	153	Ⓐ Ⓑ Ⓒ Ⓓ	163	Ⓐ Ⓑ Ⓒ Ⓓ	173	Ⓐ Ⓑ Ⓒ Ⓓ	183	Ⓐ Ⓑ Ⓒ Ⓓ	193	Ⓐ Ⓑ Ⓒ Ⓓ
104	Ⓐ Ⓑ Ⓒ Ⓓ	114	Ⓐ Ⓑ Ⓒ Ⓓ	124	Ⓐ Ⓑ Ⓒ Ⓓ	134	Ⓐ Ⓑ Ⓒ Ⓓ	144	Ⓐ Ⓑ Ⓒ Ⓓ	154	Ⓐ Ⓑ Ⓒ Ⓓ	164	Ⓐ Ⓑ Ⓒ Ⓓ	174	Ⓐ Ⓑ Ⓒ Ⓓ	184	Ⓐ Ⓑ Ⓒ Ⓓ	194	Ⓐ Ⓑ Ⓒ Ⓓ
105	Ⓐ Ⓑ Ⓒ Ⓓ	115	Ⓐ Ⓑ Ⓒ Ⓓ	125	Ⓐ Ⓑ Ⓒ Ⓓ	135	Ⓐ Ⓑ Ⓒ Ⓓ	145	Ⓐ Ⓑ Ⓒ Ⓓ	155	Ⓐ Ⓑ Ⓒ Ⓓ	165	Ⓐ Ⓑ Ⓒ Ⓓ	175	Ⓐ Ⓑ Ⓒ Ⓓ	185	Ⓐ Ⓑ Ⓒ Ⓓ	195	Ⓐ Ⓑ Ⓒ Ⓓ
106	Ⓐ Ⓑ Ⓒ Ⓓ	116	Ⓐ Ⓑ Ⓒ Ⓓ	126	Ⓐ Ⓑ Ⓒ Ⓓ	136	Ⓐ Ⓑ Ⓒ Ⓓ	146	Ⓐ Ⓑ Ⓒ Ⓓ	156	Ⓐ Ⓑ Ⓒ Ⓓ	166	Ⓐ Ⓑ Ⓒ Ⓓ	176	Ⓐ Ⓑ Ⓒ Ⓓ	186	Ⓐ Ⓑ Ⓒ Ⓓ	196	Ⓐ Ⓑ Ⓒ Ⓓ
107	Ⓐ Ⓑ Ⓒ Ⓓ	117	Ⓐ Ⓑ Ⓒ Ⓓ	127	Ⓐ Ⓑ Ⓒ Ⓓ	137	Ⓐ Ⓑ Ⓒ Ⓓ	147	Ⓐ Ⓑ Ⓒ Ⓓ	157	Ⓐ Ⓑ Ⓒ Ⓓ	167	Ⓐ Ⓑ Ⓒ Ⓓ	177	Ⓐ Ⓑ Ⓒ Ⓓ	187	Ⓐ Ⓑ Ⓒ Ⓓ	197	Ⓐ Ⓑ Ⓒ Ⓓ
108	Ⓐ Ⓑ Ⓒ Ⓓ	118	Ⓐ Ⓑ Ⓒ Ⓓ	128	Ⓐ Ⓑ Ⓒ Ⓓ	138	Ⓐ Ⓑ Ⓒ Ⓓ	148	Ⓐ Ⓑ Ⓒ Ⓓ	158	Ⓐ Ⓑ Ⓒ Ⓓ	168	Ⓐ Ⓑ Ⓒ Ⓓ	178	Ⓐ Ⓑ Ⓒ Ⓓ	188	Ⓐ Ⓑ Ⓒ Ⓓ	198	Ⓐ Ⓑ Ⓒ Ⓓ
109	Ⓐ Ⓑ Ⓒ Ⓓ	119	Ⓐ Ⓑ Ⓒ Ⓓ	129	Ⓐ Ⓑ Ⓒ Ⓓ	139	Ⓐ Ⓑ Ⓒ Ⓓ	149	Ⓐ Ⓑ Ⓒ Ⓓ	159	Ⓐ Ⓑ Ⓒ Ⓓ	169	Ⓐ Ⓑ Ⓒ Ⓓ	179	Ⓐ Ⓑ Ⓒ Ⓓ	189	Ⓐ Ⓑ Ⓒ Ⓓ	199	Ⓐ Ⓑ Ⓒ Ⓓ
110	Ⓐ Ⓑ Ⓒ Ⓓ	120	Ⓐ Ⓑ Ⓒ Ⓓ	130	Ⓐ Ⓑ Ⓒ Ⓓ	140	Ⓐ Ⓑ Ⓒ Ⓓ	150	Ⓐ Ⓑ Ⓒ Ⓓ	160	Ⓐ Ⓑ Ⓒ Ⓓ	170	Ⓐ Ⓑ Ⓒ Ⓓ	180	Ⓐ Ⓑ Ⓒ Ⓓ	190	Ⓐ Ⓑ Ⓒ Ⓓ	200	Ⓐ Ⓑ Ⓒ Ⓓ

ANSWER SHEET: Practice Test One

Name ____________________

Listening Comprehension

Part 1 | Part 2 | Part 3 | Part 4

	Answer (A B C D)		Answer (A B C D)		Answer (A B C)		Answer (A B C)		Answer (A B C)		Answer (A B C D)		Answer (A B C D)		Answer (A B C D)		Answer (A B C D)		Answer (A B C D)
1	Ⓐ Ⓑ Ⓒ Ⓓ	11	Ⓐ Ⓑ Ⓒ Ⓓ	21	Ⓐ Ⓑ Ⓒ	31	Ⓐ Ⓑ Ⓒ	41	Ⓐ Ⓑ Ⓒ	51	Ⓐ Ⓑ Ⓒ Ⓓ	61	Ⓐ Ⓑ Ⓒ Ⓓ	71	Ⓐ Ⓑ Ⓒ Ⓓ	81	Ⓐ Ⓑ Ⓒ Ⓓ	91	Ⓐ Ⓑ Ⓒ Ⓓ
2	Ⓐ Ⓑ Ⓒ Ⓓ	12	Ⓐ Ⓑ Ⓒ Ⓓ	22	Ⓐ Ⓑ Ⓒ	32	Ⓐ Ⓑ Ⓒ	42	Ⓐ Ⓑ Ⓒ	52	Ⓐ Ⓑ Ⓒ Ⓓ	62	Ⓐ Ⓑ Ⓒ Ⓓ	72	Ⓐ Ⓑ Ⓒ Ⓓ	82	Ⓐ Ⓑ Ⓒ Ⓓ	92	Ⓐ Ⓑ Ⓒ Ⓓ
3	Ⓐ Ⓑ Ⓒ Ⓓ	13	Ⓐ Ⓑ Ⓒ Ⓓ	23	Ⓐ Ⓑ Ⓒ	33	Ⓐ Ⓑ Ⓒ	43	Ⓐ Ⓑ Ⓒ	53	Ⓐ Ⓑ Ⓒ Ⓓ	63	Ⓐ Ⓑ Ⓒ Ⓓ	73	Ⓐ Ⓑ Ⓒ Ⓓ	83	Ⓐ Ⓑ Ⓒ Ⓓ	93	Ⓐ Ⓑ Ⓒ Ⓓ
4	Ⓐ Ⓑ Ⓒ Ⓓ	14	Ⓐ Ⓑ Ⓒ Ⓓ	24	Ⓐ Ⓑ Ⓒ	34	Ⓐ Ⓑ Ⓒ	44	Ⓐ Ⓑ Ⓒ	54	Ⓐ Ⓑ Ⓒ Ⓓ	64	Ⓐ Ⓑ Ⓒ Ⓓ	74	Ⓐ Ⓑ Ⓒ Ⓓ	84	Ⓐ Ⓑ Ⓒ Ⓓ	94	Ⓐ Ⓑ Ⓒ Ⓓ
5	Ⓐ Ⓑ Ⓒ Ⓓ	15	Ⓐ Ⓑ Ⓒ Ⓓ	25	Ⓐ Ⓑ Ⓒ	35	Ⓐ Ⓑ Ⓒ	45	Ⓐ Ⓑ Ⓒ	55	Ⓐ Ⓑ Ⓒ Ⓓ	65	Ⓐ Ⓑ Ⓒ Ⓓ	75	Ⓐ Ⓑ Ⓒ Ⓓ	85	Ⓐ Ⓑ Ⓒ Ⓓ	95	Ⓐ Ⓑ Ⓒ Ⓓ
6	Ⓐ Ⓑ Ⓒ Ⓓ	16	Ⓐ Ⓑ Ⓒ Ⓓ	26	Ⓐ Ⓑ Ⓒ	36	Ⓐ Ⓑ Ⓒ	46	Ⓐ Ⓑ Ⓒ	56	Ⓐ Ⓑ Ⓒ Ⓓ	66	Ⓐ Ⓑ Ⓒ Ⓓ	76	Ⓐ Ⓑ Ⓒ Ⓓ	86	Ⓐ Ⓑ Ⓒ Ⓓ	96	Ⓐ Ⓑ Ⓒ Ⓓ
7	Ⓐ Ⓑ Ⓒ Ⓓ	17	Ⓐ Ⓑ Ⓒ Ⓓ	27	Ⓐ Ⓑ Ⓒ	37	Ⓐ Ⓑ Ⓒ	47	Ⓐ Ⓑ Ⓒ	57	Ⓐ Ⓑ Ⓒ Ⓓ	67	Ⓐ Ⓑ Ⓒ Ⓓ	77	Ⓐ Ⓑ Ⓒ Ⓓ	87	Ⓐ Ⓑ Ⓒ Ⓓ	97	Ⓐ Ⓑ Ⓒ Ⓓ
8	Ⓐ Ⓑ Ⓒ Ⓓ	18	Ⓐ Ⓑ Ⓒ Ⓓ	28	Ⓐ Ⓑ Ⓒ	38	Ⓐ Ⓑ Ⓒ	48	Ⓐ Ⓑ Ⓒ	58	Ⓐ Ⓑ Ⓒ Ⓓ	68	Ⓐ Ⓑ Ⓒ Ⓓ	78	Ⓐ Ⓑ Ⓒ Ⓓ	88	Ⓐ Ⓑ Ⓒ Ⓓ	98	Ⓐ Ⓑ Ⓒ Ⓓ
9	Ⓐ Ⓑ Ⓒ Ⓓ	19	Ⓐ Ⓑ Ⓒ Ⓓ	29	Ⓐ Ⓑ Ⓒ	39	Ⓐ Ⓑ Ⓒ	49	Ⓐ Ⓑ Ⓒ	59	Ⓐ Ⓑ Ⓒ Ⓓ	69	Ⓐ Ⓑ Ⓒ Ⓓ	79	Ⓐ Ⓑ Ⓒ Ⓓ	89	Ⓐ Ⓑ Ⓒ Ⓓ	99	Ⓐ Ⓑ Ⓒ Ⓓ
10	Ⓐ Ⓑ Ⓒ Ⓓ	20	Ⓐ Ⓑ Ⓒ Ⓓ	30	Ⓐ Ⓑ Ⓒ	40	Ⓐ Ⓑ Ⓒ	50	Ⓐ Ⓑ Ⓒ	60	Ⓐ Ⓑ Ⓒ Ⓓ	70	Ⓐ Ⓑ Ⓒ Ⓓ	80	Ⓐ Ⓑ Ⓒ Ⓓ	90	Ⓐ Ⓑ Ⓒ Ⓓ	100	Ⓐ Ⓑ Ⓒ Ⓓ

Reading

Part 5 | Part 6 | Part 7

	Answer (A B C D)		Answer (A B C D)		Answer (A B C D)		Answer (A B C D)		Answer (A B C D)		Answer (A B C D)		Answer (A B C D)		Answer (A B C D)		Answer (A B C D)		Answer (A B C D)
101	Ⓐ Ⓑ Ⓒ Ⓓ	111	Ⓐ Ⓑ Ⓒ Ⓓ	121	Ⓐ Ⓑ Ⓒ Ⓓ	131	Ⓐ Ⓑ Ⓒ Ⓓ	141	Ⓐ Ⓑ Ⓒ Ⓓ	151	Ⓐ Ⓑ Ⓒ Ⓓ	161	Ⓐ Ⓑ Ⓒ Ⓓ	171	Ⓐ Ⓑ Ⓒ Ⓓ	181	Ⓐ Ⓑ Ⓒ Ⓓ	191	Ⓐ Ⓑ Ⓒ Ⓓ
102	Ⓐ Ⓑ Ⓒ Ⓓ	112	Ⓐ Ⓑ Ⓒ Ⓓ	122	Ⓐ Ⓑ Ⓒ Ⓓ	132	Ⓐ Ⓑ Ⓒ Ⓓ	142	Ⓐ Ⓑ Ⓒ Ⓓ	152	Ⓐ Ⓑ Ⓒ Ⓓ	162	Ⓐ Ⓑ Ⓒ Ⓓ	172	Ⓐ Ⓑ Ⓒ Ⓓ	182	Ⓐ Ⓑ Ⓒ Ⓓ	192	Ⓐ Ⓑ Ⓒ Ⓓ
103	Ⓐ Ⓑ Ⓒ Ⓓ	113	Ⓐ Ⓑ Ⓒ Ⓓ	123	Ⓐ Ⓑ Ⓒ Ⓓ	133	Ⓐ Ⓑ Ⓒ Ⓓ	143	Ⓐ Ⓑ Ⓒ Ⓓ	153	Ⓐ Ⓑ Ⓒ Ⓓ	163	Ⓐ Ⓑ Ⓒ Ⓓ	173	Ⓐ Ⓑ Ⓒ Ⓓ	183	Ⓐ Ⓑ Ⓒ Ⓓ	193	Ⓐ Ⓑ Ⓒ Ⓓ
104	Ⓐ Ⓑ Ⓒ Ⓓ	114	Ⓐ Ⓑ Ⓒ Ⓓ	124	Ⓐ Ⓑ Ⓒ Ⓓ	134	Ⓐ Ⓑ Ⓒ Ⓓ	144	Ⓐ Ⓑ Ⓒ Ⓓ	154	Ⓐ Ⓑ Ⓒ Ⓓ	164	Ⓐ Ⓑ Ⓒ Ⓓ	174	Ⓐ Ⓑ Ⓒ Ⓓ	184	Ⓐ Ⓑ Ⓒ Ⓓ	194	Ⓐ Ⓑ Ⓒ Ⓓ
105	Ⓐ Ⓑ Ⓒ Ⓓ	115	Ⓐ Ⓑ Ⓒ Ⓓ	125	Ⓐ Ⓑ Ⓒ Ⓓ	135	Ⓐ Ⓑ Ⓒ Ⓓ	145	Ⓐ Ⓑ Ⓒ Ⓓ	155	Ⓐ Ⓑ Ⓒ Ⓓ	165	Ⓐ Ⓑ Ⓒ Ⓓ	175	Ⓐ Ⓑ Ⓒ Ⓓ	185	Ⓐ Ⓑ Ⓒ Ⓓ	195	Ⓐ Ⓑ Ⓒ Ⓓ
106	Ⓐ Ⓑ Ⓒ Ⓓ	116	Ⓐ Ⓑ Ⓒ Ⓓ	126	Ⓐ Ⓑ Ⓒ Ⓓ	136	Ⓐ Ⓑ Ⓒ Ⓓ	146	Ⓐ Ⓑ Ⓒ Ⓓ	156	Ⓐ Ⓑ Ⓒ Ⓓ	166	Ⓐ Ⓑ Ⓒ Ⓓ	176	Ⓐ Ⓑ Ⓒ Ⓓ	186	Ⓐ Ⓑ Ⓒ Ⓓ	196	Ⓐ Ⓑ Ⓒ Ⓓ
107	Ⓐ Ⓑ Ⓒ Ⓓ	117	Ⓐ Ⓑ Ⓒ Ⓓ	127	Ⓐ Ⓑ Ⓒ Ⓓ	137	Ⓐ Ⓑ Ⓒ Ⓓ	147	Ⓐ Ⓑ Ⓒ Ⓓ	157	Ⓐ Ⓑ Ⓒ Ⓓ	167	Ⓐ Ⓑ Ⓒ Ⓓ	177	Ⓐ Ⓑ Ⓒ Ⓓ	187	Ⓐ Ⓑ Ⓒ Ⓓ	197	Ⓐ Ⓑ Ⓒ Ⓓ
108	Ⓐ Ⓑ Ⓒ Ⓓ	118	Ⓐ Ⓑ Ⓒ Ⓓ	128	Ⓐ Ⓑ Ⓒ Ⓓ	138	Ⓐ Ⓑ Ⓒ Ⓓ	148	Ⓐ Ⓑ Ⓒ Ⓓ	158	Ⓐ Ⓑ Ⓒ Ⓓ	168	Ⓐ Ⓑ Ⓒ Ⓓ	178	Ⓐ Ⓑ Ⓒ Ⓓ	188	Ⓐ Ⓑ Ⓒ Ⓓ	198	Ⓐ Ⓑ Ⓒ Ⓓ
109	Ⓐ Ⓑ Ⓒ Ⓓ	119	Ⓐ Ⓑ Ⓒ Ⓓ	129	Ⓐ Ⓑ Ⓒ Ⓓ	139	Ⓐ Ⓑ Ⓒ Ⓓ	149	Ⓐ Ⓑ Ⓒ Ⓓ	159	Ⓐ Ⓑ Ⓒ Ⓓ	169	Ⓐ Ⓑ Ⓒ Ⓓ	179	Ⓐ Ⓑ Ⓒ Ⓓ	189	Ⓐ Ⓑ Ⓒ Ⓓ	199	Ⓐ Ⓑ Ⓒ Ⓓ
110	Ⓐ Ⓑ Ⓒ Ⓓ	120	Ⓐ Ⓑ Ⓒ Ⓓ	130	Ⓐ Ⓑ Ⓒ Ⓓ	140	Ⓐ Ⓑ Ⓒ Ⓓ	150	Ⓐ Ⓑ Ⓒ Ⓓ	160	Ⓐ Ⓑ Ⓒ Ⓓ	170	Ⓐ Ⓑ Ⓒ Ⓓ	180	Ⓐ Ⓑ Ⓒ Ⓓ	190	Ⓐ Ⓑ Ⓒ Ⓓ	200	Ⓐ Ⓑ Ⓒ Ⓓ

ANSWER SHEET: Practice Test Two

Name ____________________

Listening Comprehension

Part 1 (1–10) · Part 2 (11–40) · Part 3 (41–70) · Part 4 (71–100)

	Answer A B C D		Answer A B C D		Answer A B C		Answer A B C		Answer A B C		Answer A B C D		Answer A B C D		Answer A B C D		Answer A B C D		Answer A B C D
1	Ⓐ Ⓑ Ⓒ Ⓓ	11	Ⓐ Ⓑ Ⓒ Ⓓ	21	Ⓐ Ⓑ Ⓒ	31	Ⓐ Ⓑ Ⓒ	41	Ⓐ Ⓑ Ⓒ	51	Ⓐ Ⓑ Ⓒ Ⓓ	61	Ⓐ Ⓑ Ⓒ Ⓓ	71	Ⓐ Ⓑ Ⓒ Ⓓ	81	Ⓐ Ⓑ Ⓒ Ⓓ	91	Ⓐ Ⓑ Ⓒ Ⓓ
2	Ⓐ Ⓑ Ⓒ Ⓓ	12	Ⓐ Ⓑ Ⓒ Ⓓ	22	Ⓐ Ⓑ Ⓒ	32	Ⓐ Ⓑ Ⓒ	42	Ⓐ Ⓑ Ⓒ	52	Ⓐ Ⓑ Ⓒ Ⓓ	62	Ⓐ Ⓑ Ⓒ Ⓓ	72	Ⓐ Ⓑ Ⓒ Ⓓ	82	Ⓐ Ⓑ Ⓒ Ⓓ	92	Ⓐ Ⓑ Ⓒ Ⓓ
3	Ⓐ Ⓑ Ⓒ Ⓓ	13	Ⓐ Ⓑ Ⓒ Ⓓ	23	Ⓐ Ⓑ Ⓒ	33	Ⓐ Ⓑ Ⓒ	43	Ⓐ Ⓑ Ⓒ	53	Ⓐ Ⓑ Ⓒ Ⓓ	63	Ⓐ Ⓑ Ⓒ Ⓓ	73	Ⓐ Ⓑ Ⓒ Ⓓ	83	Ⓐ Ⓑ Ⓒ Ⓓ	93	Ⓐ Ⓑ Ⓒ Ⓓ
4	Ⓐ Ⓑ Ⓒ Ⓓ	14	Ⓐ Ⓑ Ⓒ Ⓓ	24	Ⓐ Ⓑ Ⓒ	34	Ⓐ Ⓑ Ⓒ	44	Ⓐ Ⓑ Ⓒ	54	Ⓐ Ⓑ Ⓒ Ⓓ	64	Ⓐ Ⓑ Ⓒ Ⓓ	74	Ⓐ Ⓑ Ⓒ Ⓓ	84	Ⓐ Ⓑ Ⓒ Ⓓ	94	Ⓐ Ⓑ Ⓒ Ⓓ
5	Ⓐ Ⓑ Ⓒ Ⓓ	15	Ⓐ Ⓑ Ⓒ Ⓓ	25	Ⓐ Ⓑ Ⓒ	35	Ⓐ Ⓑ Ⓒ	45	Ⓐ Ⓑ Ⓒ	55	Ⓐ Ⓑ Ⓒ Ⓓ	65	Ⓐ Ⓑ Ⓒ Ⓓ	75	Ⓐ Ⓑ Ⓒ Ⓓ	85	Ⓐ Ⓑ Ⓒ Ⓓ	95	Ⓐ Ⓑ Ⓒ Ⓓ
6	Ⓐ Ⓑ Ⓒ Ⓓ	16	Ⓐ Ⓑ Ⓒ Ⓓ	26	Ⓐ Ⓑ Ⓒ	36	Ⓐ Ⓑ Ⓒ	46	Ⓐ Ⓑ Ⓒ	56	Ⓐ Ⓑ Ⓒ Ⓓ	66	Ⓐ Ⓑ Ⓒ Ⓓ	76	Ⓐ Ⓑ Ⓒ Ⓓ	86	Ⓐ Ⓑ Ⓒ Ⓓ	96	Ⓐ Ⓑ Ⓒ Ⓓ
7	Ⓐ Ⓑ Ⓒ Ⓓ	17	Ⓐ Ⓑ Ⓒ Ⓓ	27	Ⓐ Ⓑ Ⓒ	37	Ⓐ Ⓑ Ⓒ	47	Ⓐ Ⓑ Ⓒ	57	Ⓐ Ⓑ Ⓒ Ⓓ	67	Ⓐ Ⓑ Ⓒ Ⓓ	77	Ⓐ Ⓑ Ⓒ Ⓓ	87	Ⓐ Ⓑ Ⓒ Ⓓ	97	Ⓐ Ⓑ Ⓒ Ⓓ
8	Ⓐ Ⓑ Ⓒ Ⓓ	18	Ⓐ Ⓑ Ⓒ Ⓓ	28	Ⓐ Ⓑ Ⓒ	38	Ⓐ Ⓑ Ⓒ	48	Ⓐ Ⓑ Ⓒ	58	Ⓐ Ⓑ Ⓒ Ⓓ	68	Ⓐ Ⓑ Ⓒ Ⓓ	78	Ⓐ Ⓑ Ⓒ Ⓓ	88	Ⓐ Ⓑ Ⓒ Ⓓ	98	Ⓐ Ⓑ Ⓒ Ⓓ
9	Ⓐ Ⓑ Ⓒ Ⓓ	19	Ⓐ Ⓑ Ⓒ Ⓓ	29	Ⓐ Ⓑ Ⓒ	39	Ⓐ Ⓑ Ⓒ	49	Ⓐ Ⓑ Ⓒ	59	Ⓐ Ⓑ Ⓒ Ⓓ	69	Ⓐ Ⓑ Ⓒ Ⓓ	79	Ⓐ Ⓑ Ⓒ Ⓓ	89	Ⓐ Ⓑ Ⓒ Ⓓ	99	Ⓐ Ⓑ Ⓒ Ⓓ
10	Ⓐ Ⓑ Ⓒ Ⓓ	20	Ⓐ Ⓑ Ⓒ Ⓓ	30	Ⓐ Ⓑ Ⓒ	40	Ⓐ Ⓑ Ⓒ	50	Ⓐ Ⓑ Ⓒ	60	Ⓐ Ⓑ Ⓒ Ⓓ	70	Ⓐ Ⓑ Ⓒ Ⓓ	80	Ⓐ Ⓑ Ⓒ Ⓓ	90	Ⓐ Ⓑ Ⓒ Ⓓ	100	Ⓐ Ⓑ Ⓒ Ⓓ

Reading

Part 5 (101–140) · Part 6 (141–152) · Part 7 (153–200)

	Answer A B C D		Answer A B C D		Answer A B C D		Answer A B C D		Answer A B C D		Answer A B C D		Answer A B C D		Answer A B C D		Answer A B C D		Answer A B C D
101	Ⓐ Ⓑ Ⓒ Ⓓ	111	Ⓐ Ⓑ Ⓒ Ⓓ	121	Ⓐ Ⓑ Ⓒ Ⓓ	131	Ⓐ Ⓑ Ⓒ Ⓓ	141	Ⓐ Ⓑ Ⓒ Ⓓ	151	Ⓐ Ⓑ Ⓒ Ⓓ	161	Ⓐ Ⓑ Ⓒ Ⓓ	171	Ⓐ Ⓑ Ⓒ Ⓓ	181	Ⓐ Ⓑ Ⓒ Ⓓ	191	Ⓐ Ⓑ Ⓒ Ⓓ
102	Ⓐ Ⓑ Ⓒ Ⓓ	112	Ⓐ Ⓑ Ⓒ Ⓓ	122	Ⓐ Ⓑ Ⓒ Ⓓ	132	Ⓐ Ⓑ Ⓒ Ⓓ	142	Ⓐ Ⓑ Ⓒ Ⓓ	152	Ⓐ Ⓑ Ⓒ Ⓓ	162	Ⓐ Ⓑ Ⓒ Ⓓ	172	Ⓐ Ⓑ Ⓒ Ⓓ	182	Ⓐ Ⓑ Ⓒ Ⓓ	192	Ⓐ Ⓑ Ⓒ Ⓓ
103	Ⓐ Ⓑ Ⓒ Ⓓ	113	Ⓐ Ⓑ Ⓒ Ⓓ	123	Ⓐ Ⓑ Ⓒ Ⓓ	133	Ⓐ Ⓑ Ⓒ Ⓓ	143	Ⓐ Ⓑ Ⓒ Ⓓ	153	Ⓐ Ⓑ Ⓒ Ⓓ	163	Ⓐ Ⓑ Ⓒ Ⓓ	173	Ⓐ Ⓑ Ⓒ Ⓓ	183	Ⓐ Ⓑ Ⓒ Ⓓ	193	Ⓐ Ⓑ Ⓒ Ⓓ
104	Ⓐ Ⓑ Ⓒ Ⓓ	114	Ⓐ Ⓑ Ⓒ Ⓓ	124	Ⓐ Ⓑ Ⓒ Ⓓ	134	Ⓐ Ⓑ Ⓒ Ⓓ	144	Ⓐ Ⓑ Ⓒ Ⓓ	154	Ⓐ Ⓑ Ⓒ Ⓓ	164	Ⓐ Ⓑ Ⓒ Ⓓ	174	Ⓐ Ⓑ Ⓒ Ⓓ	184	Ⓐ Ⓑ Ⓒ Ⓓ	194	Ⓐ Ⓑ Ⓒ Ⓓ
105	Ⓐ Ⓑ Ⓒ Ⓓ	115	Ⓐ Ⓑ Ⓒ Ⓓ	125	Ⓐ Ⓑ Ⓒ Ⓓ	135	Ⓐ Ⓑ Ⓒ Ⓓ	145	Ⓐ Ⓑ Ⓒ Ⓓ	155	Ⓐ Ⓑ Ⓒ Ⓓ	165	Ⓐ Ⓑ Ⓒ Ⓓ	175	Ⓐ Ⓑ Ⓒ Ⓓ	185	Ⓐ Ⓑ Ⓒ Ⓓ	195	Ⓐ Ⓑ Ⓒ Ⓓ
106	Ⓐ Ⓑ Ⓒ Ⓓ	116	Ⓐ Ⓑ Ⓒ Ⓓ	126	Ⓐ Ⓑ Ⓒ Ⓓ	136	Ⓐ Ⓑ Ⓒ Ⓓ	146	Ⓐ Ⓑ Ⓒ Ⓓ	156	Ⓐ Ⓑ Ⓒ Ⓓ	166	Ⓐ Ⓑ Ⓒ Ⓓ	176	Ⓐ Ⓑ Ⓒ Ⓓ	186	Ⓐ Ⓑ Ⓒ Ⓓ	196	Ⓐ Ⓑ Ⓒ Ⓓ
107	Ⓐ Ⓑ Ⓒ Ⓓ	117	Ⓐ Ⓑ Ⓒ Ⓓ	127	Ⓐ Ⓑ Ⓒ Ⓓ	137	Ⓐ Ⓑ Ⓒ Ⓓ	147	Ⓐ Ⓑ Ⓒ Ⓓ	157	Ⓐ Ⓑ Ⓒ Ⓓ	167	Ⓐ Ⓑ Ⓒ Ⓓ	177	Ⓐ Ⓑ Ⓒ Ⓓ	187	Ⓐ Ⓑ Ⓒ Ⓓ	197	Ⓐ Ⓑ Ⓒ Ⓓ
108	Ⓐ Ⓑ Ⓒ Ⓓ	118	Ⓐ Ⓑ Ⓒ Ⓓ	128	Ⓐ Ⓑ Ⓒ Ⓓ	138	Ⓐ Ⓑ Ⓒ Ⓓ	148	Ⓐ Ⓑ Ⓒ Ⓓ	158	Ⓐ Ⓑ Ⓒ Ⓓ	168	Ⓐ Ⓑ Ⓒ Ⓓ	178	Ⓐ Ⓑ Ⓒ Ⓓ	188	Ⓐ Ⓑ Ⓒ Ⓓ	198	Ⓐ Ⓑ Ⓒ Ⓓ
109	Ⓐ Ⓑ Ⓒ Ⓓ	119	Ⓐ Ⓑ Ⓒ Ⓓ	129	Ⓐ Ⓑ Ⓒ Ⓓ	139	Ⓐ Ⓑ Ⓒ Ⓓ	149	Ⓐ Ⓑ Ⓒ Ⓓ	159	Ⓐ Ⓑ Ⓒ Ⓓ	169	Ⓐ Ⓑ Ⓒ Ⓓ	179	Ⓐ Ⓑ Ⓒ Ⓓ	189	Ⓐ Ⓑ Ⓒ Ⓓ	199	Ⓐ Ⓑ Ⓒ Ⓓ
110	Ⓐ Ⓑ Ⓒ Ⓓ	120	Ⓐ Ⓑ Ⓒ Ⓓ	130	Ⓐ Ⓑ Ⓒ Ⓓ	140	Ⓐ Ⓑ Ⓒ Ⓓ	150	Ⓐ Ⓑ Ⓒ Ⓓ	160	Ⓐ Ⓑ Ⓒ Ⓓ	170	Ⓐ Ⓑ Ⓒ Ⓓ	180	Ⓐ Ⓑ Ⓒ Ⓓ	190	Ⓐ Ⓑ Ⓒ Ⓓ	200	Ⓐ Ⓑ Ⓒ Ⓓ

ANSWER SHEET: Practice Test Three

Name ____________________

Listening Comprehension

Part 1 (1–10) · Part 2 (11–40) · Part 3 (41–70) · Part 4 (71–100)

	Answer		Answer		Answer		Answer		Answer		Answer		Answer		Answer		Answer		Answer
	A B C D		A B C D		A B C		A B C		A B C		A B C D		A B C D		A B C D		A B C D		A B C D
1	Ⓐ Ⓑ Ⓒ Ⓓ	11	Ⓐ Ⓑ Ⓒ Ⓓ	21	Ⓐ Ⓑ Ⓒ	31	Ⓐ Ⓑ Ⓒ	41	Ⓐ Ⓑ Ⓒ	51	Ⓐ Ⓑ Ⓒ Ⓓ	61	Ⓐ Ⓑ Ⓒ Ⓓ	71	Ⓐ Ⓑ Ⓒ Ⓓ	81	Ⓐ Ⓑ Ⓒ Ⓓ	91	Ⓐ Ⓑ Ⓒ Ⓓ
2	Ⓐ Ⓑ Ⓒ Ⓓ	12	Ⓐ Ⓑ Ⓒ Ⓓ	22	Ⓐ Ⓑ Ⓒ	32	Ⓐ Ⓑ Ⓒ	42	Ⓐ Ⓑ Ⓒ	52	Ⓐ Ⓑ Ⓒ Ⓓ	62	Ⓐ Ⓑ Ⓒ Ⓓ	72	Ⓐ Ⓑ Ⓒ Ⓓ	82	Ⓐ Ⓑ Ⓒ Ⓓ	92	Ⓐ Ⓑ Ⓒ Ⓓ
3	Ⓐ Ⓑ Ⓒ Ⓓ	13	Ⓐ Ⓑ Ⓒ Ⓓ	23	Ⓐ Ⓑ Ⓒ	33	Ⓐ Ⓑ Ⓒ	43	Ⓐ Ⓑ Ⓒ	53	Ⓐ Ⓑ Ⓒ Ⓓ	63	Ⓐ Ⓑ Ⓒ Ⓓ	73	Ⓐ Ⓑ Ⓒ Ⓓ	83	Ⓐ Ⓑ Ⓒ Ⓓ	93	Ⓐ Ⓑ Ⓒ Ⓓ
4	Ⓐ Ⓑ Ⓒ Ⓓ	14	Ⓐ Ⓑ Ⓒ Ⓓ	24	Ⓐ Ⓑ Ⓒ	34	Ⓐ Ⓑ Ⓒ	44	Ⓐ Ⓑ Ⓒ	54	Ⓐ Ⓑ Ⓒ Ⓓ	64	Ⓐ Ⓑ Ⓒ Ⓓ	74	Ⓐ Ⓑ Ⓒ Ⓓ	84	Ⓐ Ⓑ Ⓒ Ⓓ	94	Ⓐ Ⓑ Ⓒ Ⓓ
5	Ⓐ Ⓑ Ⓒ Ⓓ	15	Ⓐ Ⓑ Ⓒ Ⓓ	25	Ⓐ Ⓑ Ⓒ	35	Ⓐ Ⓑ Ⓒ	45	Ⓐ Ⓑ Ⓒ	55	Ⓐ Ⓑ Ⓒ Ⓓ	65	Ⓐ Ⓑ Ⓒ Ⓓ	75	Ⓐ Ⓑ Ⓒ Ⓓ	85	Ⓐ Ⓑ Ⓒ Ⓓ	95	Ⓐ Ⓑ Ⓒ Ⓓ
6	Ⓐ Ⓑ Ⓒ Ⓓ	16	Ⓐ Ⓑ Ⓒ Ⓓ	26	Ⓐ Ⓑ Ⓒ	36	Ⓐ Ⓑ Ⓒ	46	Ⓐ Ⓑ Ⓒ	56	Ⓐ Ⓑ Ⓒ Ⓓ	66	Ⓐ Ⓑ Ⓒ Ⓓ	76	Ⓐ Ⓑ Ⓒ Ⓓ	86	Ⓐ Ⓑ Ⓒ Ⓓ	96	Ⓐ Ⓑ Ⓒ Ⓓ
7	Ⓐ Ⓑ Ⓒ Ⓓ	17	Ⓐ Ⓑ Ⓒ Ⓓ	27	Ⓐ Ⓑ Ⓒ	37	Ⓐ Ⓑ Ⓒ	47	Ⓐ Ⓑ Ⓒ	57	Ⓐ Ⓑ Ⓒ Ⓓ	67	Ⓐ Ⓑ Ⓒ Ⓓ	77	Ⓐ Ⓑ Ⓒ Ⓓ	87	Ⓐ Ⓑ Ⓒ Ⓓ	97	Ⓐ Ⓑ Ⓒ Ⓓ
8	Ⓐ Ⓑ Ⓒ Ⓓ	18	Ⓐ Ⓑ Ⓒ Ⓓ	28	Ⓐ Ⓑ Ⓒ	38	Ⓐ Ⓑ Ⓒ	48	Ⓐ Ⓑ Ⓒ	58	Ⓐ Ⓑ Ⓒ Ⓓ	68	Ⓐ Ⓑ Ⓒ Ⓓ	78	Ⓐ Ⓑ Ⓒ Ⓓ	88	Ⓐ Ⓑ Ⓒ Ⓓ	98	Ⓐ Ⓑ Ⓒ Ⓓ
9	Ⓐ Ⓑ Ⓒ Ⓓ	19	Ⓐ Ⓑ Ⓒ Ⓓ	29	Ⓐ Ⓑ Ⓒ	39	Ⓐ Ⓑ Ⓒ	49	Ⓐ Ⓑ Ⓒ	59	Ⓐ Ⓑ Ⓒ Ⓓ	69	Ⓐ Ⓑ Ⓒ Ⓓ	79	Ⓐ Ⓑ Ⓒ Ⓓ	89	Ⓐ Ⓑ Ⓒ Ⓓ	99	Ⓐ Ⓑ Ⓒ Ⓓ
10	Ⓐ Ⓑ Ⓒ Ⓓ	20	Ⓐ Ⓑ Ⓒ Ⓓ	30	Ⓐ Ⓑ Ⓒ	40	Ⓐ Ⓑ Ⓒ	50	Ⓐ Ⓑ Ⓒ	60	Ⓐ Ⓑ Ⓒ Ⓓ	70	Ⓐ Ⓑ Ⓒ Ⓓ	80	Ⓐ Ⓑ Ⓒ Ⓓ	90	Ⓐ Ⓑ Ⓒ Ⓓ	100	Ⓐ Ⓑ Ⓒ Ⓓ

Reading

Part 5 (101–140) · Part 6 (141–152) · Part 7 (153–200)

	Answer		Answer		Answer		Answer		Answer		Answer		Answer		Answer		Answer		Answer
	A B C D		A B C D		A B C D		A B C D		A B C–D		A B C D		A B C D		A B C D		A B C D		A B C D
101	Ⓐ Ⓑ Ⓒ Ⓓ	111	Ⓐ Ⓑ Ⓒ Ⓓ	121	Ⓐ Ⓑ Ⓒ Ⓓ	131	Ⓐ Ⓑ Ⓒ Ⓓ	141	Ⓐ Ⓑ Ⓒ Ⓓ	151	Ⓐ Ⓑ Ⓒ Ⓓ	161	Ⓐ Ⓑ Ⓒ Ⓓ	171	Ⓐ Ⓑ Ⓒ Ⓓ	181	Ⓐ Ⓑ Ⓒ Ⓓ	191	Ⓐ Ⓑ Ⓒ Ⓓ
102	Ⓐ Ⓑ Ⓒ Ⓓ	112	Ⓐ Ⓑ Ⓒ Ⓓ	122	Ⓐ Ⓑ Ⓒ Ⓓ	132	Ⓐ Ⓑ Ⓒ Ⓓ	142	Ⓐ Ⓑ Ⓒ Ⓓ	152	Ⓐ Ⓑ Ⓒ Ⓓ	162	Ⓐ Ⓑ Ⓒ Ⓓ	172	Ⓐ Ⓑ Ⓒ Ⓓ	182	Ⓐ Ⓑ Ⓒ Ⓓ	192	Ⓐ Ⓑ Ⓒ Ⓓ
103	Ⓐ Ⓑ Ⓒ Ⓓ	113	Ⓐ Ⓑ Ⓒ Ⓓ	123	Ⓐ Ⓑ Ⓒ Ⓓ	133	Ⓐ Ⓑ Ⓒ Ⓓ	143	Ⓐ Ⓑ Ⓒ Ⓓ	153	Ⓐ Ⓑ Ⓒ Ⓓ	163	Ⓐ Ⓑ Ⓒ Ⓓ	173	Ⓐ Ⓑ Ⓒ Ⓓ	183	Ⓐ Ⓑ Ⓒ Ⓓ	193	Ⓐ Ⓑ Ⓒ Ⓓ
104	Ⓐ Ⓑ Ⓒ Ⓓ	114	Ⓐ Ⓑ Ⓒ Ⓓ	124	Ⓐ Ⓑ Ⓒ Ⓓ	134	Ⓐ Ⓑ Ⓒ Ⓓ	144	Ⓐ Ⓑ Ⓒ Ⓓ	154	Ⓐ Ⓑ Ⓒ Ⓓ	164	Ⓐ Ⓑ Ⓒ Ⓓ	174	Ⓐ Ⓑ Ⓒ Ⓓ	184	Ⓐ Ⓑ Ⓒ Ⓓ	194	Ⓐ Ⓑ Ⓒ Ⓓ
105	Ⓐ Ⓑ Ⓒ Ⓓ	115	Ⓐ Ⓑ Ⓒ Ⓓ	125	Ⓐ Ⓑ Ⓒ Ⓓ	135	Ⓐ Ⓑ Ⓒ Ⓓ	145	Ⓐ Ⓑ Ⓒ Ⓓ	155	Ⓐ Ⓑ Ⓒ Ⓓ	165	Ⓐ Ⓑ Ⓒ Ⓓ	175	Ⓐ Ⓑ Ⓒ Ⓓ	185	Ⓐ Ⓑ Ⓒ Ⓓ	195	Ⓐ Ⓑ Ⓒ Ⓓ
106	Ⓐ Ⓑ Ⓒ Ⓓ	116	Ⓐ Ⓑ Ⓒ Ⓓ	126	Ⓐ Ⓑ Ⓒ Ⓓ	136	Ⓐ Ⓑ Ⓒ Ⓓ	146	Ⓐ Ⓑ Ⓒ Ⓓ	156	Ⓐ Ⓑ Ⓒ Ⓓ	166	Ⓐ Ⓑ Ⓒ Ⓓ	176	Ⓐ Ⓑ Ⓒ Ⓓ	186	Ⓐ Ⓑ Ⓒ Ⓓ	196	Ⓐ Ⓑ Ⓒ Ⓓ
107	Ⓐ Ⓑ Ⓒ Ⓓ	117	Ⓐ Ⓑ Ⓒ Ⓓ	127	Ⓐ Ⓑ Ⓒ Ⓓ	137	Ⓐ Ⓑ Ⓒ Ⓓ	147	Ⓐ Ⓑ Ⓒ Ⓓ	157	Ⓐ Ⓑ Ⓒ Ⓓ	167	Ⓐ Ⓑ Ⓒ Ⓓ	177	Ⓐ Ⓑ Ⓒ Ⓓ	187	Ⓐ Ⓑ Ⓒ Ⓓ	197	Ⓐ Ⓑ Ⓒ Ⓓ
108	Ⓐ Ⓑ Ⓒ Ⓓ	118	Ⓐ Ⓑ Ⓒ Ⓓ	128	Ⓐ Ⓑ Ⓒ Ⓓ	138	Ⓐ Ⓑ Ⓒ Ⓓ	148	Ⓐ Ⓑ Ⓒ Ⓓ	158	Ⓐ Ⓑ Ⓒ Ⓓ	168	Ⓐ Ⓑ Ⓒ Ⓓ	178	Ⓐ Ⓑ Ⓒ Ⓓ	188	Ⓐ Ⓑ Ⓒ Ⓓ	198	Ⓐ Ⓑ Ⓒ Ⓓ
109	Ⓐ Ⓑ Ⓒ Ⓓ	119	Ⓐ Ⓑ Ⓒ Ⓓ	129	Ⓐ Ⓑ Ⓒ Ⓓ	139	Ⓐ Ⓑ Ⓒ Ⓓ	149	Ⓐ Ⓑ Ⓒ Ⓓ	159	Ⓐ Ⓑ Ⓒ Ⓓ	169	Ⓐ Ⓑ Ⓒ Ⓓ	179	Ⓐ Ⓑ Ⓒ Ⓓ	189	Ⓐ Ⓑ Ⓒ Ⓓ	199	Ⓐ Ⓑ Ⓒ Ⓓ
110	Ⓐ Ⓑ Ⓒ Ⓓ	120	Ⓐ Ⓑ Ⓒ Ⓓ	130	Ⓐ Ⓑ Ⓒ Ⓓ	140	Ⓐ Ⓑ Ⓒ Ⓓ	150	Ⓐ Ⓑ Ⓒ Ⓓ	160	Ⓐ Ⓑ Ⓒ Ⓓ	170	Ⓐ Ⓑ Ⓒ Ⓓ	180	Ⓐ Ⓑ Ⓒ Ⓓ	190	Ⓐ Ⓑ Ⓒ Ⓓ	200	Ⓐ Ⓑ Ⓒ Ⓓ

PRACTICE TEST SCORE CONVERSION

HOW TO CONVERT YOUR PRACTICE TEST SCORES

To convert your practice test scores, use the table on page 349. Follow these simple steps.

1. Take a practice test.
2. Total the number of correct answers in the listening section.
3. Match the total number of correct listening answers with the corresponding practice score.
4. Total the number of correct answers in the reading section.
5. Match the total number of correct reading answers with the corresponding practice score.
6. Add the two scores together. This is your estimated total practice score.

Sample

Number of correct listening answers	56	= Practice listening score	290
Number of correct reading answers	82	= Practice reading score	+ 405
Estimated total practice score			695

Your score on Practice Test 1

Number of correct listening answers	____	= Practice listening score	______
Number of correct reading answers	____	= Practice reading score	+______
Estimated total practice score			______

Your score on Practice Test 2

Number of correct listening answers	____	= Practice listening score	______
Number of correct reading answers	____	= Practice reading score	+______
Estimated total practice score			______

Your score on Practice Test 3

Number of correct listening answers	____	= Practice listening score	______
Number of correct reading answers	____	= Practice reading score	+______
Estimated total practice score			______

Practice Test Estimated Score Conversion Table

# CORRECT	PRACTICE SCORE LISTENING	PRACTICE SCORE READING
0	5	5
1	5	5
2	5	5
3	5	5
4	5	5
5	5	5
6	5	5
7	10	5
8	15	5
9	20	5
10	25	5
11	30	5
12	35	5
13	40	5
14	45	5
15	50	5
16	55	10
17	60	15
18	65	20
19	70	25
20	75	30
21	80	35
22	85	40
23	90	45
24	95	50
25	100	60
26	110	65
27	115	70
28	120	80
29	125	85
30	130	90
31	135	95
32	140	100
33	145	110
34	150	115
35	160	120
36	165	125
37	170	130
38	175	140
39	180	145
40	185	150
41	190	160
42	195	165
43	200	170
44	210	175
45	215	180
46	220	190
47	230	195
48	240	200
49	245	210
50	250	215
51	255	220
52	260	225
53	270	230
54	275	235
55	280	240
56	290	250
57	295	255
58	300	260
59	310	265
60	315	270
61	320	280
62	325	285
63	330	290
64	340	300
65	345	305
66	350	310
67	360	320
68	365	325
69	370	330
70	380	335
71	385	340
72	390	350
73	395	355
74	400	360
75	405	365
76	410	370
77	420	380
78	425	385
79	430	390
80	440	395
81	445	400
82	450	405
83	460	410
84	465	415
85	470	420
86	475	425
87	480	430
88	485	435
89	490	445
90	495	450
91	495	455
92	495	465
93	495	470
94	495	480
95	495	485
96	495	490
97	495	495
98	495	495
99	495	495
100	495	495

CD-ROM CONTENTS

MP3 AUDIO FILES FOR THE COMPLETE AUDIO PROGRAM:

Listening Comprehension Practice (CD 1, track 2–CD 2, track 11)
Listening Comprehension Review (CD 3, tracks 2–28)
Practice Test 1, Listening Parts 1–4 (CD 4, tracks 2–28)
Practice Test 2, Listening Parts 1–4 (CD 5, tracks 2–28)
Practice Test 3, Listening Parts 1–4 (CD 6, tracks 2–28)

PDF FILES FOR:

Complete Audioscript
Complete Answer Key (in specified editions only)